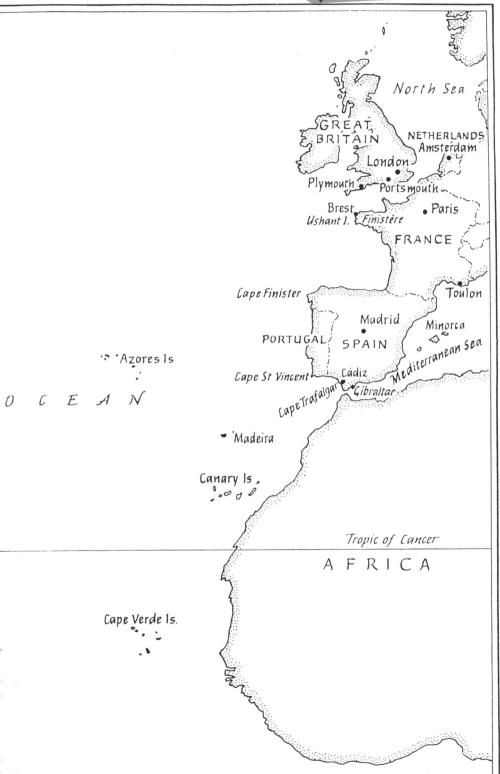

THE GOLDEN ROCK

THE GOLDEN ROCK

An Episode of the American War
of Independence 1775–1783

by
RONALD HURST

NAVAL INSTITUTE PRESS
ANNAPOLIS, MARYLAND

First published in Great Britain in 1996
by LEO COOPER, 190 Shaftesbury Avenue, London WC2H 8JL
an imprint of Pen & Sword Books Ltd,
47 Church Street, Barnsley, South Yorkshire S70 2AS

Published and distributed in the United States of America and Canada
by the Naval Institute Press,
118 Maryland Avenue,
Annapolis, Maryland 21402-5035

Library of Congress Catalog Card No. 96-67492
ISBN 1-55750-338-9

For Phyllis

Real solemn history, I cannot be interested in . . . the quarrels of Popes and Kings, with wars or pestilences in every page: the men all so good for nothing, and hardly any women at all.

Jane Austen

CONTENTS

MAP

AUTHOR'S NOTE AND ACKNOWLEDGEMENTS

A journey such as this owes much to the kindness and talent of those met along the way. My first tribute therefore must be to the late Barbara Tuchman who not only showed me the fascination and delight of historical research, but whose book, *The First Salute – A view of the American Revolution* also inspired this work with her own reference to the St Eustatius Affair.

It will be clear that I have drawn on a great fund of sources. However, it will be of interest to mention here the key studies and material now amplified in these pages. The general course of Rodney's life and campaigns therefore – with the exception of my own interpretation of the events at St Eustatius – is to be found in David Spinney's *Rodney*, (George Allen and Unwin Ltd., London 1969). Rodney's other biographers, Munday, Hannay and McIntyre must be mentioned for their collective esteem for their subject but not alas, for any useful illumination on the events on St Eustatius.

Much detail and correspondence is derived from the *Rodney Papers*, held in the Public Record Office in London, under PRO 30/20/1–26 and the *Letter Books and Order Books of Admiral Lord Rodney, 1780–1782*, published by the Naval History Society, New York 1932. In 1787 and in extenuation of his own and Sir John Vaughan's conduct at St Eustatius, Rodney published his *Plain State of Facts Relative to the Capture of St Eustatius*. This was followed in 1789 by the publication of Rodney's correspondence during his stay at St Eustatius, under the title of *Letters from Sir George Brydges now Lord Rodney to His Majesty's Ministers relative to the capture of St Eustatius*.

For guidance on the career and campaigns of Sir John Vaughan I have leaned heavily on the doctoral dissertation by R N McLarty: *The Expedition of Major-General John Vaughan to the Lesser Antilles 1779–1781*, published by the University of Michigan, 1951. For the very great friendship and interest shown to me by Robert Cox, Curator of Manuscripts at the William L Clements Library, University of Michigan and for his concern that I should receive much relevant material and illustrations from the Library, I now offer my sincere thanks. My original request to the William L Clements Library, swiftly granted, was for access to the *Vaughan Papers*, which arrived with the information that this collection was comprised entirely of letters to the General and did not include any *from* him. *Pace* Edna Vosper who collated the *Vaughan Papers*, I am happy to repay the Library in some part by revealing that my research in the files of the Public Record Office unearthed a batch of Vaughan's own letters, previously unpublished, the majority written from St Eustatius. These are held under Class CO5/238 and copies will usefully enhance the Vaughan archive in the Clements Library.

The *Germain Papers* in the PRO, Class 246/1 supplement the correspondence between the leading figures. This file also includes the King's Instructions to Rodney and Vaughan for the distribution of the booty following the Great Capture, the business correspondence of the American traders and agents, Samuel Curson and Isaac Governeur, and Lieutenant Rogerson's revelation on the mysterious voyage of Sergeant Gordon.

The most important single source of information on the British occupation of St Eustatius is represented by J Franklin Jameson's *St Eustatius in the American Revolution* – a lecture to the cadets of the Naval War College, Newport, Rhode Island, in 1902, published in *The American Historical Review*, Vol. 8, July, 1903. I have also consulted reports of the affair published contemporaneously in the Dutch *Nieuwe Nederlandsche Jaerboeken* and in American newspapers such as *The Newport Mercury* and *The Connecticut Gazette* and the *Universal Intelligencer*. These have been cross-referenced with the accounts which appeared in British newspapers such as *The London Chronicle*, the *Annual Register* for the period and in Hansard.

The letters of Brigadier General Christie to Lieutenant-Colonel Cockburn at St Eustatius and to Lord George Germain concerning the misdeeds of Commissary-General Forster and the aftermath of the surrender are filed under PRO references CO318/17 and /9: and although I have quoted the full range of the *Rodney Papers* above, I believe that it is worth singling out the testimony of Arthur Savage, which will be found in PRO 30/20/21/6.

All accounts of actions at sea are based on the Captains' and Masters' journals of the vessels concerned – *Alcemene, Mars, Monarch, Panther, Ranger, Sandwich, Shrewsbury, Sybil* and *Vengeance*. Captains' journals are held at the Public Record Office under ADM 51, Masters' journals under ADM 52 and Ships' Muster Rolls under ADM 36.

The fine detail of the punitive measures against the islanders and of the expropriations of their monies and property is revealed in three further primary sources. First, the narrative by Richard Downing Jennings, *The Case of an English Subject*, 1784 (in the *Vaughan Papers*), next, the *Report of the Capture and Surrender of St Eustatius and the Islands of Saba and St Maartens*, made to the Directors of the Dutch West India Company by Johannes de Graaff, 1781 and third, the Proclamations issued by the Military Governor, in Dutch and English: *Proclamaties door de Engelsche gepubliceerd na het namen van St Eustatius 1781*, in the Algemeen Rijksarchief, Den Hague, Netherlands. More detail is culled from letters and lists of the merchants' claims against Rodney and Vaughan which are included in the *Rodney Papers*.

A number of people at Oxford came to my aid on request. Alan Lodge, Librarian at Rhodes House, helped me to find Dr J Hartog's *History of St Eustatius* at an early stage. This became a valued reference throughout the research period and I took great pleasure in subsequent correspondence with this author. Dorothy Nicholson of the Bodleian Library translated the Vaughan microfilms into print-out: abstracts of these were most efficiently produced by Sarah Hurst. Ron May, of the Bodleian and Professor David Patterson of St Cross College were helpful in recommending sources for my exploration of the Jews in Colonial America and the Antilles and with my questions concerning the inscription in Hebrew in the St Eustatius census document.

My thanks are due to the Librarian of the Newport, Rhode Island Historical Society, Bertram Lippincot III for the research facilities made available to me there, and to Bernard Kusinitz for his enthusiastic co-operation. I am especially glad to record the friendship and warm hospitality extended by Bernie and Mrs Kusinitz during my stay.

More kind help was extended by Marijke Koning and Han Jordaan of Den Hague, friends and fellow students of Statia's history. Their crucial role in guiding me to Dutch-language sources and in providing English translations from the *Nieuwe Nederlandsche Jaerboeken* and from Cornelius de Jong's *Voyages to the Caribbean Islands during the Years 1780 and 1781* is most sincerely appreciated. Similarly, I am indebted to Mrs M J G A Barthels and Diederick Kortlang, Archivists of the First Section, Algemeen Rijksarchief for their ready response to my enquiries and for arranging the translation of de Graaff's Report. I also benefited from *The History of St Eustatius* by Ybeltje Attema and from her courtesy in permitting me to quote from her work.

For material on the French at St Eustatius I express my gratitude to Philippe Moret, of Paris. His concurrent research into de Bouillé's expedition for his own work, *General De Bouillé and the 'Surprise' of St Eustatius* sparked a lively exchange of views, information and illustrations sustained over a considerable period. That he shared his findings from French national archives so generously brought a happy authority to my references in this area.

To my daughter Lois, who was assistant, itinerary manager and support during some arduous field research at St Martin's, St Eustatius, St Lucia and Martinique: I admit to pulling rank to discourage her from descending into the crater of The Quill: elderly parents would prefer to read of such feats on a postcard after the event. However, she crewed the rubber dinghy piloted by that cheerful girl of Statia's Dive Shop, Kim, from which we surveyed and photographed Jenkins' Bay and the coastline down to Fort Orange. Both of these young ladies introduced me to snorkelling on that occasion, although at some risk for the future of this book.

Siegfried Lampe, who is deservedly Statia's most respected and best-known resident welcomed us into his home on Fort Orange Street. That welcome was doubly valuable to tired travellers, for Siegfried extended it so far as to fill in much historical detail and drive us over the island. With him, we visited the key locations in this story, the Fort and Doncker's house in the Upper Town, the Dutch Reformed Church, with its tombs of Brigadier General Ogilvy and Admiral Krul*, and the Synagogue, and those graveyards in which lie not only Statia's people, but also, so many of the anonymous soldiers and sailors of this book. And with Siegfried too, we stood among the fallen stones of what had once been the great warehouses along the strand and among the dismounted, rusted guns of the batteries . . . and wondered at what had passed in this tiny place, at the author's task of acquiring source material dispersed so widely over the world and indeed, if that quest should be successful, at what one would make of it.

It remains to thank so many others, among whom are the staff of the Public Record Office and HM Controller, for the quotations and excerpts from Crown copyright material from the PRO. For assistance in research at that establishment and for her valued familiarity with the Admiralty and Army files therein, I was privileged to enlist Gillian Hughes, whose perceptive selections enabled me to add spice to this narrative. From the beginning, also, some four years ago, Dr Linda Washington, Head of the Department of Printed Books at the National Army Museum, Chelsea, was unfailingly helpful and gladly arranged the microfilming of the record of James Cockburn's court martial. Thereafter, her replies were comprehensive and her suggestions always fruitful. I am grateful too, to Gwyneth Campling, Assistant Curator of Photographic Services at The Royal Library, Windsor Castle, and to Richard

*Variously offered as 'Crul'. (*See page 6*)

Callaghan of the Redoubt Museum, West Sussex Combined Services: from Richard and from Major John Ainsworth, acting for the Trustees of the Royal Sussex Regimental Association, I acquired valuable information on James Cockburn's regiment, the 35th Regiment of Foot. To complement this, The Prince Consort Library at Aldershot kindly furnished a photocopy of Richard Trimen's *Historical Memoir of the 35th Royal Sussex Regiment of Foot*.

Alan Readman of the West Sussex County Records Office, for alerting me to the location of the record of Edward Drewe's court martial and to Robert Cupido, Librarian of the Toronto Metropolitan Library for making a copy available to me and for interest and good wishes for this endeavour.

My Editor, Bryan Watkins brought a much-needed order to a turmoil of incident and chronology. I am not the first author to acknowledge that shrewd guidance and I do so with special pleasure.

The very fact of this book's existence is owed to my publisher Leo Cooper. Leo gambled on a few pages of synopsis in the belief that the project represented an exciting contribution to the literature. For that faith he underwent the anxieties of its protracted gestation with good humour and encouragement at all times for his new author. This work is offered in the sincere hope that it will justify the patience and goodwill I have enjoyed during our happy association.

Ronald Hurst
Woodley
January 1996

PROLOGUE

This book is concerned with the capture of a small island in the Caribbean in the year 1781 and with the effect of that happening on the lives of some of the people who were involved.

The British seized St Eustatius from the Dutch in order to put an end to its role as a major supplier of arms and necessities to the American rebels during the War of Independence. There could be no resistance, as will be seen, but we should not anticipate our chapters: here, it will be enough merely to identify a single episode of history and to set out time and place. What follows is a statement of intent.

The story described in this work is supported by appropriate contemporary records: that is, by documents preserved in national archives and in collections otherwise housed. The historical researcher today benefits, in addition, from the existence of a substantial and dedicated bibliography, from the opportunity for co-operation and from methods of information retrieval previously unimagined. Yet it has been this author's good fortune that others who have touched on the story of St Eustatius have generally busied themselves with a much larger canvas. Britain's attempt to stem the tide of the American Revolution enmeshed her further in war against France, Spain and Holland: it is, of course, the major issues of this period and their interplay of interests, governments, fleets and armies which have so largely influenced the literature.

So too have these issues inspired critical studies of the great figures in that contest. There are, for example, no less than four different biographies of the Commander-in-Chief in the Caribbean, Admiral Sir George Brydges Rodney. His co-Commander, Lieutenant-General Sir John Vaughan – overshadowed in this, as in so many other aspects of his partnership with Rodney – has not been as well served: but nevertheless, his Papers have been preserved in the Clements Library at Ann Arbor, Michigan and in part, in the British Public Record Office. Equally, there is no dearth of biographical information on Admiral Sir Samuel Hood and the Secretary of State for War and the Colonies, Lord George Germain – their numbers are doubtless legion but, if we are so minded, we can learn a great deal about all those who came to the forefront of public, military or naval affairs during the years of the American War of Independence.

It is more difficult to seek out the stories of individuals who have not left so deep a mark. For so many of these, there are no copious diaries, no perceptively edited Letter-Books and Order-Books and more often, no first-hand documentary record whatsoever. In the case of others, one must delve among the invoices of merchants, correspondence (where it exists), newspapers of the time, the logbooks of ships, the reports of legal actions – dustier files, too frequently asleep in more inconvenient locations and often discovered by chance rather than application. Here, indeed, are the moments when the hopeful researcher opens shabby and torn covers to be rewarded by a joyful find, rich in its reflection of human experience and significant as another, hitherto missing piece, of that jigsaw to be assembled in these pages.

− I −

'STATIA': THE GOLDEN ROCK

It is known in the region as 'Statia'. At the height of its fame in the last thirty years of the eighteenth century, the small island of St Eustatius was the richest trading centre of the Caribbean: hence it became known too as 'The Golden Rock'. Its reputation for earnest dedication to the business of making money is paralleled today by that of Hong Kong.

The island's wealth came on the one hand from the export to Europe of American and Caribbean products, mainly coffee, sugar, hides, indigo and rum, and on the other, from the sales of imported manufactures – such as iron and tinware, textiles clothing and shoes, all eagerly sought by America as well as by Statia's island neighbours. This mutually pleasing and efficient commerce however, conducted for most of the century by the Dutch, French, American and English traders of St Eustatius, and also by its fewer Swedes, Danes, Russians and Irish, came to an abrupt end on 3 February, 1781. This book is the story of how this event came about and of what happened on that day and afterwards, of the soldiers and sailors who wrought the cataclysm and of the people who suffered or profited from this tide.

The prosperity of St Eustatius as a free port, long established by the Dutch, was to be demolished by the British for two excellent reasons.

St Eustatius, on 16 November, 1776, had committed the sin of being the first foreign territory officially to recognise the Grand Union Flag of rebel America, flown by the brig-of-war *Andrew Doria*, commanded by Captain Isaiah Robinson of the one year-old Continental Navy.

The recently adopted flag was, of course, completely unknown to the officer in command of the battery at Fort Oranje, Abraham Ravene, but it was customary to acknowledge the dipped colours and gun salute of arriving vessels. With the flexibility for which the island was noted – and possibly a puzzled shrug – he therefore obliged with a formal nine shots from the Fort.

This gaffe – for it is certain that the political consequences had not been envisaged by the Commander of the island, Johannes de Graaff, who is said to have been consulted by Ravene – might have been and indeed, appeared for a short time to have been, assuaged with diplomatic apologies and censure for the Governor, who at the insistence of the British, was recalled to The Hague to answer for this resoundingly tactless gesture: but it was impossible, as relations between Britain and the Netherlands deteriorated and the struggle in America developed in all its ferocity, to ignore the second offence: namely, the crucial role of St Eustatius in sustaining the rebellion with shipments of arms and gunpowder for its troops and essentials for its upstart navy.

For this enterprise the island traders had devised their own ploys to overcome official interference: there was most certainly none from Governor de Graaff, notoriously vigilant only for his own profit. By and large it was possible for the traders to ignore anti-contraband decrees emanating from Holland: as for the inquisitive British and their patrolling vessels, the tiresome matter of clearances and papers validating ship and cargo was not regarded as an insurmountable obstacle. The Royal Navy's obsessive scrutiny of these documents – and perhaps the sense of humour of the officer intercepting an allegedly innocuous merchantman – were repeatedly tested by the outrageous falsifications endemic in the Caribbean. In this practice Statian merchants were second to none: barrels of rum and sugar according to the ship's papers were not always what they were claimed to be, and under similar guise went those lethal supplies for the rebels, ammunition as 'fruit' and gunpowder as 'grain'.

* * *

Much furious recrimination notably by the near apoplectic British ambassador at The Hague, Sir Joseph Yorke, was met with injured if transparent protest by the States General: but by its nature and because Dutch sympathies were inimical to British purposes, there was, in fact, little of effect which could be done about the contraband trade. It is a recurrent theme in history that embargoes invite profitable evasion and here, half-hearted Dutch decrees prohibiting the export of war material neither placated the British nor deterred the arms dealers and their co-operative merchant captains.

The political events of the drift to war are described in Chapter 3: for now it suffices that the unacceptable possibility that Holland might join a defensive coalition of the neutral Northern Powers and so out-gun Britain at sea forced the issue: it was a situation to be resolved in only one fashion and accordingly Britain declared war on the Netherlands on

20 December, 1780. The necessary pretext was the capture at sea of the unfortunate agent of the Continental Congress, Henry Laurens, and the discovery among his papers – in a bag which obstinately refused to sink when thrown overboard – of a draft proposing a treaty between America and Holland. The ensuing demand presented by the British ambassador that the States General should repudiate any such intent and that the Dutch correspondents should be punished, was neither issued nor received with any hope of compliance: but that formality satisfied, war followed. The Netherlands and all her possessions in the Antilles were now prey to British guns and high on that list, uneasily aware of impending crisis but nevertheless wholly preoccupied with its flagrant traffic, was the festering thorn represented by the tiny island of St Eustatius.

*   *   *

No more than five miles in length and approximately two and a half miles at its widest span, St Eustatius, known in the region as 'Statia', is, as noted above, a Dutch possession in the Caribbean. Specifically, its chief settlement, Oranjestad is in latitude 17 degrees 29 North and on the line of longitude 62 degrees 59 West. The body of the island is skewed on a north-west/south-east axis between two seas: its eastern and windward shores look on the Atlantic Ocean and its western and leeward coast, the Caribbean Sea.

St Eustatius is among the most northerly of the Leeward Islands, stationed almost at the top of that great chain, the Windward and Leeward islands. This chain begins at its most southerly with Trinidad, a mere fifteen miles off the northern coast of Venezuela: from here, it rises to the northwest in a shallow arc covering some seven hundred miles, to make its final landfall by way of the Virgin Islands at Puerto Rico.

It might be less irksome if we abandon this form of instruction: the endpaper indicates Statia's position, that of her neighbours and the long haul necessary to reach North America and Europe under sail.

*   *   *

The climate is hot and, in the summer rains, can be distressingly humid. It is, in addition, a difficult terrain: a minimal central plain permits some farming and the rearing of livestock, predominantly goats. There are cattle in small numbers and fowl and there is the sea, with its staples of fish, lobster and crab.

The plain separates two inhospitable ranges of volcanic hills, happily extinct, and clothed in dense rain forest. Over the centuries Statia's heights and bays have been identified by a fine variety of names: the larger features of the northern range, beginning at the headland and travelling south are thus, Boven, the Bomba and Gilboa hills, Bergje, Panga, or Signal Hill, of much relevance to this story.

In the south-east the plain gives on to two significant heights, the Round Hill, lodged like an off-centre buckle on Statia's girth and, at the extremity of the island, the two-thousand foot cone known as The Quill. Some few isolated houses shelter in the lee of the hills but the greater number of Statia's eighteen hundred people live in Oranjestad or in its vicinity.

* * *

With its sister islands, Saba and St Martin, St Eustatius is a component of the northern group of the Dutch Lesser Antilles. Until 1986, the southern group, 500 miles distant, included Aruba but now consists only of Curaçao and Bonaire. All three islands are huddled together above the Gulf of Venezuela: save for some unrealised ill-intent on the part of the British, these places are peripheral to the events to be described and can safely be left there.

* * *

The north-east coast has two features of importance to this story. First is the narrow strip of beach called Jenkins' Bay over which rears a wall of cliff: 300 feet of red clay and razor-edged rock, clothed by saddles of dark green and hemmed with its scree of boulders and fallen stone. This wall faithfully follows the island's contour: but at the crest barely a half-mile below Jenkins' Bay is all that remains of a battery, where the corroded barrels of cannon are strewn in the rough grass. The Dutch colonists named this post Tommelendijk, which for the English became Tumble Down Dick. But the six and eight pounders and even the eighteen pounders have surrendered at last to mere scrap dealers and souvenir hunters, so that, from the sea, there remains no sign of Tumble Down Dick's long vanished battery.

The cliff wall continues around Interloper's Bay until the face opens to reveal the harbour, the settlement of Oranjestad and its guardian, Fort Oranje dominating the sea approach. A copybook fort this, with its brave Dutch flag snapping aloft and the grey stones of its embrasured walls irregularly set and bound by a web of white mortar. Within are quarters and a powder house and, along the seaward wall, an artful disposition of cannon. Landside, a moat: dry now and bridged by a metalled walkway giving free access from town to Fort. The original drawbridge has

4

gone and only the brightly painted yellow portals remain: but over the gateway, fresh and lively, are now the arms of the Netherlands Antilles.

The dwellings about the Fort comprise the Upper Town, the most populated level of the island. Below, at sea-level is the Lower Town, now no more than a foreshore running the length of Oranjestad Bay and edged with the long, palm-lined avenue called the Bay Road.

Along the beach, for perhaps a mile are two staggered files of broken stonework, all that remains of what were once the warehouses for the island's vast sea-commerce. Enough is left of their walls to inform the curious: two or three feet high or sometimes even approaching what must have been their full height, it is possible to see the ordered siting of these buildings, the layout of rooms within, basements and the sockets of roof joists. Whatever befell them – and we shall learn something of that – has been made irreversible by two centuries of weathering and neglect: these stones make excellent ballast and building material and many tons have been taken away for these purposes. Yet there is still more than enough to carpet the length of this beach and the area of the sites with a deep layering of jumbled stones: beds now for shell and weed and all else washed up by this sea.

* * *

For this book we seek some memory of the people who lived here, or who came here in the critical year of 1781. This evocation is to be found in the Upper Town, on the road called Kerkweg, where stand the ruins of the Dutch Reformed Church. The arched entrance is graced by an iron gate but it is unlocked: it lacks only a notice saying that the eighteenth century lies within.

Strangers to this graveyard need patience. These memorials and so many of their inscriptions have also yielded to time, as indeed, has the entire fabric of the church. But in a lonely corner formed by one side of the square tower and an adjacent wall there is a simple grave topped by a cracked slab:

Brigadier General Ogilvy
Commandant of the Island
of
St Eustatius
and
Its Dependencies
. . . who died, Universally Lamented
May 31st, 1781
Aged 58 years

The cracks run deep in the stone but these words are legible:

> . . . This marble is erected by his afflicted friends of the 13th Regiment, in which he served forty years . . . as a testimony of their regard . . .

Struggling to set out his letters on that narrow slab, the sculptor found it easier to end Ogilvie's name with a 'y'. We shall see what else was set in train by this man's death: meanwhile another of our characters shares the ironic peace of this burial place.

Not far from Ogilvie's grave is the low rounded tomb of the Dutch Admiral Willem Crul . . . 'the brave Crul, last of de Ruiter's strain' . . . born in Haarlem, in 1721 and killed in action on 4 February, 1781 . . . '. . . aboard the line-of-battle ship *Mars*, near the island of Sombrero . . . while defending a convoy which had sailed from St Eustatius only to be overtaken by a superior English force . . .'

Statian earth covers a number of nameless British soldiers and sailors, the majority taken by the endemic sickness which felled Ogilvie. Perhaps death was too common among them and the grieving for them too far away, although they might be found as the individuals they once were in surviving muster rolls, if not in regimental histories. The author has so far found only those which designate the lowly fallen as 'private men' or 'NCO's'. Common sailors likewise: where such documents still exist, the ship's muster book is usually their only memorial.

In 1781 the population of St Eustatius was 'reckoned to be about 1200 whites among whom are people of all nations and about 1600 negroes'. There are traces of this white community in a later cemetery, although its rugged wildness calls for some determination. But it is possible to find, among others, the grave of Johannes Heyliger, who once commanded this island, and the larger tomb of the 18th century merchants Cuvelje, John Packard and Henry Jennings, son of that Richard Downing Jennings, who was one of Statia's richest and most remarkable residents. Much more will be heard of Richard Downing Jennings and of some of his fellow islanders; and something too, of those others who have left a legacy here. The people of all nations included a community of Jewish traders and merchants, a bubbling kettle of Sephardic Jews – Spanish and Portuguese refugees from the murderous Inquisition – and Ashkenazim, those Jews of German and East European descent who differed from the others, often to the point of violence, in matters of ritual, group culture and esoteric language. For trade or social purposes, both groups could offer a range of European languages but among themselves, the

Sephardim spoke Ladino, the admixture of old Castilian and Hebrew while the Ashkenazim made use of Yiddish: it will save us from entering a philological swamp if we agree to call this a corrupted medieval German.

Sixty-three Jewish names, meticulously separated from the names of their Christian fellow-residents, appear on the alphabetical list of Burghers drawn up by the island secretary, Alexander Lejeune on 20 February, 1781. A few names which do not appear on that list can be found in a coerced declaration of 'length of residence' made three days later.

It is estimated that this community consisted of 101 men and their families. With the material and moral assistance of their brethren of Curaçao and Amsterdam, the Jews of St Eustatius built a splendid synagogue to which they gave the title *Honen Dalim* . . . The One who is merciful to the poor. The still impressive shell of that building is here, between the Kerkweg and the lane known as the Synagogepad: some little way beyond, on the Prinsesweg, is their own goat-cropped burial place, with the great mound of The Quill for background: and, for those who pushed the bier along that sad road, a glimpse of the sea which brought them to this last haven.

These people too, are part of this story.

* * *

Statia's great day is 16 November, the anniversary of that first salute to American independence. A plaque in the courtyard of Fort Oranje commemorates the event and is the focus of an annual parade conducted with as much solemnity as Statians can manage, which is not much: therefore there is also laughter, excitement and horseplay, particularly among the children. It is interesting to quiz them or even Statian adults on the meaning of the strange procession rounding off the festivities: a mock funeral, headed by a sham clergyman, complete with beaming pall-bearers, coffin and train of swaying Statian ladies, all equally amused by their participation.

The coffin is said to contain money which is being hidden in this way from the dread figure who despoiled the island for ever. The spirit of this bogeyman also resides in the coffin and the children giggle in delicious terror of his sudden reappearance.

The name of this demon was Rodney, the British Admiral who seized and held St Eustatius in 1781. His is a splendid name in naval history, recalling 'one of Britain's greatest sea-officers'. It is, therefore, ranked with the names of the Royal Navy's most illustrious figures, Nelson,

Blake and Hawke and it is honoured in Britain, in St Paul's Cathedral and in the church of the quiet Hampshire village of Old Alresford, where he lies. Yet in St Eustatius, the name of Rodney is derided in a bathetic pantomime: it seems a paradox, but we shall find that both memorials are well earned.

– 2 –

RODNEY, VAUGHAN AND COCKBURN

The blow would fall on Statia in due course and when it did, its people would find that the reality of British might was represented by three of King George's officers. Two of these – Admiral Sir George Brydges Rodney and Major-General Sir John Vaughan, shared the command of the British expeditionary force which seized St Eustatius. The third man was Lieutenant-Colonel James Cockburn of the 35th Regiment of Foot, who was to become the Military Governor of the captured island.

Since we are concerned with the manner in which these men interpreted their duties it will be useful to learn something of them in advance of their mission to the Antilles.

*   *   *

RODNEY

Save for one revelation which will be noted, this is a familiar outline: but there is much else to relate and for our own purposes we need to find Rodney on the eve of his most controversial capture. To arrive at that year we must cover the ground in leaps.

George Brydges, the second son of Henry and Mary Rodney was baptized on 13 February, 1718, at the church of St Giles-in-the-Fields, London. George had been born into a family of the minor gentry and although his parents were in modest circumstances – which would decline into an even worse predicament – young George was to benefit from the saving grace of family connections. Thus, his father Henry, went to live

9

at Walton-on-Thames and married Mary, eldest daughter of Sir Henry Newton, a diplomat in the reign of Queen Anne and a judge of the High Court of Admiralty. Mary's sister, Catherine, chose a loftier union and married Lord Aubrey Beauclerk, son of the Duke of St Albans, a naval officer whose brother Lord Vere, was to become one of the Lords of Admiralty: with the Brydges/Chandos connection all of these ramifications gave access to the most influential quarters. And happily so: by 1724, Henry and Mary had become the parents of five children, growing progressively poorer meanwhile as the result of Henry's financial misfortunes. The couple were lucky indeed that when both credit and hope were at last exhausted, the mechanism of family 'interest' was in place to rescue the children.

* * *

There is a cloudiness about the next few years in the life of the young Rodney: it is believed that he was brought up by his godfather, George Brydges at Avington, in Hampshire and that at an appropriate age he went to Harrow. This period of his life is without firm record and it is not until his entry into the Navy in July, 1732, at the age of fourteen, that Rodney emerges with certainty as a 'King's Letter Boy' borne – nominally at least – on the books of a guardship, HMS *Sunderland*. The special entrée facilitated by the King's Letter reflects the influential connections which were to be employed on Rodney's behalf at critical stages of his career. These efforts were, of course, particularly important during the apprentice years of service: coupled with the benevolence of three of his earliest captains – Captain Medley of the *Dreadnaught* (60), who elevated Rodney to midshipman in November 1734, that useful uncle, Lord Aubrey Beauclerk, who took his nephew aboard his 24-gun frigate, *Dolphin* some five years later as an 'acting officer' and Captain Francis Holburne who succeeded Beauclerk in the *Dolphin* on 18 February, 1740. On that day Rodney, aged twenty-one, received his commission as lieutenant.

The shortcomings of his formal education were now handsomely overlaid by his professional experience. There is unfortunately no account of Rodney's first years at sea but the common lot of such newcomers is well known and we may take it that Rodney shared it. It would certainly have begun with the searing impact of the dark and rat-ridden depths within those elegant ships in which he would eat, sleep and live as best he might with other sea-smitten young gentlemen categorized as captains' servants or midshipmen.

As potential officers, these youngsters would have been spared the worst degradations of shipboard life: they might eat execrable food and grow accustomed to weevily ships' biscuit, to the stink and filth of hundreds of men jammed into their sea-going styes and to their own cramped quarters not vastly better: but they were at least separated from the ruck and, of course, protected from them by their status, though not from each other or their seniors who, for better or worse, would be their mentors. In port or at sea, in home or in foreign waters they would learn: the anatomy of a ship of war from keel to masthead, the power of its armament, the intricacies of rigging, the dynamics and handling of sail and the mathematics of navigation. Above all, they would be expected to carry out their tasks in any weather, cold, wet and with little sleep and in that state of misery which inspired Dr Johnson to liken life in the Navy to a 'life in jail with the chance of being drowned.'

But Rodney would not agree with Johnson that jail commonly offered better company. In this society the survivors would feel themselves ennobled and bonded by the ideal of the King's service, although they would become inevitably calloused by its occurrences and customs. No cat-o'-nine tails fell on their own backs but they were not spared from witnessing that punishment being used on others – retaken deserters and sailors deemed negligent, to have otherwise transgressed or to have been unwisely 'insolent' or labelled so. Peace-time or no, men fell from the yards, or drowned or died of disease or in accidents. In port, women came aboard, many of them wives but the majority prostitutes operating in the fervid, crowded rutting-house of the lower deck.

It was not ground in which a youth could be shielded or his innocence long survive: but here again, the unremitting harshness and the earthy realities of life in the Navy have been thoroughly documented. It remains only to say that by the time of his majority and in these circumstances, the erstwhile King's Letter Boy of tender age had clearly developed the necessary steel for his chosen calling. Years on, the boy become an Admiral would have no hesitation in approving the hanging of six mutineers before the eyes of his assembled fleet.

In modern eyes this represents a harsh and terrible decision: harsh and terrible indeed, but one which was entirely in the spirit of the century and specifically, of the eighteenth century Navy. That Rodney acted as a product of both does not make a monster of a man acknowledged to be one of the greatest seamen in English history, despite his marked concern with the claims of prize money.

Save for that preoccupation with money – and we shall shortly find the cause – it was, in any event, a characteristic shared then, as now, by all without aspirations for sainthood. There is another side to Rodney: '. . . Four seamen, supernumaries in the *Princess Royal*, petitioned the Admiralty to serve in the *Sheerness* under Captain Rodney. Sailors are quick to perceive the qualities, good and bad, in their officers, and later in Rodney's career such petitions recur with pleasing frequency.' *

There could be no greater compliment to anyone set in authority over others: but stern and autocratic Rodney certainly could be, although his letters show that he did not lack tact whenever that seemed advisable. One might ask what other kind of Commander-in-Chief he should have been, or in that capacity, as his great fleet lay before St Eustatius, what else he should have written to Philip Stephens at the Admiralty on 5 March, 1781:

> A dangerous conspiracy having been entered into by several men belonging to His Majesty's cutter the *Sylph*, to rise in mutiny to seize and destroy the officers, and carry the cutter either to America or to a French port, and having been happily discovered by a marine, whom they attempted to delude to join them in their villainous design, I ordered the affair to be inquired into at a court martial, when six men were found guilty and condemned to death . . .

It is brutal, but it is not Rodney's alleged brutality:

> . . . So atrocious a deed, deserving of no pardon and the very existence of the British fleet, and I may say, of the nation, depending upon the strictness of the discipline necessary to be observed in our Navy, in order to prevent treason and mutinies, and to deter others from committing so heinous a crime, determined me to let the law take its course; and this day they were executed accordingly on board the different ships in this road . . .

And before the eyes of their shipmates, some racked few of whom tailed on the ropes and at the signal, hauled those wretches to the yard-arm, high above the uncaring sea because:

> . . . to have pardoned any one after committing so heinous a crime as treason and mutiny, might have induced others to run the same risk; whereas the whole suffering, cut off all hope from men who may commit the same crime, and I am sure will have a good effect, and I hope for ever prevent it. I have long experienced, that where good discipline prevails, there is seldom occasion for punishment . . . Inclosed I transmit the minutes of the court martial, and the original sentence.

* * *

*David Spinney, Rodney, London 1968: hereinafter, Spinney.

Although the chronology of Rodney's service at sea, of his commands and the nature of their tasks is necessarily compressed in this book, since we must now be concerned with other aspects of Rodney's life, this is the outline of his development as a sea-officer.

It can be seen that although influence and connections continued to favour him they were not called on to provide him with any comfortable sinecure but rather, to keep him almost continuously employed at sea. In the context of potential advancement however, Rodney was also fortunate in his times, for Britain's declaration of war on Spain in December, 1739 had anticipated his commission as lieutenant by only a few weeks.

It had never been difficult for Britons to find cause to fight the Spanish at the first roll of a drum and the current antagonism for Spain – ironically, charged with that same interference with shipping which the British, in their turn, were to inflict on other nations – had been brought to the boil by the evidence given to the House in 1738 by a certain Captain Robert Jenkins: not only had the captain sworn to the cruel iniquities of the Spanish coast guard who had boarded his ship in the West Indies and pillaged the vessel, but they had, in addition, cut off his ear: which severed relic Jenkins then displayed to the revolted members of the Committee, lest they had forgotten that this had actually occurred seven years earlier in April 1731.

Nevertheless, the demonstration served its purpose and what then began as the War of Jenkins's Ear was to keep Britain, France and Spain involved in a series of conflicts protracted over the next half-century. It would also provide the springboard for ambitious officers: within two years of his elevation by Admiral Haddock, Lieutenant Rodney became Captain, promoted with astonishing smoothness over the heads of others with more seniority but much less in the way of patronage.

This all-important transition on 9 November, 1742, from the promotion-starved mass of deserving but unrecognised lieutenants was owed to the initiative of Admiral Thomas Mathews, then flying his flag in the 90-gun *Namur*, on service in the Mediterranean. In August, Mathews had written to the Secretary of State, the Duke of Newcastle warmly commending his first lieutenant for a minor, but useful expedition (a landing from 'HM row-boat under your command' to destroy straw and barley intended for the Spanish army) – and, on the transfer of Captain Watson from the *Plymouth*, had followed this up by appointing Rodney to the vacancy. A brief tenure this, though with an even more joyful ending, for that worn-out vessel was soon ordered home: and whatever powers had moved in Rodney's favour were still at work on his arrival at Spithead, when his acting rank of post-captain was immediately confirmed by their Lordships.

There were to be many more ships for this twenty-five-year-old captain, but at this moment we need remind ourselves only of one: it is some fifteen years on, in '57 and it is this captain, in the *Dublin*, who has brought General Amherst to that late rendezvous with Boscawen's fleet off Halifax. Like the moody soldier entrapped on one of the transports, Rodney, too, does not yet know of their impinging destinies: but for the first time he has entered the compass of Lieutenant James Cockburn of the 35th Regiment of Foot.

* * *

A little shore-leave for this sailor. Toughened and educated by the sea, he was less favoured by experiences and relationships on land, for all too many of these were to his disadvantage. Save for the four years of happiness derived from his first marriage in 1753 to Jane, daughter of Charles Compton, brother of the sixth Earl of Northampton, the record on land is blotched with disappointment, frustration and in his financial affairs, rank foolishness. But of that brief idyll there were two sons, George and James: James was to be lost at sea in 1776 while in command of the *Ferret* sloop, but in the difficult times to come for his father, the elder brother was to be the loving prop and provider until Rodney's death in 1792.

Jane died in 1757. There is much evidence of the devastation caused to her husband by this loss, not least that despite a second marriage of some twenty-eight years it is Jane who rests beside him at Old Alresford in the family vault – the entrance 'now lost' – in the sward of the parish church of St Mary the Virgin. She was, proclaims her memorial tablet '. . . an honour to her family and the delight of all who knew her.' . . . and it is transparent in Rodney's letters to Jane that for those fleeting years he shared fully in that gladness.

There is another benchmark in his life at this time. The last weeks of Jane's illness coincided with the disgrace of Admiral Byng, accused of failing in his duty before besieged Minorca and of cravenly abandoning the garrison of Port Mahon to the French.

As a friend of Byng, although critical of his conduct, Rodney could only have been distressed by the resulting summons to serve on Byng's court martial. That classic scapegoat for the ineptitude and malevolence of ministers – who had miserably failed to provide for the mission they had assigned him – paid with his life for the privilege before a firing party on the quarter-deck of the *Monarch*, then commanded by Rodney. It was perhaps the only compensation in the sickness which also laid the captain low beside his dying wife that it permitted him to plead their Lordships for exemption from their bloody design – for it was hardly to be doubted – because of 'a Violent Bilious Cholick'.

* * *

In 1759 Rodney was promoted to rear-admiral. Interest had served him, of course, but the flag also acknowledged his dedicated years of service. After his first command, the *Plymouth*, he had been appointed in '43, to the *Sheerness* (24), then to the *Ludlow Castle* (40) on service in the North Sea under Admiral Vernon, to the *Centurion* (50) and to the *Eagle* (60) . . . all of this service, whether cruising against privateers, patrolling the coast of Scotland during the rebellion of '45, escorting merchant convoys or carrying troops to the Low Countries, giving him the solid basis of seamanship, ship handling and the experience which was thereafter to support his authority. And in June, '47 just before the Peace of Aix-la-Chapelle called a temporary halt to operations – they would be resumed, formally, in '56 to continue as the Seven Years' War – the captain of the *Eagle* indeed benefited from the fortunes of war, in this case represented by two richly laden French convoys, one bound for the East Indies and the second returning from St Domingo, in the West Indies. The first of these convoys fell victim to an intercepting squadron under Admiral Anson and made that already prize-wealthy officer wealthier still. The West Indiamen enriched Commodore Fox and his captains: one of these was Rodney, who was to employ this early cornucopia, from which £8,165 and one shilling spilled into his hands – and even more would come from other prizes – possibly enjoyably but certainly unwisely among the best and the worst of London society.

* * *

In 1764 the young widower married the daughter of John Clies of Lisbon, Henrietta, who gave him three daughters and two sons. The career of the older boy, John can truly be described as 'meteoric' since his father, when Commander-in-Chief of the Leewards in 1780, promoted him from lieutenant to captain at the age of fifteen and a half and after barely one year in the Navy. True, a year filled with action for the boy: aboard his father's flagship, *Sandwich* he had seen the capture of a Spanish convoy, the defeat of Admiral Don Juan de Langara in the famed Moonlight Battle off St Vincent – in which John had commanded a gun – the relief of Gibraltar and the battle of 17 April with De Guichen (so ill-managed and indisciplined on the part of the British fleet, Rodney's instructions and signals so ill-understood by his divisional commanders and captains as to leave the admiral furious for the heads of Rear-Admirals Parker and Rowley, Commodore Hotham and Captains Carkett and Bateman).

But what was a personal disaster for these officers was fighting

15

experience for John, and Rodney, now Sir George, endorsed this in a letter of 30 July, to Lady Rodney:

> John is very well, and has been kept constantly at sea to make him master of his profession. He is now second lieutenant of the *Sandwich*, having risen to it by rotation; but still I send him in frigates; he has seen enough of great battles. All he wants is seamanship, which he must learn. When he is a seaman he shall be captain, but not until then.

Not, in fact, for another two months and a few days: and then a lightning progress in which, on 4 October, John became Master and Commander of the sloop *Pacahunta* (Pocahontas) and 'on the same day' says the DNB* – although to be fair it was ten days before he was posted – Captain of the *Fowey* (24), the guardship at Sandy Hook. But at that time Rodney was indeed Britain's saviour in the West Indies and like other commanders before and since, with enough clout to postpone politically inopportune criticism from Their Lordships: perforce, they resigned themselves to this audacity but their private views must have entertained many.

*   *   *

Yet it was on land that Rodney created and cultivated his greatest misfortune – chronic and ruinous debt. That road he travelled first as a foolhardy young captain attending London's notorious gaming club, White's. In that fashionable den he was clearly out of his depth and no match for White's clientele of wealthy, frivolous, sometimes desperate, but always hardened players risking extraordinary sums on the turn of a card. The unhappy record of his gambling debts can be traced from 1748: thereafter the harvest of insolvency sown at the tables was reaped some twenty-five years on. No matter that in the interim he had earned his place in naval annals and public esteem: that respect was not shared by his creditors and in 1775 he was forced eventually into ignominious flight to France in order to escape them.

It is chastening to see what real attainments and honours were concealed in that fugitive figure: but this was the same man who had become a rear-admiral in '59 and whose squadron of bomb-ketches and other vessels had eliminated an immediate threat to his country by promptly demolishing a French invasion fleet gathered at Havre: who in '61 became Commander-in-Chief at the Leeward Islands and from there took Martinique, St Lucia, Grenada and St Vincent: who had become a vice-admiral in '62 and who had returned to England in triumph to be

*The Dictionary of National Biography, London 1897, p.87.

16

created a baronet in '64 in recognition of his services: and who, in November of the next year, had been appointed Governor of Greenwich Hospital. This post he held for five years during which he . . . 'suggested and insisted on several measures conducive to the comfort and well-being of the (naval) pensioners.' It is to be noted that his suggestions and insistence were in the face of an entrenched administrative *laissez faire* which required all of Rodney's determination and genuine feeling for the old seamen for its undoing.

The same man. We should look now at what was a further and perhaps the most damaging contribution to that humiliation, namely Rodney's decision to contest the Northampton election of 1767–68.

* * *

To serve the nation as a member of Parliament is a prideful enough endeavour for any person. Perhaps this thought motivated many eighteenth century naval officers but there were other encouragements to explain the large number of admirals and captains with seats in the House. That 'the best club in England' was an 'agreeable' venue for men of standing was one attraction, but even better was the fact that a naval officer in Parliament was to be preferred by the Admiralty for any vacant command. Backs were obligingly scratched in this case, for in return, the minister could rely on the dutiful exercise of his nominee's vote. And nominate their sailor protégés the ministers did, precisely for this reason: for navy-struck dockyard constituencies and for all kinds of rotten boroughs with no more than a handful of voters whose allegiance by bribery or coercion could be taken for granted.

For Commodore Rodney in command of the 50-gun *Rainbow* and for the past three years Governor of Newfoundland – which title meant that he was guardian of the fisheries – the opportunity to avail himself of these advantages came as early as 1751. A convenient by-election found him nominated and then elected for Saltash in Cornwall, courtesy of his patron, John Cleveland, Clerk of the Admiralty: an elevation which eased Rodney into the successive commands of the *Kent*, the *Fougueux*, the *Prince George* and the *Monarch*. In 1751, these appointments to the guardships at Portsmouth lay in the future but the rich promise of such favours was there and, as the chronology shows, was clearly fulfilled.

His tenure in Parliament was less striking. Displaced in '54 by a more useful protégé, Admiral Clinton, the ex-member for Saltash at length became the member for Okehampton, in '59 and for Penryn, in Cornwall, in '61. The nominations for these seats had been in the gift of a patron very much more distinguished than Clevland, no less than the very head of the Government, the Duke of Newcastle, but this pleasant state of affairs yielded inevitably to the passage of time and the arrival of new men in power, whose favour was to be bestowed elsewhere. Thus, in '68 it became necessary for Rodney to find a new constituency: Northampton offered and was won, but success in this came dearly. It is estimated that the seat cost him some £30,000, crippling his fortunes beyond any possibility of redemption and thus compounding the relentless pressures and demands of his creditors which produced the man we shall find at St Eustatius.

*   *   *

The years of peace after the Seven Years' War were of little delight to men who lived and were advanced by making war. Fortunate though Rodney was to have the appointment at Greenwich, the year 1770 found him made desperate by his debts and for employment which would at once, remove him from the danger of a final and hopeless confrontation and even, by way of prize-money, relieve him for ever from that threat.

Yet it seemed, in that year, that the opportunity had arrived, created by the forcible eviction by a Spanish force of British settlers at Port Egmont, West Falkland. The subsequent preparations by which Britain signalled her readiness for yet another bout with Spain included the strengthening of the Navy in the West Indies: true, there were others anxious for this command but their cause was lost when the First Lord of the Admiralty, Sir Edward Hawke, was succeeded by Rodney's admirer of long standing, Lord Sandwich. But although happy enough to oblige Rodney in the matter of the command at Jamaica, Sandwich drew the line at the admiral's request that he might also retain his appointment at Greenwich Hospital. In consequence, as the Spanish threat and its potential for prize-money failed to materialise in the next three years and as Rodney failed in his plea to succeed the lately deceased Governor of Jamaica in that office, the Jamaica station proved to be a pleasant interlude for Sir George and his family, but a wholly unprofitable one.

Nor, he found, on his return to England in August '74, had his debts diminished or his duns become less aggressive. It might have helped had he actually received the pay due to him since his promotion to Rear-Admiral of England in '71, but this was mired in the complexities of so many of his expedients to stave off disaster. One of these had been to commit his pay to the most dangerous of his creditors, leaving him with only one recourse. To escape arrest and a debtors' prison, Sir George Brydges Rodney, the Rear-Admiral of England who had already served his country with so much honour and to such effect, must fly before them like any shabby defaulter. Accordingly, says the DNB with touching delicacy, 'he retired to France at the beginning of 1775, and for the next four years or more lived in Paris.'

The words conceal a vast humiliation which would surface at the height of his power in 1781 to provoke an even greater personal disaster.

* * *

Much of the above sketch of Rodney's career, as previously remarked, is merely a gallop through familiar sources: they will not be further raided to describe that sojourn in exile, for other characters await their entry: but during those years of skulking in Paris, much futile energy was spent by Sir George and Henrietta in soliciting the First Lord for the release of the emoluments withheld by the Admiralty.

'. . . I have enquired at the Navy Office' Sandwich replied to Lady Rodney on 1 October, 1766, '. . . and I find that Sir George Rodney has now no Imprest against him' (Rodney's less than convincing accounts for expenditure of public funds while in Jamaica had been doggedly challenged by the Navy Board) . . . 'but what there is due to him must go to those who are legally empowered to receive it and the Admiralty can no way interfere in that business, especially as I understand there are more Claimants than one . . .'

No luck either in soliciting for a command, as Sandwich told the admiral in November, 1777. '. . . however painful it must be to me I can not avoid telling you that I do not think your object of obtaining a foreign command can be met with success . . .'

It is not entirely clear how the Rodneys had lived in Paris although in that city, too, creditors would at length force the admiral to the wall. But Spinney suggests that '. . . he was sufficiently in pocket (or credit), in the autumn of 1775 to buy his son George some handsome embroidered waistcoats which were much admired when they arrived: and there is more than a suspicion that he was gambling again . . .' That suspicion reached London and brought the reproof of a friend, John Marr, who had gone out to Jamaica with Rodney as purser: '. . . a report reached the Admiralty that you was every night at a public gaming house . . . and that you played as much as ever . . .'

That year saw the beginning of armed rebellion in America, that resounding shot at Lexington's rude bridge, heard, as Emerson wrote . . . 'round the world'. The bloody nose dealt out to the British as their soldiers retreated to Boston had cost enough of their lives to signal a crisis for royal authority. Soon it was to become an unwinnable war, compounded in 1778 by the declared intent of France to join the rebel cause.

Mortified by his own inactivity as these great events unfolded before him, Sir George saw the possibility of employment at last: but by that year of '78 his debts in Paris had assumed the menace of those in England and his dilemma was plain. He could not leave France – indeed would be prevented from doing so – until those debts, – 'amounting to about £600' – were paid. And while he was trapped in Paris, the vision of a new command remained merely a vision and one that must eventually fade.

How desperate he had become and how much he hoped that he might be helped to return to serve his own country is revealed in this extract from a letter to Henrietta – now in poor health in England – dated 11th March:

> Not hearing from either you or my son by the last messenger gives me uneasyness inexpressible as the delay . . . obliges me to remain in the hotel where I am at an expense I could wish to avoid and daily adds to the sum I already owe for Board and Lodging. I beg you will desire my son to see Lord North again either at his House or Levee . . . delays are worse than Death especially at this Critical time when every hour teems with momentary expectations of war . . .

*　*　*

So much for recorded biography. We now turn to the astonishing manner in which Sir George is said to have been relieved of his financial burdens in France and here we must trespass on legend.

All of Rodney's biographers are in agreement that at this critical moment, Louis-Antoine de Gontaut, Duc de Biron and Marshal of France, came forward to advance one thousand Louis to Rodney to enable him to pay his debts: because, said the Marshal, it was an acknowledgement of French regard for Rodney's services to his country. And all are agreed on the magnificence of this gesture by the man described by Spinney as:

> . . . an alert and active old man of seventy-six, (who) represented all that was finest in the *ancien régime*. Bearer of an historic name and a professional soldier of the highest distinction . . . he was universally respected as a man of the strictest honour and undeviating principles. That he should go out of his way to smooth Sir George's path is a moving instance of disinterested generosity and chivalrous fellow-feeling: but it is also a striking testimony of the impact made by Sir George's personality upon the best society in Paris.

Hm . . . which convenient literary device must indicate a lifted eyebrow. A more realistic appraisal of this incident – and indisputedly, of its consequences – is to be found in the refreshing earthiness of the historian, Claude Manceron, writing of the arrival of Admiral de Grasse off the Chesapeake in the summer of 1781:

De Grasse is still rabid on the subject of that old imbecile of a Maréchal de Biron . . . the senile dodderer in command of the Paris military forces, whom he has to thank for the last five months on his lonesome facing Rodney-the-Death, the most dreaded fighter on the high seas. Because, four years ago Rodney was a prisoner on parole in Paris, brought to bay by a mountain of debt. A true man of the sea, a man of memorable broadsides.

But Biron wanted to play tea-party war: 'it is inadmissible that we should be deprived of an adversary of your quality. I shall stand surety for your debts.'

Proponents of the knightly courtesies might ponder Manceron's next thoughts:

Rodney didn't need to be told twice, and since that day he has been spicing up George III's navy with that incomparable punch whose secret has been handed down in the heat of battle from every admiral since Drake to every midshipman in the Royal Navy: the art of striking at the right moment with the most force. But it's de Grasse, not Biron, who's having to swallow the stuff: Biron is gazing at the flowers in the gardens of the Palais Royal*.

*   *   *

One more suggestion, conceivably bearing on de Biron's magnanimity: this time by the author, and not to be found in the DNB or in any of the four biographies of Rodney:

While in Paris Sir George Brydges Rodney became a member of a Secret Society and Masonic Club, rue Saint Nicaise. He was elected under an assumed name: on disclosing his real one, at the instance of the Duc de Biron, Marshal of France, his debts were paid and a banquet given in his honour . . .

The source of this information is of far too thunderous a title to await any bibliography. The natural curiosity of readers therefore may be satisfied by reference to the work by Robert Freke Gould (Gale & Polden, London & Aldershot, 1899) which treats of *Military Lodges 1732–1899: The Apron and the Sword, or Freemasonry under Arms, being an account of Lodges in Regiments and Ships of war and of famous soldiers and sailors (of all countries) who have belonged to the Society.*'

It is almost anticlimax to return to Sir George.

*   *   *

*Claude Manceron: *The Wind from America* (Touchstone, New York 1974) p.183.

It was now possible to leave France with dignity and a note-of-hand for that providential thousand Louis or 'twenty-four thousand livres.' That debt of honour at least, as between mutually respected gentlemen and not concerning mere tradesmen or importunate gambling partners was repaid at once, doubtless by extraordinary efforts. Such efforts were also needed to ensure that the admiral could live in London and in like case, the recognised solution was for the debtor to find a 'liberty' – a refuge in the Royal shadow and thus barred by ancient privilege to his creditors. In this, Rodney succeeded. No furtive hole, but a comfortable lodging behind one of the elegant porticos of Cleveland Row, in the very environs of St James's Palace: from where he watched the further disasters heaped on Britain by the Colonists.

More usefully, Sir George now came to some bearable agreement with his creditors and in January 1779, even saw the Navy Board at last release his Admiral's pay. Meanwhile he noted the angry schism among senior officers resulting from the dispute between Admirals Keppel and Palliser, following their unsatisfactory action off Ushant. The significance of this for Rodney was that no flag-officer of calibre would thereafter agree to serve under Lord Sandwich and while the imperative at the Admiralty was now to replace Byron in the West Indies, the First Lord could call on no alternative and equally strong candidate.

The conditions were finally to Rodney's advantage: careful cultivation of Lord George Germain in his role as Secretary of State for the Colonies and a last appeal to Sandwich bore fruit on 1 October. Indeed, his Lordship had little choice and on that day, the 61-year old former fugitive, Admiral of the White Sir George Brydges Rodney, was appointed Commander-in-Chief of His Majesty's Ships and vessels at Barbados and the Leeward Islands and the seas adjoining.

*   *   *

The euphoria would give way quickly to sober contemplation of his mission. With twenty-two ships of the line to protect the enormous convoy in his charge – including sixty merchantmen and thirty-seven supply vessels and transports that he must see safely on their way to the West Indies and Portugal (the Indies-bound convoy carried the 88th and 89th Regiments, recruits for the 60th and the newly-appointed Commander-in-Chief of the British land forces in the Lesser Antilles, Major-General Sir John Vaughan) – Rodney was to:

> . . . proceed to Gibraltar, relieve the fortress, send a convoy up the Mediterranean to Minorca, then go himself to the West Indies with four ships, leaving his second-in-command, Rear-Admiral Digby, to bring back the empty transports (and) the sick and the wounded from the garrisons.

It will be almost three months before he sails from Spithead and the weeks will be filled with frantic activity: dispositions for his private affairs, farewells for wife and children and always, the endless preparations in hand: for his own flagship, the 90-gun *Sandwich* and in addition, the exasperations of assembling and marshalling merchantmen, ordnance vessels, store-ships, transports and victuallers. In all of this, of course, was the need for endless communication with the captains of HM Ships of War who were to escort them.

To fill this cup came a fervid, ominous exhortation from the First Lord on 8 December urging him to sea in the face of winds which made that end impossible, and which, for another sixteen days, ensured the unmanning of yet another generation of queasy soldiers yearning vainly for dry land.

The business of the flagship included the matter of places aboard her and in this, Rodney made his own decisions and naturally obliged old friends and their nominees as far as was possible. The fourteen-year-old John Rodney came aboard, as we have seen, but another of the admiral's own selections was Dr Gilbert Blane as his personal physician, but later to be appointed Physician to the Fleet. Not only Rodney, but in time the entire navy, would owe this devoted man much for their welfare. And we shall certainly hear more of two other men who occupied significant posts in *Sandwich*, namely the Admiral's secretary, the Reverend William Pagett, who had first sailed with Rodney in the *Marlborough* in '61, and Rodney's flag-captain, Captain Walter Young. Pagett served his master with loyalty and energy: of Young, it is best to leave him to reveal himself in a later chapter.

On 24 December all made sail and *Sandwich* at last left Spithead, as the fulcrum of a convoy some one hundred and fifty strong.

With this voyage Rodney was to begin his greatest phase and for that beginning, all the factors were in his favour. Spain had become an ally of France for her own excellent reasons, chief of these being to wrest back Minorca and Gibraltar from the British. The Spanish declaration of war had therefore been followed by the isolation of Gibraltar from Spain by land and in June '79, by a blockade by sea which by January had produced famine, and all that is dreadfully implied in that word, among the besieged. Mahan* notes that 'At the close of the year 1779, flour in Gibraltar was fourteen guineas the barrel and other provisions in proportion.' Other sources attest that numbers depended for their daily meal on . . . 'Thistles, dandelions, wild leeks etc.' . . . but these statements barely touch on the terrible realities of the siege.

*A T Mahan, *The Major Operations of the Navies in the War of American Independence*, (1912).

23

To relieve Gibraltar therefore was to seek battle, and this opportunity, for Rodney, no brighter road to redemption. Conveniently, the West Indiamen had parted from the main body on 7 January, some three hundred miles west of Finisterre, escorted by the *Phoenix* (44) and three frigates. There were less distractions, at dawn on the 8th (and surely that hallowed prize-hungry gleam of eye in the British men of war), when a procession of strange sail was observed in the north-east. These proved to be a Spanish convoy of sixteen merchantmen escorted by one 64-gun ship of the line and six frigates, all of which made a pathetic show of fight before conceding the impossible odds represented by Rodney's force and sensibly striking their colours.

There was a much better destination for the naval stores and provisions carried by twelve of the merchantmen: the Spanish fleet at Cadiz would mourn but these vessels were now to sail to Gibraltar, their shepherd the erstwhile escort-leader, the *Guipuzcoana*, now renamed *Prince William*, commissioned into British service and manned accordingly. One 74, the *America* and the *Pearl* (32) would be detached from the fleet in order to return to England with the prizes.

The few feeble shots of defiance from the sixty-four represented the first noises of war Sir George had heard since his triumphs in the West Indies seventeen years earlier. Those reports and perhaps even a whiff of powder could only have been relished: but when a number of enemy sail was sighted at one pm on the 16th, as Rodney's fleet was rounding the Cape of St Vincent, the Admiral was abed, the victim of gout afflicting his feet and hands.

It is because of this indisposition that we hear the first of Captain Young in the role of Sir George's mentor. At this time, Young relayed events to his bed-bound superior and credited much to himself for the conduct of the action which followed. It may have been so: Doctor Blane, in attendance on his patient, speaks of 'discussion between the Admiral and the Captain.' But whatever the truth of the matter, the outcome was still a disaster for Spain.

The sighting was that of a Spanish squadron guarding the ring about Gibraltar – a force of eleven sail of the line and two frigates under Admiral Don Juan de Langara, all now aware of their imminent destruction and in the face of it, attempting to head for the sanctuary of Cadiz, one hundred miles to the south-east. They were however, clearly at the mercy of Rodney's eighteen of the line (plus the latest acquisition, *Prince William*) and once again, the disparity made the result inevitable. In the course of the 'general chase' signalled by Rodney, accompanied by his audacious order to engage to leeward, the dangers of a lee shore were deliberately risked to cut off the Spaniards' escape to landward: and meanwhile two further developments added to the drama – the coming of night and of a 'tempestuous' storm throughout those hours.

The encounter is remembered as the Moonlight Battle:

> At 4 pm the signal for battle was made, and a few minutes later the four headmost of the pursuers got into action. At 4.40, one of the Spanish ships, the *Santo Domingo*, 80, blew up with all on board, and at 6 another struck. By this hour, it being January, darkness had set in. A night action therefore followed, which lasted until 2 am when the headmost of the enemy surrendered and all firing ceased . . .

Mahan's dispassionate sentences also spare us too close a view of those shattered vessels: '. . . of the eleven hostile ships of the line, only four escaped. Besides the one blown up, six were taken . . .' These were the *Fenix*, (80), flagship of the Spanish Admiral and five 70-gun ships, the *Monarca, Princesa, Diligente, San Julian* and *San Eugenio*. 'The latter two drove ashore and were lost. The remaining four were brought into Gibraltar and were ultimately added to the navy. All retained their old names, save the *Fenix*, which was renamed *Gibraltar*.'

Their Lordships' instructions had been fulfilled and Spain grieved while Gibraltar rejoiced as only those reprieved can rejoice. In London, Rodney's despatches of 27 January brought the public a new and long-wanted popular hero: the worthies of London conferred on him the Freedom of the City (in a gold casket), while both Lords and Commons declared their admiration and thanks.

Lord Sandwich added his own congratulations, first for Rodney: '. . . you have taken more line-of-battle ships than have been captured in any one action in either of the two last preceding wars . . .' . . . and next, for himself, for his own sagacity in 'pitching upon' such an outstanding commander: and one moreover, who had carried out his mission with brilliance and thereby done so many of the Royal Navy's dissident Admirals in the eye.

Rodney had arrived at Gibraltar on 26 January. The immediate task was completed by sending the storeships and their escorts on to Minorca: following their return, Sir George sailed for the West Indies on 13 February, his squadron now reduced to four 74's – *Sandwich, Ajax, Montagu* and *Terrible*, the *Pegasus* (32) and the captured *San Vincente* (10). His prizes were on their way back to England, but he had permitted one seventy-four, the *Edgar* to remain at the Rock: for which decision their Lordships, alas, tempered their delight – but probably not Sir George's – with a surly admonition for ignoring specific instructions in his orders to do no such thing. '. . . It has given us the trouble and risk of sending a frigate on purpose to order her home immediately . . .'

It could not have troubled the triumphant Admiral overmuch and it is a happy note on which to take leave of him. Rodney arrived at Barbados on 17 March and it is in those waters that we shall meet him again at the end of the year. He gives place now to Major-General Sir John Vaughan, delivered at Barbados on 15 February by the West India convoy, along with his sea-weary troops. In total and intent he would command a corps of 3,500 men, but in this, as in so many other human aspirations, the realities of conditions in the West Indies would have the last word.

*   *   *

VAUGHAN

History has been arbitrary with this man. Nevertheless we need know this largely overlooked General because he will become Rodney's partner in their future embarrassment: but in Vaughan's case there are no distinguished biographers and only a column or so in the Dictionary of National Biography to sum a life noted chiefly for two allegations to his discredit – the burning of Kingston in the State of New York and known as Esopus in 1777 and the grimy business at St Eustatius in '81. This paucity of material is confirmed by a footnote in McLarty, mentioned below, which categorically states that: '. . . The only printed estimates of Vaughan appear in Edna Vosper, *Report on the Sir John Vaughan Papers* in the William L Clements Library (Ann Arbor, 1929) and in the Dictionary of National Biography.' This is cheerful news for the author, about to offer additional material. Some reference to the sources already quoted and to the new discoveries adding weight to this chapter will therefore be helpful.

John Vaughan is saved from obscurity by one chronicler, Robert Neil McLarty, whose 1951 thesis fully explores this soldier's campaign in the West Indies and includes correspondence between Vaughan and Germain and with others. Similarly noted above is the large collection of Vaughan's incoming correspondence known as the Vaughan Papers, which is housed in the William L Clements Library, of the University of Michigan. In 1929 these Papers were collated by Edna Vosper, who stressed however, that all of the letters were written to Vaughan by fellow-officers, family and friends and that, in the absence of his own replies, Vaughan's reasonable and accommodating character must be inferred from the tone of these correspondents.

The present author has been lucky enough to unearth a further group

26

of letters written by Vaughan in the West Indies and at St Eustatius. There is also George W Pratt's valuable monograph on the British operations above the Hudson*, which describes the burning of Kingston. With this material and in the course of this story we might draw a more detailed picture of Vaughan.

* * *

There is a portrait, in fact, but despite the uniform, the face is surprisingly unwarlike. Here is none of the intimidating hauteur of Rodney, or of Rodney's second-in command, Hood. There is nothing of the patrician features, those disdainful steely eyes, eagle noses and bitter mouths with which the obliging Sir Joshua Reynolds endowed both men as if from an Identity-Kit labelled 'British Admiral'. His sailors were accurately mirrored, of course. These were formidable men and they look the part.

No such implications here and not even an allegorical cannon in the background. In uniform, true, but there is no jaunty tilt to the cockaded hat sitting square over that florid, jowled face. This is the mild expression of a middle-aged alderman who could as well be the Mayor of a small country town; save that it is worn by one committed to war and greatly experienced in its hardships. More to this man, it seems. Indeed, it may be that this mildness will tell us as much of John Vaughan as all of Reynolds' fierceness tells us of Rodney and Hood.

* * *

John Vaughan was the younger son of Wilmot Vaughan, third Viscount Lisburne and Elizabeth, eldest daughter of Thomas Watson, of Berwick-on-Tweed. That area, Britain's Border country, will produce another soldier of concern to us, one James Cockburn, soon to make his entry.

Vaughan was born in 1737. There is, in fact some doubt as to the actual date of his birth but it appears from the DNB that he '. . . entered the service in the old 52nd Regiment, or Colonel Pawlett's 9th Regiment of Marines, from which on 9 April, 1748, he was transferred to the cornetcy in the 10th Dragoons wherein he served in England and Scotland, and in Germany during part of the Seven Years' War.'

His subsequent promotions were no doubt eased by a ready purse and the necessary connections but here again – as in Rodney's case – each elevation brought the privilege of dangerous service, although unlike the Admiral, no wife suffered melancholy on his account; Vaughan was never to marry.

Vaughan came to North America in 1761 as the Seven Years' War turned at last in Britain's favour, in command of the newly-raised 94th

---

*George W Pratt: *An Account of the British Expedition above the Highlands of the Hudson River* (Ulster County Historical Society Vol I, 1860)

Foot. He left the regiment in that year to serve with Major-General Robert Monckton's expedition against the French in the West Indies, and it is after the taking of Martinique, that scene of Rodney's major triumph in the campaign, that Vaughan earned Monckton's praise and first comes to significant notice.

> . . . the grenadiers of the army headed by Lt. Colonels Fletcher, Massey and Vaughan, the light infantry and the rangers . . . distinguished themselves particularly, the warmest part of the service having fallen to their lot . . .

A lengthy fallow period ensues. After Martinique, Vaughan took command of the 46th Regiment of Foot (in November 1762) and with them, spent five years in North America before returning to Ireland for a further eight years. He had become the Member of Parliament for Berwick in 1774 and from 1776 was also an MP in the Irish parliament. There is probably a rich seam of incident during this phase of his army service but only one event is noted in the regimental history – the appointment of Colonel the Honourable William Howe by his Majesty King George III '. . . from the Fifty-Eighth to the colonelcy of the Forty-Sixth regiment on the 21st November, 1764, in succession to Lieut.-General the Honourable Thomas Murray, deceased.'

The rebellion of the American Colonists brought new promotions – Howe to the command of the British Army in North America and, early in 1776, the return of Colonel Vaughan with the 46th and other reinforcements. Granted the rank of Major-General under Lord Cornwallis, Vaughan – again leading the grenadiers – took part in the British landing at Long Island in August and in the battle which secured it. In October however, he was wounded in the thigh at the battle of White Plains after which, he returned briefly to England with Cornwallis. A year later he was back in America – a Major-General under Sir Henry Clinton, who was about to mount a marauding expedition up the Hudson in support of Burgoyne. This endeavour would afford Vaughan a reputation for bravery and much useful credit: but it would also earn him the evergreen detestation of the Colonists and the withering title of 'General Esopus' for his association with that place.

In the course of Clinton's advance Vaughan's force had turned for Kingston, being reinforced en route by a further party of British troops which had taken a different road. It is alleged that at this point Vaughan was approached by a New York Loyalist, Jacobus Lefferts with news of Burgoyne's surrender at Saratoga. That did not become fact until the following day, the 17th, but the grapevine proved to be reliable and the news not unexpected. It followed that the expedition was reproached by the Americans for not being deterred from further operations by the

28

knowledge that Burgoyne and his men were lost: yet it might have added to their rage, for in the event, Vaughan and his troops descended on the village, destroying arms, munitions, flour, provisions and such property as could not be carried away, then systematically burned every house with only two exceptions – a house and barn belonging to Tobias Van Steenburgh and – possibly because it stood at some remove from the village or possibly because the recall was fortuitously sounded – the house of Jacobus Lefferts.

* * *

That first casualty of war, truth, is also to be found bleeding in this affair. Vaughan wrote his own account for Clinton 'On board the *Friendship*, Off Esopus (on) Friday, October 17th, 10 o'clock, Morning . . .'

> Sir: I have the Honor to inform you that on the Evening of the 15th Instant I arrived off Esopus; finding that the Rebels had thrown up Works and had made every Disposition to annoy us, and cut off our Communication, I judged it necessary to attack them, the Wind being at that time so much against us that we could make no Way. I accordingly landed the Troops, attacked their Batteries, drove them from their Works, (and) spiked and destroyed the Guns . . .'

More will be heard of Vaughan's next phrase: he will find occasion to use it again:

> Esopus being a Nursery for almost every Villain in the Country, I judged it necessary to proceed to that Town. On our Approach they were drawn up with Cannon which we took and drove them out of the Place (but) . . . on our entering the Town they fired from their Houses, which induced me to reduce the Place to Ashes, which I accordingly did, not leaving a House. We found a considerable Quantity of Stores of all kinds which shared the same Fate . . .
>
> Sir James Wallace has destroyed all the Shipping except an armed Galley, which run up the Creek with every Thing belonging to the Vessels in Store . . .
>
> Our loss is so inconsiderable that it is not at present worth while to mention . . . I am, &c.,*

* * *

Some of the lustre faded from this cheerless triumph when Vaughan found himself pondering a stinging reproach from General Gates.

*London Gazette, 2 December, 1777.

Written from Albany and dated 19 October, 1777, it accompanied Burgoyne's forlorn last Dispatch to Clinton:

> Sir: . . . With unexampled cruelty you have reduced the fine village of Kingston to Ashes, and most of the wretched Inhabitants to ruin. I am also informed that you continue to ravage, and burn all before you on both sides of the River. Is it thus your King's General thinks to make Converts to the Royal Cause?
> It is no less surprising than true that the measures they adopt to serve their master have quite the contrary effect. Their Cruelty establishes the glorious act of Independency upon the broad basis of the general resentment of the people . . .'

Bearable indignation this. But Gates's letter ended with a threat, impossible for Vaughan to ignore while he served in America:

> . . . Other Generals and much older officers than you can pretend to be are now by the fortune of War in my hands; their fortune may one day be yours, when Sir, it may not be in the power of anything human to save you from the just vengeance of an injured people.

> I am, Sir, Yr most obedt Servt. Horatio Gates.'

The reverberations of Burgoyne's surrender at Saratoga muffle Vaughan's footsteps for the next year. What was left of Burgoyne's army – and their women and children – continued, ill-sheltered and ill-fed, into a miserable captivity not, of course, shared by their commander. Burgoyne gave his parole and went home to survive political criticism and the displeasure of the King, who stripped him of his regimental command and so presented the Opposition with an embittered recruit. His payment for this support came with the fall of North's government at the end of the war, when the incoming Marquess of Rockingham appointed him Commander-in-Chief in Ireland: Burgoyne held this command for perhaps a year before abandoning the army for private life in fashionable London society and a new and successful role as a playwright. To this day, so many have relished that lasting comedy 'The Heiress', without identifying its author with the defeated British commander at Saratoga.

Howe had also seen enough of this war: his successes dated from Bunker Hill and New York: he had beaten the Americans at Brandywine and at Germantown and had occupied Philadelphia. But he had failed at Valley Forge and failed again in the face of Burgoyne's peril thereafter. In his own estimation he had not been supported by the government and desired therefore that he should be recalled: and in this flux of affairs in America, even as France, soon to be followed by Spain endorsed her own entry into the war with a treaty of Alliance with the rebels, command of the British forces devolved from the disappointed to the unwilling: Sir Henry Clinton – soon to begin his own series of demands to be relieved of this impossible task – was appointed Commander-in-Chief on 4 February, 1778.

Vaughan remained under Clinton's eye. There would be problems enough for the new commander, beginning with the urgent need to get the army and its Loyalist wards out of Philadelphia and overland, to New York. This operation began on 18 June but its purpose was achieved only at the cost of some three hundred killed in battle with Washington's forces en route – at Monmouth Courthouse, after ten days march – and the loss of six hundred who became prisoners of war or who deserted.

Vaughan is not mentioned, but his future was being mapped for him in London, where the government grappled with the new facts of war with France and the threat thus posed to the British sugar islands in the Caribbean. Ships and troops, therefore, were required for the West Indies: the naval command went to Rodney, and as we have seen, he delighted in the opportunity. But not so Vaughan at the possibility that he might be chosen for the military command and initially, lead an expedition for the recapture of St Lucia. Martinique and the Caribbean were not so remote in his memory that he had forgotten anything of what had been endured.

He wrote to Clinton on 5 June, 1778, therefore, in an attempt to discourage the General from any thoughts in that direction, 'flattering' himself that . . . 'what I have already suffered from that climate will be an excuse for me not to be thought of, as I could not muster health on such an occasion . . .'

The assault on St Lucia took place on 13th December, but Vaughan, is next noted as having returned to England in 1779. In December of that year we find him digesting the orders he had just received. Despite his reluctance, he was indeed to command in the West Indies and for this purpose, he was to embark with Rodney's great fleet now gathering at Spithead. In Vaughan's charge was the security of the British islands, but he was also enjoined to take the war to the enemy. Reservations as to his fitness for the task at this point would have been only human: but on 29 December the fleet sailed and Vaughan, whatever his inner feelings, was firmly committed.

*   *   *

Like Rodney, Vaughan owed his current elevation and his resigned presence within the West India convoy to an ogre only fitfully at rest since the Peace of '63. Now French aggression was again become a reality made plain by the French capture of Dominica in September barely two months after their declaration of war.

Of only minor significance in military terms, this event was nevertheless to ignite the greatest alarm in the British islands. All of them were as poorly defended and could well share the fate of Dominica. Their representatives therefore combined in vigorous expostulation and protest, in the Caribbean by the planters and merchants and in England, by the pressure-groups of the West India interest. All of this engulfed the chastened and much harassed Germain, already concerned with plans to ensure that vital British domination of the West Indies.

It was this need that made it so necessary to seize French St Lucia, most windward of their islands. In British hands, St Lucia's magnificent harbour, the Carenage, secure under the fortified heights of Morne Fortune, offered a prime and sheltered naval base for the protection of St Vincent, Barbados, Grenada and Tobago. It would challenge French command of the sea from nearby Martinique and it would at the same time, put an end to the Royal Navy's wearisome reliance on Antigua, that inconveniently located station, more than 200 miles to the north and well to the leeward of the proposed operations.

It was ironic that St Lucia had fallen to the British during the Seven Years' War but had been returned to France in the Peace. Rodney, with his own experience in the Caribbean and his great share in the capture of Martinique in '62 had strongly opposed that settlement for its disastrous implications for British naval strategy. His prescience was now justified by the realisation in Whitehall, a mere fifteen years on, that all was to do again: a task for which Germain required troops from the only source available, North America.

Thus it was that in March, 1778, the newly appointed Commander-in-Chief, Sir Henry Clinton, had been ordered to provide the expeditionary force of five thousand troops with artillery, for that operation and for further service in the West Indies. And thus it was that Vaughan, scenting the preparations for this adventure and not in the least attracted by that too-evocative whiff of the Caribbean, had made his plea to Clinton in June that he should be overlooked for the command. Clearly, it served to postpone his entry into that theatre. The command went to Major-General Grant but the project had first to surmount some considerable hurdles – the business of evacuating the whole of the army from Philadelphia, of fighting their way back to New York, of reorganisation, of finding ships of war and transports and of holding all back in the light of reports of an intruding French fleet under d'Estaing. The

Royal Navy's thirst for ship-to-ship action was not shared by the military. The prisons of rebel America awaited those British soldiers who would be taken at sea in their hundreds and of whom the American naval historian Maclay was to write:

> . . . Every reader of American history is familiar with the capture of Stony Point and its British garrison of five hundred and forty three men; of Ticonderoga, with its garrison of fifty men; of the battle of Trenton, with nearly one thousand prisoners. But it is doubtful if many have heard of the capture of three hundred British soldiers, with their colonel, in two transports, by the little State cruiser *Lee*, of the two hundred Highlanders and twenty officers of the Seventy-First Regiment by our *Andrea Doria*, of twenty four British army officers by Captain John Burroughs Hopkins' squadron, of the two hundred and forty Hessians captured by the privateer *Mars*, of the company of Dragoons taken by the privateer *Massachussetts*, of the sixty three Hessian chasseurs made prisoner by the privateer *Tyrannicide*, of the capture of a colonel, four lieutenant-colonels, and three majors by the privateer *Vengeance*, and of the capture of one hundred soldiers by the privateer *Warren* . . .*

Maclay notes that to the date of the final drama of the war at Yorktown in October 1781 '. . . fully sixteen thousand prisoners were made by our sea forces . . .' but by '78, the Continental Navy and the privateers had already made their impact. It was clear that more was to be expected and the reported appearance of d'Estaing was an effective reminder. The army could not, in any case, be transported during the hurricane months of the summer and autumn and all these factors determined that the expeditionary force would not sail before November. St Lucia lay ahead: but at this point, national interest and grand strategy settle on the shoulders of another character of importance to this story.

Among the soldiery selected for the expedition was the Thirty-Fifth Regiment of Foot, quartered in New York and now under the command of Lieutenant-Colonel James Cockburn.

*   *   *

COCKBURN

No single character will play a more prominent part in this tale of the seizure of St Eustatius than James Cockburn, both as Quartermaster-General to General Vaughan and later, as Military Governor of the

---

*E S Maclay, *A History of the American Privateers* (London, 1900) p. ix.

island. Though a highly professional officer, his flawed personality bedevilled much of his career. With Rodney and Vaughan, James Cockburn completes the trio who presided over one of the most bizarre episodes in British military history. We shall learn much of Cockburn's contribution to that affair and it is therefore important that we should take a close look at this soldier's background.

There is a picture. It commemorates the most critical moment of Cockburn's career but it is also unintentionally symbolic. While paying much attention to a hugely improbable Palladian background – it is, after all, a remote Caribbean island which is depicted – the artist has chosen a pose, appropriately dramatic but entirely hiding Cockburn's face.

Cockburn was a person of substance and one of no inconsequential name. The bleak coastal areas of north-east Britain are richly veined with Cockburns, who have also given their name to a town, Cockburnspath, in the Border country, and a mountain, Cockburn Law. It is an association with an area and its culture generating a proper pride and in this case, a pride sustained by some useful and compelling connections.

The status of Cockburn's father, Dr James Cockburn, is self-evident enough but there is something impressive about his grandfather, Dr William Cockburn – Physician-General to the army of the Duke of Marlborough and himself the second son of Sir William, baronet, of Ryslaw and Cockburn, in Berwickshire.

The soldier James Cockburn earns only a modest place in a genealogical maze described in Foster's Baronetage as 'chaotic', but the baronetcy and estates were tangible enough and passed, eventually, to Cockburn's eldest son, William. There was indeed substance there but Cockburn himself must clearly have been in more marginal circumstances, as we shall see. Nevertheless, there were sufficient means to buy him his first commission in the Army in 1747, though they were not sufficient for his advancement to field rank. Cockburn found his own solution to this difficulty, in 1776 and in doing so, displayed some of the less attractive facets of his character.

However, given his social eligibility, it was still no light matter to gain entry as a regimental officer. The board of general officers which had been set up by King George III to decide on the vexed question of an equitable purchase price for commissions, as between those who served in Europe and those who soldiered elsewhere – the source of much bitterness among the brotherhood of arms – had fixed the price of a captaincy in the 'Marching Regiments of Foot' at fifteen hundred pounds and that of a major's commission at two thousand six hundred pounds. This pernicious system, protested vainly by many but blessed for the most part at the highest levels of political, social and military life for its crude advantage to all participants, clearly lent itself to practical as well as moral corruption.

Cockburn, like every aspirant to a commission – and even those better connected than himself – would have had no option but to pay the going rate imposed by the competition, nepotism and greed which combined to inflate considerably these allegedly 'fixed' figures.

It seems clear that he was by no means averse to a little nepotism on his own account. The Army Lists for 1780 and '81 show that the officers of the 35th Regiment of Foot included his son, William, beneficiary of the above-mentioned estates, born 'in a camp' in 1768 and now a Lieutenant, all of twelve years old. The entry into military life of the even younger William is noted in the exultant opening of his father's letter of 25 October 1778, to Lieutenant-General Campbell . . .

> . . . I have the pleasure to tell you that my Boy is appointed an Ensign in the Regiment, the 17th Instant.

In some thirty years of soldiering Cockburn has learned a thing or two about shaping the regulations to his needs. He is about to send young William home from New York to England and confidently appeals to Campbell to offer the child 'the usual indulgence upon his arrival . . . that he might be properly educated . . .' 'I am told' adds Cockburn '. . . that the smoothest way will be of Lt-Colonel Townshend to return him "Recruiting" as one of the additional Companies, which I hope, he will not hesitate at, particularly on your application . . .'

They are plainly present but there is something more than mere artifice here and the pulling of influential strings. At least nominally, William is an officer of the 35th and therefore entitled to a passage which would keep him under a supervision chosen by his father: a returning family, perhaps, or one of the soldiers' widows shipped home in their scores. A Muster taken in New York shortly after this letter was written shows that the 9,686 British troops and 10,250 German mercenaries had with them an 'official' 3,615 Women and 4,127 Children, suggesting that William's placement in such care would not have been difficult.

The Army was after all well used to its corps of infants and the wry observations of a contemporaneous soldier, Private James Aytoun of the 58th Regiment of Foot, indicate that Cockburn's son need not have lacked a suitable command:

> . . . Here I have to remark a practice at that time in the Army, viz: an officer having command of a regiment contrived to put his sons on the muster rolls of the regiment as sergeants, corporals or privates although not three feet high. This accounts for Major Brawen being the only field officer who was continually with the regiment, because, had he been under the immediate command of a senior field officer, he could not have had baby sergeants,

corporals and privates in the muster rolls . . . he had a large family and I believe, nothing to depend on but his and his children's pay . . .*

The Army List also contains an intriguing entry which shows that a Peter Cockburn joined the 35th Regiment as an Ensign on 1 February, 1781, but while the familial link is suggested, the relationship is not clear. Cockburn's marriage to Letitia Little, heiress of the Irish houses of Rossiter and Devereux, produced 'several children'. William, however, is described variously in the Dictionary of National Biography as the 'only son' and again, as the 'eldest son': but while Peter Cockburn's span was brief – he is noted as 'retired or died in 1783* – William, by no means unique in this, founded an illustrious military career on his seniority to become, some four decades later and after seeing service during the War of Independence and in India, both a Lieutenant-General and a knight.

* * *

James Cockburn's progress to St Eustatius was a matter in which he took a fierce pride. The Army knew too many officers who had purchased merely the privilege and social advantages of a splendid uniform and who, on their reluctant appearances on parade, relied on the muttered promptings of NCO's for the simplest words of command. In contrast, Cockburn applied himself with utter dedication to the business of soldiering, willingly accepting its demands on his patience as well as on his undoubted courage. As adjutant of the regiment from 1757 to 1772 he dealt with its endless administrative needs, earning impressive testimonials to his competence and gift for organisation. These talents were coupled with the experience he was to gain as a fighting soldier and the good fortune, not always granted to the deserving, that these qualities were recognised to his advantage. Cockburn himself was aware of them to the point of assertiveness: in maturity, his was a personality to be reckoned with and one hardened by participation in a succession of terrible events.

It was true enough that his introduction to military life had not been unduly taxing although it is clear that he had readily absorbed the lessons of policing a cowed population. The 35th Regiment had been raised in Belfast by Colonel Arthur Chichester, 3rd Earl of Donegal, little more than a decade after the crushing of Catholic hopes at the Boyne in 1690 and for forty-eight brooding, but largely peaceful years thereafter, had served in Ireland as a further insurance against its smouldering people. The years since Cockburn had joined the Regiment had been spent in putting down the occasional – but brief – flowerings of rural revolt and,

*James Aytoun, *Redcoats in the Carribean* (East Lancashire Regimental Museum, Blackburn) p.4.

36

with all necessary pomp, making manifest the brute steel upholding the domination of the country by the Protestant Ascendancy.

It was politic, in this endeavour, to move the regiments periodically to different locations, that the example of the Boyne should remain in Catholic minds. In fulfilment of this role the 35th, known after its long-serving commanding officer as 'Otway's Foot', had accordingly been stationed at times at Limerick, Athlone, Kinsale and Dublin but, beyond their prime purpose, had found themselves with little more to do than enjoy some social opportunity for the officers, the perennial drunkenness and brawling of their men and for both, some periodic involvement in local rioting.

But there had in addition, been much concern with ceremonial duties, with the new Royal Warrant numbering all the regiments of the army and settling details of colours, uniform, equipment, the styling of hair and even the correct cock of their tricorne hats. They had also found time to attend to their drill and even, for one man of each company to go to Dublin to learn the gun exercise '. . . it being contemplation that a field piece might be attached to every regiment . . .' In the face of what was to come, Cockburn and those with him must bitterly have regretted that this remained only a worthy idea.

*   *   *

The familiar routine of barracks life in Ireland came to an end in April 1756, when the Regiment, in company with the 42nd Highlanders, was embarked for North America to reinforce the only two British regiments of Foot on that soil, the 44th and 48th.

Arriving at New York in June, the troops knew only that they were to fight the trespassing French and their strange allies, the Indians. History would know better: this was to be the French and Indian War, the onset of the Seven Years War and the beginning of the end of French power, if not of ambition, in Canada.

It was also the beginning of Cockburn's seasoning in active service. By the end of the war, in 1763, the Regiment had taken part in seven sieges and battles, Cockburn himself being wounded at Louisbourg in '58 and again at Quebec one year later. He was, of course, luckier than Wolfe, who died there, leaving not only an immortal memory but in addition, the following order of 24 July 1759:

> . . . the General strictly forbids the inhuman practice of scalping, except when the enemy are Indians, or Canadians dressed like Indians . . .

Cockburn endured the squalor and the nauseating unease of the packed transports which brought the regiments to America and there-

37

after deployed them for further afflictions. There is an infinite catalogue of the miseries of active service and all this represented a fearsome education. Of necessity it was a violence to be absorbed with a professional impassivity but the need for that discipline may also have been at the root of Cockburn's notable brusqueness and acerbity. The words used by fellow-officers to describe him are 'efficient' – '. . . a good officer, diligent and intelligent'. There are no tributes to his popularity and no evidence that Cockburn exerted himself to this end. To the contrary, he coupled his bid for a majority with an unwarranted presumption on his friendship with Campbell who quite properly took offence at this and at the spite Cockburn showed towards the incumbent, Major Gaul. Yet Gaul was fortunate: in May, 1780, Cockburn's malice helped to cashier a brother-officer, Major Edward Drewe. Moulded by the most harsh circumstances, James Cockburn emerges from the record as a brave solider and a tough and waspish survivor: an opportunist, a difficult man with his peers, and even a dangerous one.

But it is a very human paradox that he emerges, also, as a concerned father. We know nothing of his life with Letitia, save that Cockburn had taken his family to be with him at New York and that in 1779 he was obviously mindful of their welfare when the regiment was ordered for the West Indies. Clearly, he succeeded in establishing his charges safely in London, which must have called for no small effort on his part.

Sadly, there is a dearth of evidence of Letitia's regard for her husband: only the decorous perhaps even prompted letter which she wrote to Major-General Vaughan on his appointment to Vaughan's Staff:

. . . Greenwich March 18th, 1781 . . .

Permit me Dr Sir to Congratulate you most sincerely on your late glorious success against the Dutch, and sincerely wish you may meet with the reward and gratitude from your Country which your eminent services and merit so truly deserve . . .

In the last Letter I received from Mr Cockburn he inform'd me you had been so kind as to appoint him QM General, for which mark of favour I return my sincere thanks, and shall ever have a most grateful sense of your goodness, and am Dr Sir with wishing you Health happiness and safe return to England, your Obliged And most Humble Servant, L Cockburn . . .

*   *   *

Cockburn saw his first action in North America in '57 at Fort William Henry and it was to produce its echoes some twenty-five years on. This

38

was a saga which became deeply etched in army legend*: when Cockburn at length faced his most dire professional challenge it was this service, above all others, which he offered in proof of his integrity.

Fort William Henry, 1757

In the summer of '56 Lieutenant James Cockburn had found himself in garrison with the 35th at Fort William Henry, the stronghold established by the army commander, the Earl of Loudoun: a rude place, but one of importance for its location at the southern tip of Lake George.

The vital role of the lakes provoked some of the bloodiest fighting of the war. For both armies, impeded by rugged country, much of it hostile forest, mastery of the lakes spelled mobility, surveillance, if not always control, of vast territories and the ability to supply those in the field. These advantages were proclaimed and defended by fiercely contested forts at every artery and at Lake George, William Henry guarded the long waterway which began at Lake Champlain, on the borders of Canada and ran – with only one moderate portage – to the head waters of the Hudson.

Having demonstrated his strength, Loudon felt it unnecessary to retain his ten-thousand strong army at the fort during the coming winter. Late in November, therefore, the army was sent into winter quarters, the security of the fort being entrusted to a detachment made up of the 35th and 60th regiments plus the Loyalist New Jersey Militia – the whole numbering less than two thousand men.

The garrison was commanded by Lieutenant-Colonel George Monro of the 35th, who might also have taken some comfort from the proximity of a British force at Fort Edward, only fifteen miles to the south, commanded by Brigadier General Webb.

Campaigning weather came with the spring of '57 and with it, the elated French, their columns reinforced by their painted partners but much aggravated by their capricious nature. One year earlier, under the Marquis de Montcalm, this army had forced the surrender of the British at Oswego, adding Lake Ontario to the strategic waters under French command. Now, to the east another lake beckoned, temptingly exposed by the departure of Lord Loudoun with the main body of the army for a first and quarrelsomely abortive expedition to Louisbourg.

The existence of a British fort or so in the vicinity of Lake George could be discounted: with forces drawn additionally from Crown Point and Ticonderoga, plus some two thousand Indians, the French could pit some

---

*. . . and which, in 1826, provided the setting for a classic of American literature: *The Last of the Mohicans* by James Fenimore Cooper.

eleven thousand men against the inferior numbers of the British. Given the continued misfortunes of the British in this campaign, Montcalm could have every reason for confidence.

The first three probing attacks on Fort William Henry were driven off. Accordingly, in the first days of August, Montcalm invested the Fort, the revelation of his powerful artillery a painful reminder to the 35th of the field-piece they might themselves have owned.

Monro rejected the opportunity of an honourable surrender, for despite the odds against his force, there remained the possibility of relief from Fort Edward. In that direction lay the only hope of raising the siege or of forcing supplies of ammunition and provisions into the garrison. As the firing began, therefore, and while the siege continued, both sides kept an eye open – the British with hope, the French with prudence – for the appearance of General Webb: who, in fact had only fifteen hundred men and little hope, once he learned of Monro's plight and the enemy numbers, of useful intervention.

For the British, as for many of the New Jersey Militia, these attacks also brought them their first sight of the Indians. Since their arrival in North America, the soldiers had learned something of these people and their frightful war trophies, but it was one matter to listen to such accounts in the security of camp or billet and another to witness the Indians in the flesh. Alien and barbaric in paint and ornamentation, near naked or in their motley of uniform scraps donated contemptuously by the French or posthumously by the British, theirs was an ominous presence to behold. For Cockburn and his fellow officers, as for all of the troops so lately come from Ireland, it was one for which the rituals of guard-mounting at Clare Castle could have been no fitting preparation.

Implicit in Montcalm's courteous offer to avoid bloodshed had been the understanding that the Fort might otherwise be battered into submission. Rendered inevitable by Monro's defiance, this achievement would not, in fact, take long.

The seven days of siege and unremitting bombardment which followed left three hundred of the garrison dead at their posts and the Fort systematically reduced to a pocked, smoking ruin. Periodically, between the sniping and the cannon-fire, Monro's men looked with increasing despair for succour from General Webb. Equally mystified but greatly encouraged by Webb's continued failure to appear, the French made full use of their opportunity, finally demolishing any hope of rescue by sending in an intercepted letter in which Webb advised Monro to surrender. Bereft of food, ammunition and now of spirit, the defence of Fort William Henry came to an end, signalled by an urgent and improvised flag of truce.

Generous in victory, Montcalm assured Monro of his respect for that gallant resistance. In token of this, the survivors, Cockburn among them, would be permitted to march out with all the honours of war. They would be escorted by a French detachment to Fort Edward in order to ensure their safety en route and they might keep with them one six pounder. And of course, they would be bound not to serve against the French for eighteen months from that day.

The men of the garrison gathered their packs and contrived the dignity of formation. Behind them trundled the sick and wounded and after them, clutching their own bundles and possessions, shuffled the dependent hundreds – a multitude of women, children and civilians, among these, Indians and black slaves in the service of the British: but no sooner was this humiliated procession clear of the Fort than Montcalm's Indians fell on them, at first snatching what little they possessed, then singling out and attacking Monro's Indians and blacks and finally, proceeding to a general scalping, slaughter and abduction reported to number 'several hundreds' of victims.

Captain Richard Trimen's *Historical Memoir of the 35th Royal Sussex Regiment*, published in 1873, claims that '. . . the French looked coolly on . . . while this unfortunate and helpless band was butchered . . .' However, the indignation of the report in the Annual Register for 1758, when the event was still fresh in mind, is focused elsewhere. Noting that the Indians committed 'a thousand outrages and barbarities, from which the French commander endeavoured in vain to restrain them', it adds that '. . . All this was suffered by 2000 men with arms in their hands, from a disorderly crew of savages. The greatest part of our men, though in a bad condition, got to Fort Edward, some by flight; some, having surrendered themselves to the French, were by them sent home safe.'

Trimen reports that Monro hastened to the French camp to plead for the promised protection and there remained, anguished and impotent in the face of their alleged failure to intervene: but at long last, Brigadier General Webb sent a detachment under its own flag of truce to obtain Monro's release and bring him back to Fort Edward. It comes as no surprise to learn that Monro died six weeks later, at Albany '. . . of a broken heart . . .'

* * *

Cockburn would need to come to terms with this early introduction to defeat and broken faith: he would need also, to satisfy himself as to his own part in this inglorious tragedy, even if that could only be done by a renewed determination for distinction in the future. What can be seen as a first step toward this came one year on, at Albany, where the shattered remnant of the Regiment licked their wounds. Cockburn expressed no doubt as to where the blame for this disaster should lie. Through the Commander-in-Chief, Major-General Jeffrey Amherst, he petitioned the King for release from the parole he had given to the French. In securing this annulment – subsequently extended to cover all officers and soldiers of the Fort's garrison – Cockburn accepted that from the day this was granted, he would serve in a double jeopardy. Added to the hazard of combat was now the real possibility that, if he were captured once more, he would be assured of a rope about his neck.

1758–63, Cheers for King George

Cockburn is now to be hurried through his next years of service. The pace is not meant to diminish anything of the events he saw but some broad strokes are needed to round out his background. It is not until 1766 that there is any traceable personal testimony and it is at that point that Cockburn comes centre-stage.

*　*　*

Much more would be added to Cockburn's experience of war but he was fortunate in that he participated in successive victories. Albany gave place in 1758 to Halifax, Nova Scotia, where the regiment, under Lieutenant-Colonel Henry Fletcher (who would become Lieutenant-General and then Major-General Henry Fletcher Campbell), successor to the tragic Monro, was sent to join the army assembling for the renewed operation against Louisbourg. Far in the future lay the strains which Cockburn would put upon a friendship with Fletcher, developed, or professed, over years of service as brother officers.

There, in Halifax, incorporated in a Brigade formed of three other regiments – the 15th, 40th and 78th – the troops embarked on their assigned transports, then waited, all fourteen thousand of them, crammed into one hundred and twenty vessels miserably weatherbound in harbour. It will be instructive to wait with them for, by coincidence, another of our characters comes close enough to be named at this time.

It was not only the weather which hindered their progress: the expedition was also temporarily headless and its fuming officers undecided. Somewhere to the east and more than two months at sea, a weary and far more weather-worn King's ship, the *Dublin* (74), laboured doggedly in their direction, bearing the urgently appointed Commander-in-Chief, Major-General Jeffrey Amherst for whom this landfall could not come too quickly.

But on 28 May Amherst was at last united with his army, albeit at sea, since the fleet, escorted by twenty-two ships of the line and fifteen frigates, the whole armada commanded by Admiral the Hon. Edward Boscawen could delay no longer. Finally committed, Amherst or no, the ships had cleared Halifax when *Dublin* met them.

Cockburn may have noted the approach of the strange sail and its flutter of signals heralding the General's transfer but would be unaware of the significance of that moment for the course of his own life. The Captain of *Dublin* was a certain forty year-old George Brydges Rodney who alone was to make possible Cockburn's ultimate steps to disaster.

*   *   *

In two months of fighting and siege, General Amherst's more competent direction enabled the British to seize Louisbourg, where that French haven on barren Cape Breton stood sentinel over the approaches to the St Lawrence. Thus exposed, the most bitter defence (in which Cockburn's antagonist Montcalm died), could not save Quebec: that capture, in turn, permitted Amherst to engineer the triple-jawed pincers which finally closed on Montreal in September, 1760. The junction of sixteen thousand British troops before the city left its Governor, the Marquis de Vaudreuil, with only the option of a surrender which ensured the end of the French challenge in Canada: a timely relief for Cockburn, twice wounded in all this fighting. But little enough time was given for the soldiers' cheers for the conclusion of that war and the accession, the following month, of King George the Third. France was disarmed in North America only: her menace to British interests in the Caribbean was still potent and the British troops would spend the next fourteen months, first in being transported to New York and then, in being marshalled at Staten Island for the expedition against Martinique. The wounds which Cockburn had taken at Louisbourg and Quebec did not keep him from joining Major-General Robert Monckton's thousands who would yet again fill the transports. Among these thousands was Lieutenant-Colonel John Vaughan, who was to share the command of the grenadiers with Lieutenant-Colonels Fletcher and Massey: and lower down, squeezed into the dark hold of another vessel, Private William Gordon of Cockburn's 35th Regiment of Foot. We shall see something more of Cockburn for this initial portrait – it will then be in a later war – but before we return to him, there is reason to note the lowly William Gordon.

Gordon

Private William Gordon's association with Cockburn was to develop into an unusual complicity. There would come a time when Cockburn's Law would stand for something other than a peak in Berwickshire and Gordon would then be Cockburn's enthusiastic beadle, his willing herald and strong arm in a situation ripe with opportunity for some deft enterprise of his own.

A partnership such as this bridged tremendous disparities in rank and cultural background, but it was logical enough that Gordon, who had by then accompanied his commanding officer through more than twenty years of vicissitude, should have been chosen as Cockburn's right hand. Cockburn's reward for those years was to succeed to the command of the 35th and, in 1779, to be given his fateful appointment as Quartermaster-General to Sir John Vaughan. It was not long before Gordon, in attendance, assumed the title and the prerogatives of 'Assistant to the QMG.'

Gordon had, after all, been through much with the Regiment. He seems however, to have lingered in his station as a private, for it was not until the 26 November 1775, in the dreadful aftermath of Bunker Hill, that greatness in the form of a Corporal's stripes, was thrust upon him, to be followed by his promotion to Sergeant at Halifax, after the evacuation of Boston.

By that time both men had outlived most of the Regiment and had attained the highest rank they would reach. The Lieutenant-Colonel and the Sergeant would keep their proper distance but they would know each other very well: which fact may be registered for further reference.

Field Officer

There are further glimpses of Cockburn in the making: one of them is revealed in a letter written from Boston and dated 25th January 1776.

In the bitter winter after Bunker's Hill and among all the wretchedness of an exposed and impotent army hemmed in by jeering rebels so confident as to offer potential British deserters '. . . seven Dollars a month, fresh provisions in plenty, Health and . . . Freedom, ease affluence, and a good farm . . .' in contrast with the condition of the troops at Bunker's Hill . . . '. . . Threepence a day, Rotten salt pork, Scurvy, Starving, beggary and want . . .' Captain Cockburn devoted some effort to his own advancement.

The unfortunate provider of this opportunity was Major William Gaul who had served the regiment since 1767. Gaul had seen sufficient carnage in his day and had weathered it bravely, but in a turmoil which increasingly became more difficult to contain. His dilemma was finally resolved during the assault on Bunker Hill and the dreadful count thereafter: four hundred and fifty Americans dead and two hundred and twenty six British, who also suffered eight hundred and twenty eight wounded . . . 'General Howe's white silk stockings being quite red with the blood of his men . . .'

It was quite enough for Gaul, who now made it known that he proposed to relinquish his commission – a declaration which came as music to Cockburn's ears. Ambitious for a promotion so long beyond his means, blocked by the presence of Gaul as his superior officer, this was an opportunity not to be lost. It required only audacity and a helpful touch of character assassination: Cockburn most certainly possessed a propensity for both and worked assiduously to prepare his ground before presenting Major-General* Campbell, tongue in cheek, with something of a *fait accompli* . . .

'My good Sir,   Boston 2th Jan.ry 1776
                                                            Duplicate

Notwithstanding the many letters I wrote you from hence, yet I have not had the pleasure of hearing once from you, which would have given me much uneasiness had I not heard by Ogilvie† that you were well.

We are in the same kind of distress'd situation as when I last wrote you, but are in hopes of a powerful reinforcement in the Spring, sufficient to put an end to the Affair at one blow, which I believe those villains will never face, when they see a formidable-force sent against them at different Quarters . . .

The niceties so smoothly satisfied, Cockburn turns to the serious purposes of his letter. Clearly, they are to diminish poor Gaul . . .

. . . Mr Gaul has at last taken off the mask and desired Leave to retire, which I'm exceedingly sorry for at this time as I could have wish'd rather that he had continued this campaign . . .

*He was promoted to Lieutenant-General in 1777.

†David Ogilvie, who in 1781, as Brigadier General Ogilvie, would become the first British Military Governor of St Eustatius.

45

. . . and to sugar for Campbell the next announcement which Cockburn correctly senses might need that treatment:

> . . . General Howe sent for me to talk to me about the Succession, which I told him I was averse to at this time, particularly as I had no money of my own. But he calling to mind the old Friendship that the World knew you had for me, and the efforts you made in England to procure me the Majority then, which were recent in his mind, as well as many others at home, concluded that I would by no means answer your friendly intentions if I missed this opportunity of becoming your Major, a Point you so ardently wish'd for; but more particularly as he did not know when he could serve me; Upon considering the matter maturely, I ventured to become the Purchaser, and the General has declared me in Orders accordingly . . .'

It is not difficult to see Campbell's brow furrow as he reads, or Cockburn grit his teeth for the following sentences:

> . . . Upon this occasion, Sir, I have taken the Liberty to draw upon you in favour of Ogilvie, for £800, the other 300, I have raised otherwise as I would not wish to be more burdensome to you than necessity compells me; and I hope by the blessing of God, and the help of the Paymaster's Place, (which is now become better), that I shall be able to Discharge my Debt rapidly . . .

Cockburn may have felt a momentary qualm, for at this point he added a rash promise:

> . . . Should this measure not meet with your Entire approbation, I solemnly promise you that I shall without hesitation, sell out, in order to reimburse you . . .

This pledge was to be of importance to Cockburn's future: but it is almost as if he wished neither Campbell nor himself to dwell on its possibilities that he hurried to overlay the sentence with loftier assurances:

> . . . I now have it in my own Power to take care of your interest in the Regiment, without Control, which I was ever inclined to do, So shall I continue to do, if possible, with more Warmth than ever, the Good effects of which I hope you'll soon see.
> . . . I never thought it possible, that a Regiment, even tolerably founded, could have tumbled down as the poor 35th has, owing to the Indolence of the one, and the Ignorance of the other. The Work I have now upon my hands is an heavy one; but the same Principle that ever Actuated me, the

Honour and Reputation of the Regiment, and the Glory of our Prince, I hope will enable me to effect my Design.

. . . As you have ever had, so shall you continue to have, the sincere Prayers of a Grateful Family, for every Happiness to attend You and Yours, and believe me ever . . . Your Faithful Servant, Jas. Cockburn. PS.

. . . Simcoe* has got the Purchase of a Company in the 40th and Lamb is become Adjutant. Lieut. Smelt of the 14th succeeds me and Fitzgerald is now your eldest Captain . . .

Campbell replied from Stirling, on 26 March in a letter in which he took little trouble to disguise his anger.

He was at loss, he wrote, that two letters he had already 'sent by different opportunities' had apparently failed to reach Cockburn. He knew of Major Gaul's intentions before Cockburn's letter of 25 January. As to other matters . . .

. . . General Howe would in course offer you the Purchase: but I should think from what has lately happened in Ireland, on Major Sherwood's resignation, that you might have formed a Judgement with respect to the mode of purchasing the Majority without troubling the Commander-in-Chief with a Train of unnecessary recollections, which was rather uncommon, could answer no purpose, exclusive of being Disagreeable to me . . .

Struggling for civility, Campbell added:

. . . I am very glad of your being appointed Major to the 35th Regiment but could have wished, and I think I had a right to expect, that the Purchase had been managed with a more Delicate manner with respect to me, with whom you wanted all Ceremony – Your Draft upon me for £800 pounds Stirling without any previous directions from me for so doing, did not a little surprise me, Sir, and as it happened, found me unprepared, being engaged in a contract for Rebuilding my house. However, I have remitted Five hundred pounds tho I had little Time given me to prepare that sum – and Mr Ogilvie is to endeavour to get Mr Gray or Mr Ross to find you the remaining Three hundred . . .'

Which was all Cockburn wished to hear. An angry Major-General at the safe remove of a few thousand miles . . . a disrupted friendship even, were facts he could live with. What mattered to Cockburn was that he had achieved his field rank and found others to put up the money.

*John Graves Simcoe (1752–1806). MP for St Mawes, Cornwall 1790. In 1791 appointed Lieutenant Governor of Upper Canada (now Ontario).

Delighted by this stroke, he was not immediately exercised at the thought of repayment: Campbell closed his letter with an exasperated reference to this omission and another blunt rebuke by way of goodbye . . .

. . . In a former letter from you during the Sale of Sherwood's Majority you mentioned that your Scheme was to pay off so much every year, which you hoped I would approve. As therefore you take no Notice of this matter in your Duplicate, I have ordered Mr Ogilvie to write to you thereanent . . .'

. . . You may remember that I formerly mentioned to you when in Dublin, That Reflections of all kinds upon the Commanding Officer of the Regiment were not only Disagreeable but unfit for me to hear. I am, Sir, With best Wishes for Your & Family's Welfare, etc . . .'

– 3 –

CASUS BELLI

Having considered the principal characters in our story we must now turn to its focal point – the island of St Eustatius and the reasons for the British determination to seize it. For the British, France and Spain were their familiar enemies and the intervention of those countries in the American war was accepted as the latest of their challenges. But by 1779 the elements of a wider conflict had long been at work.

AT ODDS WITH THE DUTCH

Neither the century of peace between them, the conclusion of a treaty of commerce in 1674 and of alliance in 1678, not even England's ties with the Netherlands through Dutch King William, could prevent the steady worsening of the relationship since the beginning of the American war. From that time on, violent incidents and accusations of broken faith had raised ill-feeling on both sides. The pressures of the war and the opportunism of men could be relied on continually to abuse neutrality and after every offence, each government quoted the obligations of the other in respect of the treaties. Both, however, did so in the full knowledge that compliance, under the circumstances of the day, would have been detrimental to Britain and nothing less than suicidal for the Dutch.

The dilemma was exemplified by King George's disappointment that the ships and troops – the 'succours' – promised by the Dutch under the treaty of 1678 and now urgently required for the American war – would not be forthcoming. In the view of the Dutch, this reinforcement applied only in the case of war with another country: rebellion was an internal matter and it was for the British government to deal with it themselves.

This disappointment was compounded by Britain's failure to circumvent the treaty by borrowing the Scots Brigade, the British force which had been garrisoned in the Netherlands since 1685. Despatched there

49

originally to defend Dutch independence, the Brigade had been twice recalled to assist Britain in her own extremity during the Jacobite uprisings of 1715 and 1745. But although the request was on firmer ground here, since it was not for Dutch forces, it nevertheless foundered in Holland in a welter of dissent, conditions, objections and finally, in outright rejection by the States General.

The fiasco was of political, rather than military importance: King George had better luck with his German connections who obligingly – and at a price – filled the gaps in the British Army with the Hessian and other German mercenaries who were to serve him so well: nevertheless, Dutch obduracy in this matter rankled and was to become the platform on which Britain would heap each new resentment.

But Holland's denial owed much to the proximity of a France in arms, given to invasion and not to be lightly provoked. This possibility and what might follow from the event were spelled out for the British government by the opposition:

> . . . the States General, in not complying with the requisition, had not only acted wisely under the circumstances of the time, but had done us . . . a very great service. The immediate consequence would have been that Holland would have been invaded and probably over-run by a powerful French army.
>
> And if Holland, in her turn, had then called on Britain for help . . .' we must, overborne as we already were, have encountered the whole force of France in a land war, upon her own borders . . .'

Unpalatable as it was to the British government, the logic of the Dutch position had to be swallowed: but the frustration would be remembered and, while tact and patience drained away during the months of 1780, the breach would figure frequently in their exchanges. It was not, unfortunately, the only subject for bitterness and reproach. That perennial grievance, the flow of contraband supplies to the King's enemies had simmered for long enough and as far as Britain was concerned, had now reached boiling point.

It was vital to resolve it: the issue of America might still be in doubt although voices in Britain warned that victory was immoral of purpose and impossible of achievement. That was not yet conclusive, but it was basic that its achievement would be painfully delayed and even become less likely with every shipment collected by the rebels; for, as an English customs official in Boston recorded, 'Daily arrivals from the West Indies but most from St Eustatius, every one of which brings more or less of gunpowder.'*

*Barbara Tuchman, *The First Salute*, (London 1989) p.20.

There appeared to be no possibility that the trade could be effectively outlawed by the Dutch and the glaring example of St Eustatius and the undeterred industry of smugglers and blockade runners reflected that impotence. Even worse: this was only one destination for a damaging traffic. In European waters the naval might of France and Spain was being sustained in similar fashion with cargoes of timber from the Baltic for shipbuilding and masts, carried in neutral Scandinavian and Baltic vessels. British endeavours to seal off these sources would shortly bring about the crisis for which only one solution offered: Britain would choose her moment but once again, there would be war with the Dutch, who did their best, for the remaining months of that now threadbare peace, to tread carefully.

In no condition to fight, yet dependent on an uninterrupted commerce by sea, the Dutch sought to placate where they could, to shrug off where they could not and always, to argue the terms of the treaty of 1674. This guaranteed the unhindered passage of merchant ships of both nations bound for countries with which either of them might be at war, and permitted them to carry all goods save for war supplies. Powder and shot clearly fell into this category, but 'naval stores', although exempted from the ban, were of equally dire significance for the British. Whatever had been in their minds when that clause of the treaty had been agreed, it had not encompassed the provision of masts and shipbuilding timber for the French, nor of rope, hemp, ironwork or anything else that might conceivably be of use to them at sea. Treaty or no treaty, therefore, ships carrying such cargoes were prey to the Royal Navy and almost certainly would be taken in to British ports as prizes and their cargo sold. Naturally enough, since it helped to have legality on their own side, the same treaty was invoked by the British for the right of the Royal Navy to inspect neutral merchant ships and to seize therefrom any warlike supplies destined for enemy ports.

What was seen in London as the weighted neutrality of the Dutch in favour of Britain's enemies was spurred by much more than the massive scale of finance and commerce involved in these activities: what was at stake, in addition, was the assertion of sovereignty and the viability of the whole of Dutch maritime commerce and neither of these could be bent to British needs. There was clearly a very good case for not provoking the British by continuing the trade, but if this meant permitting the Royal Navy to interfere with Dutch merchant ships it was impossible to do otherwise. The complaints, if not worse, would come from all sides: from the belligerents, France and Spain, of course from America, hungry for everything that could be carried by Dutch ships, from Dutch bankers and merchants, from shipmasters and from clients whose goods and cargoes had suffered arbitrary seizure. More: the complaints would come from the Baltic nations whose friendship and commerce were equally necessary.

Under these imperatives, the possibility of war could be clearly foreseen: and while it frightened the Hague – for the Dutch, long past their fighting days, were without naval and military strength worthy of consideration – it could be safely entertained and designed in London. From there, the pressures, the advantages and the justification for war indicated no better course of action.

One of those pressures was inherent in the very nature of the Dutch Republic. The British people were certainly not alone in their bewilderment, but the individuality and influence of the Dutch provincial states, Zeeland, Utrecht, Gelderland, Overijssel, Friesland and Groningen was largely lost on them: it was less taxing that they should lump the seven United Provinces together in an entity which they called 'Holland' and its people 'Dutchmen'. Thus, 'the Dutch' in the persons of their High Mightinesses, those deputies of the States General who debated policy at the Hague, took the full impact of the anger so forcefully expressed by Britain's ambassador, Sir Joseph Yorke. But in reality and as Yorke was well aware, the sovereignty of William V, Prince of Orange and titular chief of state as Stadtholder was notional. The political structure of the Netherlands diffused the authority of the States General – and hence its powers of decision – through the fiercely argumentative provincial States assemblies, each with its hierarchy of Stadtholder and his chief advisor, the Pensionary, and with its municipal and regional governance in the hands of aristocratic councillors known as the Regents.

When Britain decided at last that she was ready for something more than diplomacy, this was a situation to be exploited by Yorke for the benefit of his own masters in Whitehall. It meant that the nominal rulers of that nation could do very little to control the enterprises of Dutch merchants outside their own jurisdiction, even if they had the will: and of all the merchant interests, none were more jealously guarded than those of Amsterdam, the richest, most energetic of all the offending cities and the very engine of the contraband trade. That being the case, 'Dutch' relations with Britain degenerated into pained attempts to appease London with words only, in the hope of damping down each new eruption transmitted by the British ambassador.

Thin ice, this, and doomed to be broken by the end of that year. In the interim, the exchanges between London and the Hague grew increasingly threatening on the one hand and alarmed on the other but, fanning the flames throughout the dialogue, Dutch merchants continued to trade with France and Spain and with America through the conduit of St Eustatius, where four thousand miles of sea between the island and the British and the absence of hard news from Europe, guaranteed that business that fateful year would go on with rather more vigour than previously. As long as this commerce represented such a vital strand of economic activity, then prohibitive edicts from the Hague directed at Dutch merchants, shippers and captains could be taken with a very large pinch of salt. The notorious precedent of the pathetic attempts by the Heren of the Dutch West India Company to ban the arms trade in 1775 had produced no noticeable effect except to inspire the ingenuity and the derision of all concerned with these transactions. A by-product of this had been the assurance that the demand and of course, the profit from the American purchasers would become even greater.

By the end of the year the situation was irredeemable. Yorke's acid letters to their High Mightinesses, uninhibited in their bullying, elicited no satisfactory replies and indeed, were not written in that expectation. Dutch traders may have fanned the flames but Yorke, too, stoked them with all the fervour necessary to the British purpose – which was not to obtain further half-hearted promises of good behaviour from the Dutch, but to prepare for the moment when they would finally be swept from the chessboard. Until that time came, the policy of interceptions, searches and seizures now being so peremptorily exercised, would continue.

* * *

None of this heavy-handed treatment had been taken meekly by the maritime nations at risk but while the resentment voiced by Sweden, Denmark and Russia was as yet without leadership, it was left to two naval officers to bring matters to a head. On 31 December, 1779, in the waters off the Isle of Wight, Captain Fielding of the Royal Navy, cruising with a squadron of six ships, challenged a Dutch convoy escorted by four men-of-war under the flag of Admiral Van Byland. Far from being a chance meeting, Fielding's presence in force resulted from intelligence received in London that a number of merchant ships laden with timber and naval stores for the French were gathered in the Texel. With no hope of disguising such a cargo and at best, only a blind eye from the States of Holland, it was hoped that these ships would find protection from the British by joining Van Byland's convoy, bound for the Mediterranean.

Fielding's orders were to intercept, to search and to seize any contraband discovered. Since Van Byland's orders were to resist any such attempt, the results were to be expected: Van Byland refused to allow his ships to be boarded, fired warning shots over the approaching boats and replied to Fielding's own warning shot with a broadside, which was promptly returned.

Further defiance was useless: outnumbered, outgunned and as a neutral, unwilling to precipitate a major battle, Van Byland struck his colours. Many of the Dutch ships had escaped during the encounter under cover of the winter darkness and by keeping close to the shore, but the rest of his vessels and the Admiral himself, stoutly refusing to be parted from his charges, were taken into Spithead.

And there Van Byland fumed as the British assessed and sold their prizes, took a grim satisfaction in the discomfiture of the Dutch and prepared themselves for the next step on the road to a wider war.

* * *

Unfortunately for the British, it was not to be dictated by themselves, but by the intervention of Catherine II, Empress of all the Russias. Not minded to see her own vessels stopped at sea, Catherine announced her proposals for a League of Armed Neutrality and invited the collaboration of Holland, Sweden, Denmark and Portugal. The purposes were to declare the limits of free trade, to specify what was to be regarded as contraband and blockade and to fight if necessary, to preserve the right to operate within these bounds. And that all parties might be aware of the rules, she did not neglect to appraise the Courts of London, Versailles and Madrid of her resolution.

As the primary target of this development, Britain viewed it with great concern: French and Spanish sea-power, it appeared, was now to be augmented by an enhanced coalition of the Northern powers. In that anticipation and with so much to gain from the situation, France and Spain could happily afford their promises of cooperation in respect of neutral inspection. The Spanish King, however, in acknowledging Catherine's declaration and, in effect, pledging his support, could not resist the sideswipe that interference by Spanish ships – they had recently taken a couple of Russian merchantmen proposing to enter Gibraltar – was brought upon themselves by the neutrals' habit of '. . . furnishing themselves with double papers and other artifices, to prevent the capture of their vessels: from which have followed captures and detentions innumerable and other disagreeable consequences . . .'

But these were not necessarily as bad as they were pretended, added the King:

> '. . . on the contrary, some of these detentions have turned to the advantage of the proprietors, as the goods, being sold in the port where they were condemned, have frequently gone at a higher price than they would have done at the place of their destination . . .'

Nevertheless, the King would observe the conduct of the English navy and that of their privateers: and in respect of her complaint about that rough usage at Gibraltar, reminded Catherine of Article 4 of her declaration, wherein '. . . a blocked-up port was to be understood as one which is so well kept in by the ships of the power that attacks it, and which keep their places, that it is dangerous to enter into it . . .'

Thus the pressures on Britain increased. The strength of the partners meant that there was nothing at all to be done against the Northern members of the League: but it was urgent to ensure that there would be no contribution from Holland. The list of Dutch offences went back a long way, from their contraband trade in the West Indies and that unforgiveable recognition of the rebel flag: from the refusal of the Scots Brigade, their flagrant protection of 'the pirate' John Paul Jones* and the equally flagrant illicit commerce with the French and Spanish – and now, in 1780, to this. If the British hoped to put a righteous face on any drastic measures necessary to end their problems with the troublesome Dutch, then they needed to find an additional straw, one which they could claim to be final.

✢   ✢   ✢

The Packet Mercury

It was presented to them one day early in September, in the grey seas of the Atlantic, somewhere off the Newfoundland Banks. On 3 September, 1780, the Congress packet *Mercury*, bound for Holland from Philadelphia, was intercepted by His Majesty's 32-gun frigate *Vestal*. The British blockade of the American coast had produced scores of similar incidents and for *Vestal*'s commander, Captain George Augustus Keppel, this matter-of-fact routine was only rarely enlivened by any serious challenge from the quarry.

This event, however, was to be distinguished by the presence aboard *Mercury* of a passenger named Henry Laurens, a South Carolina merchant and planter who had served as President of the Continental Congress: and by his bungled attempt, on the approach of *Vestal*'s boarding party – and in full view of her boat's crew – to dispose of certain documents which he had enclosed in a weighted bag and thrown overboard. The bag, however, remained afloat long enough to be retrieved by the 'boldness and dexterity' of a British seaman. He remains unnamed, but the quick eye and sure grasp of this naval cipher surely places him among those who have given history a nudge at a critical moment.

But for Laurens and the failure of his curiously maladroit action – sceptics later alleged that failure was indeed its purpose – the meeting might otherwise have had only the usual consequences of these operations.

---

*Appointed Captain in the Continental Navy in 1776. Thereafter conducted sea actions against British coastal towns and vessels. Jones was later being sheltered by the Dutch after capturing HM Ship *Sevapis* (50) on 23 September, 1779, off Flamborough Head.

55

Loss of ship and cargo for the owners, the questioning of crew and passengers, cursory apologies for neutrals and impressment or imprisonment for others: another prize for Captain Keppel to report . . .

It became instead, Britain's long-sought opportunity.

Laurens had been on his way to Holland to relieve the redoubtable John Adams as the Congress envoy to the Netherlands. His mission empowered him to negotiate a loan of ten million dollars to the Congress but among his papers – 'most of them recovered from the effects of the water' – was revealed an intent of even greater significance – the draft of a proposed treaty of amity and commerce between America and Holland, agreed with the Congress commissioner, William Lee and signed by Englebert Francis Van Berkel, Counsellor and Pensionary of the city of Amsterdam and Jean de Neufville, one of its most prominent citizens. Additionally named in the document were the two American Agents of the Congress who operated from St Eustatius, Samuel Curson and Isaac Gouverneur, names which were duly noted in Whitehall for a future reckoning.

That the treaty was dated September, 1778, and was to take effect only on the eventual recognition of American independence mattered little (although Burke was later to point this out to the House, reiterating that it was no more than 'a speculative essay. Had the King's servants obtained a copy of any treaty actually entered into and executed'?)

It made no difference. The design was clear. Here was evidence of Holland's long collusion with the rebels to be added to the accumulated bile. It mattered little, too, that their High Mightinesses, the States General of the Seven United Provinces of Holland had not actually been consulted by Lee, Van Berkel and de Neufville although the treaty had been drawn up in their name: but in this respect, the three men were confident that the weight and influence of Amsterdam would ensure the general support. So were the Americans, who had taken it most seriously and entrusted Laurens with a copy of the treaty: and so were the British, or so they chose to imply in what was described as a Memorial, but was in reality an ultimatum, presented by the implacable Joseph Yorke to the States General on 10 November.

Save for its opening sentence, courtesy was given short shrift:

'The King, my master, has throughout the whole course of his reign shewed the most sincere desire for preserving the union which has subsisted for upwards of and age between his Crown and the Republic . . . etc . . .': but from there on, Yorke concentrated on reproof and threat. 'The friendship of the two nations', he wrote, 'was being undermined by a faction aiming to dominate the Republic for its own selfish interest. Its intrigues were at the root of every affront to the King offered by their High

Mightinesses – beginning, of course, with that ever-open wound, the refusal of the stipulated succours – and accounting for every violation since: but in the latest matter of the treaty exposed by the capture of Mr Laurens '. . . who styles himself' – and the sneer was almost audible – '. . . President of the pretended Congress and whose papers furnish the discovery of a plot unexampled in the annals of the Republic . . .', the King demanded a prompt satisfaction. Only a formal disavowal of the treaty and the 'exemplary punishment of Van Berkel and his accomplices as disturbers of the peace and violators of the law of nations' would suffice.

More: His Majesty expected that the reply would be speedy and satisfactory in all respects. To refuse his proper demands or to attempt to take refuge in silence would be to indicate Holland's support for the outrages and in that unhappy event, the King would find it necessary '. . . to take measures to preserve his own dignity and the essential interest of his people . . .'

The speedy and satisfactory reply was not, and could not possibly be forthcoming. Yorke, with his knowledge of Holland's cumbersome machinery of government had made sure of that by insisting on a reply the same day, promising that if it was not received 'he should find himself obliged to acquaint his Court thereof by an extraordinary courier.'

Beyond threat, this bordered on assault. Nervously, their High Mightinesses – and never could such a title have given its bearers less comfort – despatched their recorder to Yorke to assure him that his demands had been taken *ad referendum*, that the memorial would be considered by the deputies of the provinces, that they had even resolved immediately to consult their court of justice on the matter of punishment and that he should have his answer as soon as possible thereafter.

Tragically, that humiliating epigram of the 20th century, 'peace at any price' has its antithesis: war at any price. The momentum now was such that British purposes would not have been served by Holland's surrender in this matter. Yorke refused to transmit the resolve, describing it as 'illusive'. It was urgently sent on by their High Mightinesses to the Dutch Minister in London, Count Welderen who attempted to lay it before Secretary of State Lord Stormont: but by that time all ministerial contact between them had been broken and Welderen's packet was therefore returned, unopened.

Informed by his secretary that it had been rejected as 'inadmissible', the Count offered a wry comment in a valedictory letter to Stormont before his own departure for Holland at the end of December: '. . . Give me leave to observe to your Lordship that it is impossible to know whether a proposition is admissible or not before it has been seen and examined . . .'

What might have been meant as a delaying action arrived one week later in the form of a sorrowful resolution taken by the States General on 16 November. This concerned the '. . . Insults and Violences . . .' committed by the British at the island of St Martin on 9 August when His Majesty's ships of war had seized American vessels sheltering in that neutral port, while threatening to raze the fort and village should there be any resistance.

The plaint failed to raise an eyebrow. Yorke shrugged it off as an irrelevance in a final letter to the States General on 12 December in which he equated the proposed treaty with the rebels as a declaration of war by its authors. They had '. . . raised the buckler' on the part of Holland and unless Their High Mightinesses wished to associate themselves with this, the offenders must be punished by them and reparation made: or the King, his master, would take it upon himself to exact these penalties.

Five weeks had elapsed before the States General ground out their reply to Yorke's first Memorial, but by then it was too late. Yorke had been withdrawn from his post at the Hague and Britain had declared war on the Dutch.

The tone of the proclamation issued from the Court of St James's on 20 December typified the public attitudes struck by both parties during their correspondence. They had, it seemed, expected better from each other in order to continue in peace and friendship: but the common aim had been fatally obstructed, in Holland by the evil 'factions' and in Britain, claimed their High Mightinesses, by her stubborn refusal to recognise the strict demands of neutrality governing Dutch actions . . .

The declaration brimmed with tears for what might have been. Nevertheless, the allegations of injury omitted nothing, from the first failure of the States General to support Britain against her enemies, to Holland's 'facilitation' of naval stores to France: from the insult of the haven given to the American pirate whose name was still too vile for inscription*, to the mischief fomented against the King in the East Indies. As for the West Indies, there '. . . every protection has been given to our rebellious subjects, their privateers openly received in Dutch harbours and allowed to refit there: supplied with arms and ammunition and their crews recruited and their prizes brought in and sold . . .'

Indisputably, it was the work of the 'factions, the sinister magistrates of Amsterdam whose secret correspondence with the rebels, long suspected was now exposed . . .'

It was a gratifying tribute to the vigilance of Captain Keppel who could be justifiably impressed by this consequence. But even as the King's

---

*But not here: this was naturally Britain's official view of John Paul Jones.

manifesto was being committed to paper, his ministers, not losing a moment, had ordered the first acts of war. All Dutch vessels in British ports were seized. Letters of marque and reprisal were written for eager applicants and within a few days, came the first actions at sea. The Dutch man of war *Princess Caroline* (54) was taken in the Channel by His Majesty's ship *Bellona*, the *Rotterdam* (50) was taken by the *Warwick* and a Dutch East Indiaman with other merchant vessels made to join the ignominious procession into a British port.

*   *   *

Indeed, His Majesty's ministers had not lost a moment on that eventful 20th December. The King's instructions to his Commander-in-Chief in the West Indies, Admiral Sir George Brydges Rodney had that day been given under the hands of the Lords of the Admiralty, Sandwich, Lisburn and Bamber Gascoyne and dispatched to Barbados by Philip Stephens, Secretary of the Admiralty, in the care of His Majesty's sloop of war, *Childers*:

> You are therefore . . . required and directed to consult with Major-General Vaughan . . . upon the best means of attacking and subduing the Possessions of the States General of the United Provinces within your Command . . . and when subdued, in keeping possession thereof, if you and he shall judge it necessary and proper to do so . . .
> The Islands which present themselves as the first Objects of Attack are St Eustatius and St Martin, neither of which it is supposed are capable of making any considerable Resistance against such a Land and Sea Force as you and the General can send against them, if the Attack be suddenly made . . . And as the Enemy have derived great Advantages from those Islands, and it is highly probable considerable Quantities of Provisions and other Stores are laid up there, or are upon their Way thither, which may fall into our hands if we get Possession speedily, it is His Majesty's pleasure that we should . . . and we do hereby accordingly recommend to you the immediate Attack and reduction of those Islands, as of very great Importance to His Majesty's Service . . .

*   *   *

THE MISDEEDS OF ST EUSTATIUS

Retribution for the misdeeds of St Eustatius lay in the future. Its coming would be described as a thunderclap but that was true only of the chosen moment. Statia clings still to the legend of its eighteenth century self as a mercantile Paradise brutally demolished by sudden assault, but in fact, the threatening rumblings of upheaval had troubled the islanders long in advance. News of war from America and of discord in Europe was the currency of all and seriously to be pondered. It was one tendril of a grapevine seeded by newspapers brought in by the stream of arriving vessels and nurtured by the shrewd comments of their captains, by trade associates and by relatives and friends in the islands: and it was freshened often by accounts from those – of whom Samson Mears was but one – who had fled to Statia from one army or another.

For by this time, at the turn of 1780 and within the space of the two years since France and then Spain had entered the war, the whole of the Eastern Caribbean had become a battle zone. Nobody could be deaf and blind to what had been happening around them and Statia's traders and planters, like all dwellers in the embattled sugar islands – although Statia was as yet not so seriously harmed as those others – had felt some of the effects. Many of these had caused inconvenience and hardship: but not enough to prevent Statia's men of business from profiting vastly from the hostilities.

But from the very beginning of the rebellion they had been damaged by the drying up of supplies from America. Without self-sufficiency in food or materials, the islands were heavily dependent on North America for lumber for building, shingles, staves and hogsheads for their own produce, for horses and hides and for provisions of all kinds; beef in hogsheads, fish, flour, tea, potatoes, beans, rice . . . The dearth of provisions had brought Barbados and the British Leewards to starvation and Governor Burt had informed Germain of the deaths from this cause of close on three thousand negroes there.

Throughout the region this distress had been accompanied by a rapid decline in the sugar trade until it had fallen to little more than half of the previous shipments. Seizures and losses at sea of vessels unprotected by convoys had caused insurance and freight rates to escalate: their own trade in molasses, sugar and rum to America and in tobacco from Virginia and Maryland was pursued only at increasing risk to shipper and customer: there may well have been a thunderclap brewing over St Eustatius but the storm warnings flew everywhere. What they saw plainly before them, even as the *Childers* still sought the Trades, was a scene of violent disruption with every promise of more in the near future.

* * *

The first tremor had come with the taking of British Dominica in September, 1778, by de Bouillé, of which we shall read in the next chapter. December had seen Grant's capture of St Lucia and February, 1779, the French repossession of St Martin and St Bartholomew. Presented with an opening by the unfortunate Admiral Byron, d'Estaing, operating from Martinique, had followed quickly with the capture in June of St Vincent and in July, of Grenada.

There had been a lull of sorts for almost a year, although filled with preparation. Rodney's great war fleet now paraded before them and in August, had shown something of its power with that contemptuous and intimidating thrust into Dutch waters at nearby St Martin. It was no novelty now for any watcher with a tolerably good glass on Statia to make out the British men of war at St Kitts: and by this time, to have heard of their procession of Admirals; first Young, then Barrington followed by Byron, then Hyde Parker and now Rodney, who would very shortly be joined by Hood.

But in addition to the grapevine, the residents had their own sources of information and received it and made use of it according to their leanings. Samson Mears, for example, had but recently returned to Statia in August and as the agent of the wealthy Jewish merchant shipper Aaron Lopez, had re-established contact with his employer, now at Leicester, Connecticut, despite their mutual dislocations, for Lopez himself had fled the British occupation of his home town, Newport, Rhode Island. Mears had first-hand experience to relate, having hurriedly abandoned home and business at Norwalk during the destruction of that town by General Tryon's incendiarists in July, '79. Morosely he had written to Lopez in November from his temporary shelter at Newport apologising first for his failure to call on the Lopez family: '. . . the difficulty of procuring a horse proved that disagreeable disappointment'. But in an endeavour to salvage something from the wreckage in the hope of a new start he went on:

> '. . . desirous of availing myself of your being at Boston and of your friendly services, I am induced to beg the favour of you, to let me know if there is a probability of disposing of 100 Boxes of Spermacity Candles deliverable at Norwalk for Hard Money, or good Bills of Exchange, and what price may be obtained . . .'

He would be highly obliged, wrote Mears, if Lopez would afford him an early reply '. . . as I am making some preparations to leave the Continent in pursuit of better fortune than I have met on it . . .'

Samson Mears' next refuge was St Eustatius and Fortune's messenger was on his way.

Such men as Texier and his step-son Charles-André Chabert maintained intricate family links with France – where the young Chabert had been educated – with Martinique, where Texier's brother had settled after his marriage to a creole girl of St Pierre and with Guadeloupe, the seat of the prominent Chabert family of planters. Charles-André had been debarred from claiming an inheritance in Guadeloupe since his father had left that island in 1739, married and settled in Statia and chosen the privileges conferred by Dutch citizenship. In French law, Charles-André was, therefore, a 'foreigner' and as such, his claim was invalidated – although he contested it for the best part of five years – but the disappointment had not shaken his fierce attachment to France or any of the zeal for the French interest which he shared with his step-father.

In contrast, the Bermudan, Richard Downing Jennings, would attempt to serve the British, or at least, to ingratiate himself with them. There were inevitably, in this strangely diverse society, many conflicting attachments, causing among their holders an insatiable eagerness for news. Indeed, rumour became so fervent an industry on Statia that sceptics, wrote one resident, coined the phrase 'St Eustatius news' for every new item borne on the wind: but it was not all rumour and Rodney was not the only officer to fume that his dispositions were frequently common knowledge.

Shortly after his arrival in the Leeward Islands the Admiral had himself been offered such services and by the same resident. The lengthy letter containing this proposal is dated 31, March, 1780 and is unsigned, although the writer refers to himself as a 'man of business' who would . . . 'be happy to serve the cause of (his) country'. The description and the resources claimed for this 'plan for acquiring intelligence at St Eustatius', as well as subsequent correspondence, all point to Richard Downing Jennings as the author: the stamp of his audacity, style and genius for planning in great detail, as well as the suggested use of an intermediary will become familiar.

Describing the unique importance of Statia as a catchment for important information despite its reputation for hearsay and wild invention, the proposal continues:

. . . It will at all events be necessary to have a more certain and speedy resource of intelligence from the island of Martinico, which is the grand rendezvous of the enemy in this part of the world – to which all their reinforcements come and where their plans of offence and defence are laid . . .'

To this end it is observed that:

. . . As a very extensive trade is carried on from this island of St Eustatius to the French islands, and as the Dutch being neutrals are freely admitted to trade among them, the agent appointed to collect intelligence must endeavour to discover a person proper to go constantly from St Eustatius to Martinico in a small trading vessel. This person and no other on board his vessel must be made party to the service he is sent upon: and under the colour of carrying on a trade, he is to endeavour to procure all the intelligence that is to be acquired . . .

And this, it was promised, would be transmitted to the Admiral. The appalling risk for 'this person' is nowhere mentioned, but it was not thought that the task might be difficult for:

. . . his coming as a Dutchman or a Frenchman from St Eustatius will not only shield him from all suspicion of being attach'd to Great Britain but will likewise, if he conduct himself with proper caution, open him a way into the confidence of the French . . . It will be found then, upon a just examination, that the only proper person to acquire intelligence at St Eustatius must be some merchant who resides there or at St Kitts . .

The advantages were pressed:

. . . Some vessels do not arrive at St Eustatius from the French islands or from America or from Europe and there are many of these vessels that bring intelligence of an interesting nature. Certain accounts sometimes come from the French islands of their force, expected supplies, etc. and these accounts could not be unimportant to the ear of the British Admiral. From America, intelligence of consequence is often brought. Lastly, vessels may frequently arrive from Europe, bringing some important news. The English vessels often come to St Eustatius without touching at any English islands on their way – vessels from Holland are coming in almost daily: and from these circumstances, there is hardly a French or English reinforcement coming out that previous notice is not received at St Eustatius before it arrives . . .'

When and how Rodney actually received the letter and how much use he made of the offer contained therein is not clear, since he was at that juncture at Gros Islet Bay preparing to give battle to De Guichen: but it is unquestionably among his papers and it was indeed Jennings who was much later to hound Rodney for recognition of his services and reimbursement of payments made to a mysterious spy, presumably with the acquiescence or even on the instruction of the Admiral.

* * *

At the beginning of February, Statia's Dutch residents took some reassurance from the latest news from Holland brought by Count Van

63

Byland. Bad as the situation was, he informed them, it would not come to war. His frigate, the *Mars*, of 38 guns and with 300 men was now at anchor before Fort Oranje amid a great concourse of more than one hundred and fifty merchantmen and vessels 'of all denominations.' Statia's crowded Road had been only marginally relieved by the departure on the 1st of the month of a homeward-bound convoy of twenty-three merchant sail. This cumbersome flock of Dutch snows, pinks, flutes and hookers, each with its idiosyncratic captain, was escorted by another national vessel named *Mars* (but of 62 guns) which had arrived in September under the command of Rear-Admiral Krul. Among his officers was a perceptive young Lieutenant, Cornelius de Jong, whose fluent pen will enrich this account.

It seemed, then, that Statia was in no immediate danger and despite his previous experience of British anger, Governor de Graaff appeared to be unworried. The island had been sheltered for so long by its *de facto* neutrality that he may well have believed in the ability of the States General to defend it, even though others voiced their doubts. It was clear that the islanders, even with their garrison at Fort Oranje of fifty men commemorated as 'the worst men in the service of the West India Company', could do little in that direction themselves. The business of Statia was to make money, allegedly for the West India Company but primarily for the Governor and the traders. This vocation and the Company's grudging and erratic provision of armament – for they had been known to overlook such small matters as gun-carriages and round-shot for them – had always ruled out efforts to make Fort Oranje, with its decaying wooden quarters and its damp powder-house, better fitted for its pretensions.

As for the batteries: de Jong cast a professional eye on them and reported that of the twenty-five guns in Fort Oranje it was possible to use only five: that Fort Nassau, on the south-western coast had three 'untrustworthy' cannon, Fort de Windt, protecting the south had four 'manned by a constable, a small boy and a black maid'* and what was probably Fort Tommelendijk, although de Jong called it Fort Tietchy, covered Jenkins' Bay with another ten guns. And of course, there was his own frigate, *Mars*.

It was against this unconvincing defiance that the weight of the Royal Navy and His Majesty's Land Forces was about to be directed.

The position of the island Dutch, although precarious, was at least clear, as it was indeed, for the rest of the island's odd assortment of neutrals –

---

*Ypie Attema, *St Eustatius: a short history of the island and its monuments*, (Zutphen 1976) p.41

the Swedes, Prussians and Hungarians and those individuals who claimed Corsica, Genoa, Danzig and Venice as their birthplace. Whenever it became necessary, all of these could claim and expect immunity: it was, however, a much more clouded crystal for the British and American merchants of Statia. Given the nature of their dealings, some of the British had sound reasons for troubling themselves about the movements of His Majesty's ships and for wishing them to be in other seas: while the Americans were either staunch supporters of the rebellion and as such, knew what to expect from any confrontation with the British, or Loyalists, who in those circumstances might have an equally hard time proving it. As for the Jews, those veterans of ill-usage, pessimism was bred in the bone and repeatedly justified by experience. They were truly grateful and loyal to their Dutch hosts but suspicious and fearful of all others and of what might be brought by every unknown vessel appearing on Statia's horizons.

Nevertheless, as yet the accustomed pattern of life on St Eustatius continued. Ships' boats in their scores pulled or sailed between their vessels and the warehouses, slaves unloaded and stacked bales and casks and, when there was no longer space within the walls, piled the goods beside them until the foreshore was covered as far as the buildings stretched. The captains and the traders earnestly laboured at their money-making and the merchant crewmen at their traditional pleasures. It was now the second day of February and the furious pace of the island had reached its peak. But so too had the unease we find mirrored in the correspondence of the Congress agents, Curson and Gouverneur who, in concert with their mission for the rebels and possibly as part of it, conducted a substantial business with clients in America and Holland.

TRAIT'ROUS COMMERCE

The business correspondence of the Congress agents Samuel Curson and Isaac Gouverneur is a rare view of the trading activity as conducted from Statia until the moment of its violent interruption. Spanning some eighteen critical months before hostilities reached their own island, that is, from May, 1779 to January, 1780, these letters were included in the general seizure of business books and papers ordered by Rodney immediately after his arrival. Inflamed as he had been for so long against this place, its operations and all who participated in them, it was enough for the Admiral that the majority of the letters came from Amsterdam and rebel America: that he was also to find therein offers to the partners to supply 'your Government' with goods and services confirmed their treachery and added to Rodney's grim satisfaction in their immediate arrest.

Yet the Crown lawyers would eventually need to work harder for supportive detail. Those who trafficked in powder and arms for the use of the King's enemies were not so obliging as to furnish invoices and receipts for their shipments: these letters, therefore, contain no sinister references to contraband, although where Curson and Gouverneur are advised that they should 'do the needful', something obviously remains unsaid. Here, however, descriptions of goods and cargo are circumspect and clearly written with the possibility of interception in mind: indeed, the threat, and frequently the fact, of seizure by the Royal Navy or by privateers is a recurring theme, reflecting both the formidable risks and the character of those prepared to undertake them.

The transactions recorded describe conventional shipments of bales and cases, linens, lumber, shingles, hogsheads of tobacco, rum, sugar, indigo and 'sundry goods'. There are even 'loose handkerchiefs to fill up the holes' and of course, there are the reckonings – the credit and debit of this commerce, the accounts and bills of lading, all carefully noted and only rarely requiring correction. It is by the way that we are informed of the nature of goods being shipped and the identity of the business houses and merchants and captains involved that the letters illuminate as much of the partners' proceedings as they and their correspondents were prepared to commit to paper. They also convey the personal relationships and necessary trust which developed from these associations.

Over all, one senses the remarkable vigilance with which the traders kept themselves informed of contemporary events and international affairs. There are expressions of fear for the future which spring from their awareness of political and warlike activities heightened in that turbulent year by the dangerous implications for themselves of the friction between Britain and the Dutch Republic. Albeit that the information came to Statia and its neighbours weeks in arrears, each development in that quarrel was progressively reported – as previously noted – in newspapers brought in by arriving vessels and amplified by the comments of their captains.

One or two letters come from other islands – Peter Hill writes to Isaac Gouverneur from Curaçao for example on 11 April, 1780: he has heard that:

> . . . there are frequently good Bills to be procured with You or in Your Neighbourhood on New York . . . could You procure me such a one to the amount of five or six hundred pounds, made payable to my Father Mr Thomas Hill of that place which please forward to him as I am apprehensive He stands in need of some Assistance . . .'

It tells us something about Peter Hill: but it is interesting too, that he requests that the amount should be charged '. . . to the account of

Gouverneur Hill & Gouverneur' thus indicating an established, although undefined link with Curaçao. A similar link is pointed by a letter from St Croix. This, and the single letter in the batch from Curson and Gouverneur to associates in Europe, appear below.

The earliest communication to Curson and Gouverneur in this collection is from William Manning, in London, dated 15 May, 1779. The practice of sending copies by different vessels is observed: the original was entrusted to the vessel *Archdeacon* and the copy to the *William*. Manning's letter seems to be a somewhat tardy acknowledgement of the partners' own of 14 September, 1778, in which they had transmitted a Bill of Exchange for £73.1.9 issued by Richard Downing Jennings, of St Eustatius on the prestigious Amsterdam firm of Thomas and Adrian Hope and Co. This is an early reference to that dark figure, Jennings: before too long, both Rodney and Vaughan would have cause to remember him with feeling.

The American correspondence is opened by a letter of 19 October, 1779, showing that in May and again in September of the same year the partners had been of service to Captains Kilgour and Cunningham, disposing of cargoes sent by Latimer Holstead, of Portsmouth, Virginia and informing him of the state of the markets in the Antilles. In thanking Curson and Gouverneur, care of Captain Swift of the *Wilkes*, Holstead clarified a scheme which they had apparently treated with some caution:

> . . . I imagine Capt. Cunningham must have misrepresented my intention in the proposal I then made you of furnishing the Materials and fitting a Vessill I then had in the Stocks, the one half for the other, as I meant as soon as she was fitted to have Loaded and Addressed her to yourselves . . . which would have been a method of drawing your Property out, instead of leaving more in this Country, by ordering your Factors or Correspondents here to furnish a Cargo . . .

Holstead pressed the advantages of an association: Curson and Gouverneur need not put up any money since their share in the cargo, plus charges, could be funded out of the partner's 'Effects' already in America.

> . . . I should have been glad to have established a Connection with some Gentlemen of your place, in a Vessill or two, and particularly with yourselves, as by that means we might have been of mutual service to each other in the management of those Vessills, in furnishing such Cargoes as would answer with dispatch, procuring Freights and the Disposal of their return Cargoes in either place . . .

Holstead regrets that the original proposal was rebuffed but offers further opportunities. In so doing, he remarks sourly on the discretion necessarily given to, or exacted by, the merchant Captains:

> . . . and although Canvas and Cordage is exceedingly scarce & difficult to be got here at present, I am in hopes I shall in some short time get her fitted and Loaded with good Lumber, Cypress Shingles and perhaps some Naval Stores, when I shall address her to yourselves, provided we have any favourable account of your Markets . . . in the meantime, the Schooner *Molly*, Capn Swift, is now ready to Sail and is bound to St Eustatia with a Cargo of Tobacco, being as fine a crop as Virginia affords, and Lumber which I've desired Capn Swift to give you the Offer of. This giving the Skipper the Consignments is a vile practice introduced of late which prevents my Consigning to you now: but I hope it will be laid aside 'ere long, as we can but seldom find the Seaman and the Merchant in one and the same person. This practice should now end with me, was this Vessill a little larger . . .

The letter achieved the desired response. Holstead became an important link in the partners' trade with America, and a considerable source of information and comment. His last letter to Curson and Gouverneur dated 9 September, 1780, and carried by Captain Paul Owens deals with the management of their schooner *Fame*, then loading at Portsmouth with '. . . good James River Tobacco and hogsheads of Staves and Headings and Large Cypress Shingles . . .' and with the balance of accounts and cargo to be shipped back with Owens '. . . unless an Accident.'

The proviso was an indication of the latest manifestation of British naval muscle in the area, for Admiral Rodney, as we know, had arrived at Barbados in March. Holstead told of his design to send *Fame*'s cargo to Isaac Gouverneur via Curaçao '. . . a place something more out of the way of your troublesome Neighbours, or I should have addressed her to yourselves as before . . .' and included an indignant comment on the British incursion into St Martin on 6 August, to seize, as Rodney wrote to the Secretary of the Admiralty, Philip Stephens . . . 'Five Sail of His Majesty's Pyratical Rebellious Subjects Arm'd for War . . .' which had been intercepted on their voyage to St Eustatius and pursued into the shelter of St Martin.

> . . . the Pyratical Rebels had the Insolence after they were at Anchor in the Road, to Insult His Majesty's Flag in the grossest manner, by daring to hoist their Rebellious Colours with a Broad Pendant, bringing a Spring upon their Cables and pointing all their Guns into His Majesty's Sloop the *Rover* . . .

Which insolence cost the rebels dearly for they lost not only their vessels to Captain Mark Robinson's punitive squadron of frigates and the *Intrepid* (64), but also 300 hogsheads of their tobacco, unsold and left on shore, despite pleas for their retrieval by the American owners, to whom Rodney explained loftily that His Majesty's ships had been sent to '. . . Chastise their Insolence, not to Seize their Tobacco, nor make War with the Dutch . . .'

It could hardly have salved the smart, for the humiliated and apologetic Governor Heyliger, embroiled yet again in a perilous altercation over that wretched rebel flag and it was, of course, this action that provoked the complaint made by the States General on 16 November, which had been so contemptuously brushed aside by Yorke. But Holstead's letter shows us the other side of this coin and the hopes raised among the West India traders by news of the proposed League of Armed Neutrality:

> in consequence of the Violence committed by British Subjects cutting and taking our Vessills out of your and other Neutral Ports with impunity . . . I believe few of our Vessills will venture to come amongst you until they shall be sure of the Protection all free Nations hath a right to give their Neighbours who shall incline to Trade with them in a Peacible and friendly manner . . .

He instructs Curson and Gouverneur that:

> . . . if by any accident the schooner should put into St Eustatius, they are to open his letter to Gouverneur and proceed '. . . agreeable to my instructions to him, taking every the most cautious and expeditious step to secure my Property from those bold plunderers of mankind – I hope ere long all those injured Nations will adopt some salutary Plan to deter and at least prevent . . . such unwarrantable proceedings in their Ports and Harbours . . .'

The concern for the future is real enough: Holstead returns his eyes to his ledger long enough to point out two small corrections for the partners . . . 'in your Account I observe there is an Error . . . in the Article of Ticklingburgh as also an error in Cutteau Knives, having charged me with 14 instead of 12 Dozen at 10/. per Doz . . . which I have passed to your Debit . . .' but finishes on a gloomily prophetic note:

> . . . I have had the Pleasure to hear the Price of Tobacco took a Sudden rise before our Vessills had left your Port in July, but whether we shall have it in our Power long to enjoy trade with you is at present uncertain as it will depend altogether on the spirited remonstrance . . . their High Mightinesses shall make to the freedoms taken by British Men of War and Cruizers . . .

if Captain Owens should not get to Eustatia you will please to Ship the above mentioned Balance in any well Armed fast Sailing Vessill that should be bound to Virginia . . .

* * *

The tension is still there almost five months later, in January: Britain has been at war with the Dutch for three weeks but this anonymous Statian, writing on the 8th of the month, is unaware that his apprehensions have been realised:

A brig arrived last night from Rotterdam in 35 days – I have been labouring all this Morning to decypher Dutch newspapers so late as the 21st of November – it appears that Sir J York has been remonstrating very smartly about a treaty of Commerce which Mr Laurens was charged with for ratification, betwixt the 13 States and the 7 States. The matter has been carrying on for some time by some Merchants of Amsterdam under the Cloak of Private business . . .

The writer doubts that Britain will be satisfied with the formal disavowal by the Province of Holland:

. . . certain it is that Holland has acceded to the Confederacy and actually signed the Treaty. Insurance has rose in that Country to 15 per cent instead of 4 per cent. All Merchantmen have been requested to furnish for the equipment of a Fleet, every third man of their Crews. All this has the air of Hostility, yet the Dutch Captain assures me that matters were coming round again when he left Holland . . .

Letters to the partners from other merchants in America are similar in their mix of commerce, primarily in tobacco, and comment. Some are mundane: John Holloway is concerned that '. . . the mate tells me there is one hogshead less in the Vessel than I have an acct. of . . . I pray you will pay particular attention to the Tobacco when it is landed and see whose it is . . .' while Mr G Meade, of Philadelphia wished to be advised 'how far it would be Convenient for you to ship home to Holland our Tobaccos if they could not sell at such Prices as they may be received at . . .'

Captain John Harrison of the sloop *Lincoln* brought 'Respectful Compliments to Mrs Gouverneur' in a letter of 2 May, 1780, from Nicholas Martin of West River: 'sell my two hogsheads of tobacco' Martin advises, 'and send me the Net proceeds in Rum, a porter Cask of which I shall be glad to have, good . . . Such as you like your Self, in the said Sloop . . . I have sent you by the Sloops *Lincoln* and *Brigg Lively* two hams in Each which I hope you'll Except off . . . I hope the Red bird & bagg of Oysters sent by Ca. Buchannan Come Safe to hand . . .'

The copy of this letter, written the next day contains some afterthoughts: '. . . I hope to Sail by the last of June in a new Brigg of Mr Stewards bound for France . . . I must Endeavour to Steer Clear of the West Indies . . . I have not fairly got rid of illness yet. I hope Capt. Buchannan Delivers Mr Gouverneur Red bird and Bagg of Oysters Safe I sent by him . . .'

In between are further anxieties: on 27 June, Thomas Mathews of Portsmouth, Virginia, wrote to ask Curson and Gouverneur to accept a letter for Mr Kelley who '. . . has taken his Passage in the Ship *American*, Capn Collins, for your port. Should Mr Kelley be taken on his passage, you will be pleased to Open my letters and do the Needful . . .'

Mathews also mentions a large purchase he has made in the schooner *Dolphin* which he rightly fears will prove a disadvantage: a business associate at St Croix, Christopher Evvy, broke the news to Curson and Gouverneur on 9 October that the *Dolphin* had been taken by a privateer and carried into Antigua '. . . which I am sorry for . . .'

The last letter in the American correspondence is from Griffin Lamkin. Dated 5 December, 1780, it must thoroughly have compounded the hazards of business in that year. Writing from Petersburg, Virginia, a sorely tried Lamkin reported that he had:

'. . . arrived here the 29th November last but had the Misfortune to be run on shore by a 20 gun ship about 4 miles to the Southward of our Capes. We lost the Vessell & Cargo for the Wind was so light that we could not run her on Shore hard enough for her to Stick & the Enemy got her off. Capn Mosely was run on Shore immediately after us but was saved by our Military Light Horse who happened to be near the Shore. This Vessell is now Safe up the James River . . .'

To add to the trauma of Lamkin's experience, he had almost fallen foul of Captain George Gayton's command, despatched by Rodney to support General Clinton's enterprise on the Chesapeake. He notes that . . . 'a British fleet consisting of about fifty Sail arrived in Hampton Road abt. 20th October last . . .' and closes with the rueful tale of how he – and the partners' cargo – might have come to grief even earlier: '. . . there is very few boats at this place at present for the British Fleet never Sailed until the Twenty Second of November last and no Vessel was able to get in the Whole time they lay in the road . . . a person on the Sea Shore informed us of the fleets lying in the road, or else in one hour we should have been among them . . .'

71

The only letter from Curson and Gouverneur is dated 6 November, 1780, and reveals other risks besides those of hurricane and misfortune at sea. The addressee is unidentified but this is very probably a reply to a letter from Willem Helmis, of Rotterdam who had written to them on 22 July to ask them to take action against the merchants Papineau & Elholm. Helmis had sent these men a consignment of merchandise – rope, knives, stationery, ledgers, pencils, violins with bows and strings, hair powder, gloves, and anchovy – but their partnership had since dissolved.

Helmis believes that Papineau had already sold the rope and that he will never see any money for his outlay. He holds a low opinion of Papineau and urges Curson and Gouverneur to claim the rest of his goods and sell them on his behalf, after which he will do all his future business through them: as for Papineau, they were not to waste any compassion on him or accept any of his promises . . .

If the letter of 6 November is indeed a reply, the unhappy Papineau is relegated to a final paragraph: Curson and Gouverneur's letter is almost wholly concerned with more recent events, namely the widespread damage wrought by the hurricane of the previous month:

Our last respects was the 26th September, Capn M . . . via Amsterdam and Capn P . . . for your place. All vessells have since been prevented from Sailing by the very bad weather we have had of late – here it has not been as bad as to windward where they have had a worse hurricane. Barbados has suffered more than any island we have yet heard of . . . 'tis said 1500 people lost their lives there – at Martinique it was also very violent, many houses near the sea being washd away; here we have been affected in the same way, great quantitys of provision damaged, the Stores washd away – great amounts of which are lost –

At M/que [Martinique] a fleet of 52 sail had arrived the day before from France; they were all blown out & but two have got back – many were carried into the English islands – two got here dismasted & same at St Croix; 'tis thought Curaçao has been affected as it seems to have raged with greater violence to the Southward – By a vessell just from Bermuda we hear 300 houses were blown down there and all the vessells that were building . . . In consequence of the weather, provisions, particularly flour seems to look up – a few days before we were so lucky to make sale of all your wine ashore at 35 fr . . . a very good sale considering the great quantitys we have here – most of the French vessells that are taken are loaded with it – all of which will find its way here. In a few days we expect to deliver it, which shall furnish your sales.

The partners bemoan the scarcity of arrivals from Curaçao from where they have had but one letter in the past three months. (The causes may have been due, not only to the hurricane season but also to the increasing prospect of becoming a British prize – a disaster to overtake Curaçao's biggest shipowner, David Morales, who that year lost his *Koningin Ester* and her cargo in this way.) But from that letter the two agents learn that there is very little prospect of finding a freight for an unlucky investment they have at Curaçao, for them at a cost of 5,400 pesos . . . 'which is very dear a vessell we have: we would rather have put up with the first loss.'

'Pray ship us some English goods,' they request: and of the elusive Papineau . . . 'The Governor and Council have taken it upon themselves to sell the *Snow D* . . . since Mr Papineau has absconded – it seems he is at Grenada.'

TO PROTECT THE NEUTRAL TRADE

At some time in 1779 Curson and Gouverneur had planned a voyage to Europe but had first postponed their sailing and finally, in view of the uncertainties of that year, abandoned the idea. As matters transpired, they did make the crossing little more than one year later, but under circumstances and to a destination which they could not have envisaged:

> We have duly received your esteem'd favour of 12th July, but did not reply sooner to it, since we expected from time to time that you should have become adventurers this way, agreeable to your promises and favoured us with you Commands, which if you do you may depend upon our doing our utmost for your Interest . . .'

Thus the van Staphorst brothers, writing from Amsterdam on 24 December, 1779: but the aborted project provided a number of letters to the American agents during 1780 typifying Dutch feeling as the British increased the pressure.

The American tobaccos arriving at St Eustatius were transferred by Curson and Gouverneur into vessels sailing for Holland. With these were sent consignments of West India products, the sugars, coffee, indigo and rum – part and sometimes the whole of the shipment being offset by the return cargoes to Statia. The letters dealing with this phase of the partners' business come from the merchants Nicholas and Jacob van Staphorst, certainly their most prolific correspondents in 1780, and from Alexander Honingman, Rombout Van Loon, Johannes Hoffman and Jacob van Bunschoten, all of Amsterdam. Another important contact was with the firm of Hassell and Tasker, trading from Rotterdam.

Their concerns with business matters were accompanied by the same

73

worries expressed from Virginia by Latimer Holstead. But the news from Amsterdam, at the centre of these troubled currents, was more immediate and understandably even more heartfelt. The British were, after all, jostling them on their own doorstep in the North Sea, and at no great distance in the Channel, while the confusion and impotence of the States General – particularly after the ignominy of the seizures by Captain Fielding – were painful for Dutch patriots to behold. Amid the general trepidation in the Netherlands, therefore, the declaration by Catherine of Russia that there would be no more of this bullying came as a ray of hope. It gleamed, faint but consistent, in the letters which followed.

Writing on 11 March, 1780, the van Staphorsts explained a delayed cargo – the *Lady Rebecca* has put back to unload because she . . . 'has had the misfortune to Sprung a leak . . .' and nervously reported the proposals for mutual protection:

> . . . The Empress of Russia has lately declared that She is Resolved to protect the neutral Trade and Navigation and desires the assistance of our States and the Northern Powers as likewise of Portugal . . . and we have some reason to expect that they'll all join together for that purpose which certainly may make a great alteration in the Situation of Political affairs . . . we do heartily wish it may contribute to bring about an earlier Peace . . .

As far-sighted merchants, the van Staphorsts not only worried about the effect of the war on their business but were no less easy in their minds as the thought that it might end:

> . . . we don't see any great Fluctuation in the Article (tobacco) during the present Warr & as an Article of Returns or Consignment when the Sales are effected immediately it may turn to good Account if judiciously bought . . . but (we) would by no means recommend it as an object of Speculation with an Eye to a distant period: the chance of a Peace or a Reconciliation with America would prove fatal to any such idea . . .

On 5th May they reported the safe arrival of 15 hogsheads of tobacco, nine of these being acknowledged as the property of Messrs Gouverneur Hill and Gouverneur 'of Curaçao' and, '. . . if of a very good Virginia quality . . . will command a very good price . . .' But they dampened that news with the advice that:

> Our States having accepted the proposal of the Empress of Russia to protect jointly the neutral Trade, the English have declared that the Ships of this Republick should be treated in future on the same footing as those of other Nations, which occasions a general Stagnation in our Trade as our

underwriters refuse to insure at less than 10 per cent coming from hence to your Island on neutral account. We hope to hear in a few days what Steps our States will take now and that convoy will be sent to our islands ..

In fact the information was premature. The 'acceptance' mentioned had been angrily cast back in the faces of the proposers and the only Steps to be taken by the States General at this point were in the direction of retreat. The willingness of Amsterdam, with her huge trade to protect and her ambitions for future markets in America, to chance her arm by joining the League was not matched by the provinces of Gelderland, Utrecht and Zeeland: it would not be until November and until the Dutch had been left with no other recourse but abject surrender that agreement could be found. Too late, alas. One month later and however unwillingly, they were no longer neutrals, but belligerents.

A letter dated 12 May informed Curson and Gouverneur that '... the late Proclamation of England has as yet taken no Effect, as our ships for the West India have till now sailed unmolested ... which begins to make our Trade alive again and has induced our Insurers to diminish the premium of Insurance on 7 per cent ... Coffee has advanced etc ...'

Lest this cause too much rejoicing the van Staphorsts added that:

'... if a Peace between England and America should take place it is to be feared our markets will be overstocked with products of the latter which must of course lower the price of those articles ...'

On 28 June, Nicholas and Jacob confirmed the sale of the fifteen hogsheads, six being to the account of Curson and Gouverneur at St Eustatius and realising £1089.18.0 '... to be credited when the money in Cash, when we shall hold at your disposal ...' The proceeds of the other nine hogsheads were to go to Gouverneur Hill and Gouverneur and 'according to your order we shall invest in good Checks and Stripes No. 2'

... the surrendering of Charlestown has greatly surprized People here and everyone longs to See what turn Political matters will take now ... In our department of state passes little remarkably ...

The calm deceived no-one: but while Dutch ships were still unharmed, insurance was now lowered to five per cent from Statia to Holland and six per cent for the return voyage ... 'by which the trade may continue as before ... Virginia Tobacco of the prime sort being much sought for remains very high, Sugars in General ... lower ...'

In September, letters from Holland echoed the general foreboding in the wake of the seizures at St Martin. The van Staphorsts wrote on the 19th, disposing briskly of business matters and revealing that the Empress Catherine was very much in earnest . . .:

. . . the Russia fleet is at sea and our West India Ships remain unmolested; the English have lately suffered a great loss, their West India fleet . . . five Indiamen being taken by the combined fleets; the loss . . . will naturally distress the Islands where the same were Expected and it Requires some time before others can be at Sea . . .

A hurried note from Hassell & Tasker on 23rd acknowledges incoming cargo and the partners' request that their share of the proceeds should be invested in 'good Bohea Tea': the Tobacco we have just received & are busy drawing the samples . . . any little delay in the sale shall not Retard the Expedition of the Teas as it is your Interest to have them sent before the season advances too far . . .' This is followed on 23 October by a similarly brief but discouraged note from van Bunschoten: he has decided not to send any further goods until the next year – until he has seen what turn the American war will take in the winter . . .

The doughty Captain Lamkin reappears with other captains in what is the last of the informative letters from Nicholas & Jacob van Staphorst. Dated 28 October, the Amsterdam merchants say they are glad that Curson and Gouverneur are pleased with the sales of their tobacco: the ship *de Vrouw Hillegonda Christina* Capn Mels Ruling '. . . by which Mr Areson Ship'd us from Curaçao some Indigo in which you are concerned, is arrived in a Port of Zealand, near Middelburg . . . but has got a leak in his Ship which however we hope will have occasioned no damage to the Indigo . . .'

The Staphorsts note that the *Lady Rebecca*, Captain Lamkin, has arrived safely at Statia with goods the agents will pass on to addressees: then comes yet another reference which would quite soon prove to be disastrous for them. Set before the triumphant eyes of unintended and hostile readers it reinforced beyond doubt Curson and Gouverneur's importance to the rebel cause:

We also accompany you herewith a letter of Mrs Izard to her husband, the Hon. Ralph Izard Sen.r Esq. and another of his Excellency John Adams Esq, to your good selves and which please to make use of and to forward the former by the first safe conveyance . . .
. . . You'll no doubt be acquainted before this reaches you that Mr

Laurens, old President of Congress on his voyage to Europe has been taken by the English and is kept a close Prisoner in the Tower of London, . . . of which Mr A will give you some particulars . . . we are extremely sorry for this unhappy event, since we have a notion that his being in this Country would have been of great Success to the American cause. The news you gave us of the most extraordinary Conduct of the English at St Martin was known already here, before we got your letter. It should certainly be very Surprising, if experience had not Proved us sufficiently that (these) desperados are capable of doing any thing whatsoever that they think convenient . . .

But these 'desperados', Holstead's 'bold plunderers of mankind' faced nothing worse than this tearful resentment. There is hope, but little conviction in this letter, that salvation might be at hand:

Our States are at present assembled and it is Expected every day to be known what their resolutions will be with regard to the proposalls of the Northern Powers in joining with them, for the Protection of the neutral Trade and Navigation against the vexations of the English . . . which we think will have a great Influence upon Politicks: tho' the British Court Seems to be determinated to carry on the war . . .

Inclosed we do accompany you a price currant [sic] for your Speculation . . .

We have seen that in British eyes, Samuel Curson and Isaac Gouverneur were already damned as rebels by the inclusion of their names in Lauren's fated Treaty. Their business letters provided further evidence and no paragraph therein more incriminating than that which ended the final letter of 28 November from Hassell and Tasker . . .

. . . Tobacco keeps up owing to the scantiness of our late supplies . . . You have on the other side prices of sundry articles for your government & in all your commands we remain Respectfully . . .

– 4 –

WAR, TEMPEST AND TREACHERY

The declaration of war by France and Spain generated much concern among the planters and traders of the Caribbean. It was clearly not in their interests that the privateers of the belligerent nations should make free with the vessels of the inter-island trade. The commonsense proposal by the Governor of Martinique, François-Claude-Amour, Marquis de Bouillé, that merchant craft should be safe from interference in their own or their neighbours' harbours and waters – although not on the high seas – was put to the British governors and agreed, to the obvious relief of all concerned.

DE BOUILLÉ

It would not be long before the name of de Bouillé would impinge more forcefully on British minds. As de Guichen, d'Estaing, de Grasse and La Motte-Piquet were to typify French naval power in the West Indies, so de Bouillé would represent the threat of French military action in the region. This patriotic duty de Bouillé undertook with a courage that his British opponents were to acknowledge and a military genius which they would fatally underestimate. His place in the events of this time is such, however, that we should know something of his background: his achievements during his tenure as Governor of Martinique will speak for themselves.

*   *   *

François-Claude Amour, Marquis de Bouillé, was born in 1739 in his father's mansion, Le Cluzel, near the south-west boundary of Auvergne. Orphaned while yet a child, he became the charge of an uncle who was then Bishop of Autun, a small see in Burgundy. Fifty years later, at the outbreak of the Revolution, this post became famous as the springboard of a more ambitious incumbent named Talleyrand.

The boy was placed in the most prestigious college of the Jesuits in Paris, Louis-le-Grand, and remained there until he was fourteen, when he entered the Army. This popular solution discharged his guardian's responsibilities. Furthermore, the early curtailment of conventional education and boyhood and this precipitation into an adult and deadly environment made him at one with his adversary-to-be and his senior by twenty-two years, Rodney.

De Bouillé became a Dragoon captain at sixteen, but was to enjoy that splendour in peace for only three years before the Seven Years' War provided him with the ambience in which his personality was to thrive and develop. He earned Royal notice in 1761, after a furious action at Grunberg in which he routed a column led by the Duke of Brunswick '. . . taking eleven guns and nineteen flags and standards.' Despatched to Versailles to inform the King of this good news it is recorded that he passed over his own part in the fighting and . . . 'spoke only of his valiant comrades . . .'

This transparent omission caused His Majesty to observe that M de Bouillé had perhaps forgotten that he was responsible for this brilliant affair. No doubt there was much deprecatory fluttering of fingers at this but a more tangible reward was to follow: in recognition of this service de Bouillé would leave Versailles as a Colonel and with the promise that he would be given the next vacant command.

*   *   *

In 1768, five years after the end of the war and with it, perhaps, the appeal of regimental life, he was given his first colonial assignment as Governor of Guadeloupe. He was then 29 years old. He was to hold this position until 1770: by that date he had bought land in Guadeloupe and had visited all of the neighbouring islands, including St Kitts and St Eustatius in his final year. The soldier's eye with which he examined these places and his familiarity with their approaches armed him for the exploits which were to trouble the British so sorely in the next contest. Meanwhile, and as its ingredients seethed, he was recalled and served again in France.

Yet de Bouillé's experience of the Caribbean was to be remembered when, in the anticipation of a new war, France began to reinforce her own hold in that sea. The smart of her lost territories in Canada was to be considerably soothed by the prospect of damaging Great Britain in the West Indies, of inhibiting her trade by raiding or privateering and of denying her sugar islands vital supplies from North America. These and many other reasons, and somewhere among them, the stirring call to aid the rebels' bid for freedom, all motivated the Alliance of France and Spain with the colonists. The rationale was complete. It required only that in preparation, the right man should be chosen to govern France's most important bastion in the area, Martinique: and as events were to prove, the right man was de Bouillé, now in 1777 promoted Maréchal de Camp, the equivalent of Brigadier General.

His instructions were to remain alert for moves by the British and, should war come, to assume supreme military command of the French Windward Islands, although each of these, much to de Bouillé's dissatisfaction, retained its own civil administration. His reservations on the potential for conflict arising from the independence of their governors were to be given force by such disputes on the British side: here, also, to the exasperation of the commanders and the detriment of their task, the civil governors intervened in military affairs and insisted on their right to do so.

De Bouillé's appointment, however, was timely, if only just: on receipt of the declaration of war he had interceded sensibly in the matter of arranging an acceptable *modus vivendi* for the islands: but that done, there were more dramatic plans to be drawn up and put into effect.

Thus, grudging respect by the British for de Bouillé's pragmatism lasted no longer than one month before being translated into fury on the 7 September, when the Marquis mounted an invasion of Dominica and took it from them with contemptuous ease – a success ensured by four frigates and a vast flotilla of armed small craft carrying a force near three thousand strong. With the enthusiastic collaboration of the French islanders this army confronted a British garrison of forty-one regular troops and some one hundred and fifty militia: whereupon, the futility of resistance being clear, Lieutenant Governor William Stuart surrendered the island to de Bouillé.

OLD WARS AND NEW

As related, de Bouillé's exploit had ignited great alarm in the equally vulnerable British sugar islands and this had spurred the military and naval counter-measures planned in Whitehall. This urgency was later to be expressed in the most blunt terms by the King: after hearing Admiral Barrington's account of the condition of Bryon's fleet resulting from his misguided attempt on the French off Grenada on 6 July 1779, His Majesty warned Sandwich that, were Britain to lose her sugar islands ... 'it will be impossible to raise money to continue the war.'

For so critical an issue as the very fate of the empire it was essential to be supreme in the West Indies. The keystone for that aim was, of course, St Lucia, now held by the French and in sufficient force to justify that large army of five thousand British troops with artillery which had been placed under the command of Major-General James Grant. We last saw this army, snatched from a protesting General Clinton and assembling for its forthcoming voyage to the West Indies. It is at this point that national interest and grand strategy settle on the shoulders of a familiar character for among the soldiery selected for this service was the 35th Regiment of Foot, now quartered in New York under its commanding officer, Lieutenant-Colonel James Cockburn: who regarded the prospect with dismay.

Cockburn was now in his twenty-eighth year of service, established in New York with Letitia and the children and enjoying the blessed peace of garrison duty after three years of fighting begun at Bunker Hill. He had proved his courage and professional ability but he had come too far and along too rough a road to pretend anxiety for yet another campaign, especially in a region infamous for its virulent sickness. There may well have been other motives for his reluctance and doubtless, Letitia would have added to them. But that Cockburn now pleaded his impaired health in an effort to be excused from serving with Grant suggests an anxiety with good cause.

He would, of course, go wherever he was ordered and fight whenever that became necessary: but if there was an alternative it was worth exploring. Accordingly, he not only sought Grant's indulgence but also endeavoured to circumvent any possible refusal from that quarter. There was, he thought, another influential person who might be used to extricate him. The letter of 25 October to Lieutenant-General Campbell in which Cockburn reported that '... my Boy is appointed to Ensign in the Regiment...' therefore included two further paragraphs reflecting this purpose.

There are ten Battalions under Mr Grant ordered for the West Indies (the 35th, one) and we are told the Embarkation is to take place in a few days; tho' we are in hopes the next Frigate from England may Stop it. The Climate I don't like, tho' the Winter months are very tolerable ... Yet to Guard against the Worst, I should be obliged to you to make application that the King's Leave should be sent out to me, on account of my Health, least the Commander should take it into his head to refuse my personal application.

This request I hope may not be deemed extravagant, particularly when

81

my Services are Stated and that the Service we are destined for must be finish'd before that Leave can be Sent me . . .

I propose leaving my family here, 'till a proper opportunity offers for England, Where I hope, soon to join them . . .

That much-desired Leave was not forthcoming. Let us leave Cockburn savouring his disappointment in New York as he breaks the news to Letitia and prepares his regiment for their march to the wharves.

*　*　*

The death of Lieutenant-Colonel Robert Carr during the fighting at White Plains in '76 had raised Cockburn to this importance, his seniority in the regiment and his presence on the battlefield outweighing any consideration of purchase. But if that knowledge relieved him in that one very real barrier to his progress had been removed, there were others to mock the promises he had given to Campbell two years earlier.

The free hand with which he had hoped to rejuvenate 'the poor old 35th' had been stayed by vexations still unresolved. At one time it had been ambition enough to desire this command but Cockburn was now finding its achievement soured by insolence from one quarter, defiance and challenge from another, and a conspicuous lack of warmth towards him on the part of many of his long-serving officers. His pride, his sense of military propriety and his own authoritarian personality limited the opportunities for compromise even where there existed the will: which on neither side, was always the case.

An unhappy situation and no doubt seen by Cockburn as a bitter recompense for what had been endured during his long climb and the years of his initiation. The events of that journey had moulded him thus far and helped to shape the forbidding image projected at St Eustatius. Here, however, we have an advantage over the islanders to whom he came as an oppressive stranger: we are able to retrace his steps.

*　*　*

As a veteran Lieutenant, Cockburn had already seen his share of battle and in wounds taken and experience gained could count himself an equal among any of his war-hardened fellow-officers. Behind him at this time was the shambles of Fort William Henry and the fighting, wounds and privations of Louisbourg, Quebec and the campaign along the St Lawrence.

The assault on Martinique had followed – the only expedition shared in their various capacities by Rodney, Vaughan, Cockburn and Gordon, whose paths would not again merge for nearly twenty years: and after Martinique, the treacherous tranquility of Pensacola, on the Gulf of Mexico, whither the 25th and 35th Regiments, each a thousand strong, were deployed after the Floridas had been ceded to Great Britain in exchange for Havana. That sojourn of three years left its mark on James Cockburn, for the evil locality repaid the Regiments for their previous six years of hardship by wasting their ranks by disease. Brought back to England in '65, the muster of the 25th was barely one hundred and that of the 35th, a pitiful forty: among them Lieutenant James Cockburn and Private William Gordon.

It is time to find Cockburn again, now, in 1778 a Lieutenant-Colonel summoned to that other army commanded by Major-General James Grant. Five thousand souls, they regard this expedition to St Lucia without illusion: they are aware that on those beaches and heights, French cannon and musketry will greet them, and those who are not killed or wounded in the attack will face the prospect of an indeterminate stay in the sickly West Indies. Such unsoldierly introspection is not to be found in Trimen's *History of the 35th Regiment* of course, but there is good authority for supposition. Although the troops might not have known of it, one Samuel Johnson had doubtless spoken for all men in such circumstances, twelve months earlier: 'Depend on it, Sir, when a man knows he is to be hanged in a fortnight, it concentrates his mind wonderfully.'

ST LUCIA

On 3 November, 1778, the 35th Regiment was duly crowded into its allotted transport among the sixty such vessels embarking Grant's army. These, with their attendant ancillaries, the storeships and the miscellany of floating handmaidens for the force, sailed on the same day from Sandy Hook, under the protection of that energetic Hotham who had been the naval commander of Clinton's Hudson adventure.

For those soldiers not already preoccupied by the first shifting of the planks under their feet, the powerful escort promised a sobering future. Hotham's 50-gun *Preston* was accompanied by two 64's – *St Albans* and *Monmouth* and by two more 50-gun ships *Isis* and *Centurion*. It was coincidental that this was also the day on which d'Estaing, with twelve line-of-battle ships, grasped the opportunity of sailing from Boston, since his always-to-be-baffled pursuer, the unlucky Admiral Byron – who would be remembered by history as 'Foul Weather Jack' – had been driven away by a violent storm and was then nursing his twice-damaged squadron – for he had suffered during his stormy outward voyage from England – at Rhode Island. Foul weather would continue to keep him there, impotent and neutralised until 14 December: and by then, it was too late for him to influence the fate of St Lucia.

It was fortunate for Hotham's ships that d'Estaing remained unaware of their proximity and that a wild gale threw them further apart: but the smaller British force and the convoy remained intact and made Barbados on 10 December. So earnestly desired, that landfall at Carlisle Bay merely provided extra torment for the troops, rewarded for their thirty-seven bruising days at sea by only the sight of unattainable Bridgetown. At which, still imprisoned in the transports, they gazed hungrily for only two days before the new naval commander in the Lesser Antilles, Admiral Barrington, added his own squadron and led them to sea yet again.

* * *

To St Lucia, on the 13th, skirting, at the northern tip of the island, the choice locations of Pigeon Island and Gros Islet Bay, which two years on would become the base of that commander-in-waiting, Rodney. On down the western coast until they came to anchor off the great bay of the Grande Cul-de-Sac: and that evening began the assault by landing the reserve of the army under Brigadier General Meadows – the Fifth Foot and the grenadier and light infantry battalions, in which were the two flank companies of the 35th. For all of these men, this long-delayed release from those hateful ships came dearly: they were immediately employed in forcing the northern heights of the bay, held by French regulars and island militia.

This operation masked the landing of the main body of troops: five regiments under Brigadier General Prescott, one of these, Cockburn's 35th: their first task was to secure the bay and their communication with the reserve. A vigilant night on the ground thus established, and at dawn, an advance up the great slope of Morne Fortune to take that stronghold, and with it, the little town. Next, the Vigie: three miles north of the Grande Cul-de-Sac, this peninsula formed the northern boundary of the great bay of the Carénage, where Barrington had hoped to keep his transports in more security than at the Cul-de-Sac. Meadows, with 1300 troops, therefore occupied the post with its command of that arm of the bay, while Calder's four battalions held the shores and maintained the link with the fleet. In addition, detachments occupied the mountain posts overlooking the south side of the Cul-de-Sac.

But they were still a long way from victory. No sooner had the last height been taken than d'Estaing appeared off the island, urgently diverted from an expedition intended to dislodge the British from St Vincent and the Grenadines and for which he had gathered a powerful force. Twelve sail of the line, the same number of frigates and privateers and more than fifty transports carrying nine thousand troops, a great proportion of these brought from France and the remainder comprised of men from the French islands.

But these men had first to be landed. d'Estaing made two attacks on Barrington's fleet screening the mouth of the Cul-de-Sac, and in the first was severely punished for his assumption that the batteries on the heights were still in French hands. He was no more successful in his second attempt, despite a long and fierce engagement, but on the 16th, managed to land some 5000 men in Choc Bay, to the north of the Vigie peninsula. Supported by diversionary fire from the sea, this force advanced in three columns, one of them headed by d'Estaing himself, one commanded by M de Lovendahl and the third by de Bouillé, never one to forgo such an opportunity, although, on this occasion, one of a trio leading their men to utter disaster.

They were at once exposed to the enfilading fire of the British batteries and suffered greatly: but went on to make three successive frontal attacks on Meadows' entrenched soldiers, who held their fire until the attackers were at point-blank range, cut them down in their scores with a single volley, and received the others with the bayonet. Three such attacks, and each one, vide Mahan, a repetition of Bunker Hill. Shattered, routed and broken, the survivors withdrew, leaving their dead and wounded where they lay. Shortly after came common need and the human grace of compassion: by ready agreement, the dead were allowed burial and the wounded, removal to their own side.

There could be no further attacks. In the burning heat and amid the chaotic leavings of battle, British and French counted the cost since the landing at the Cul-de-Sac five days earlier. For the three assaults on the Vigie, the French had lost forty-one officers and suffered eight hundred men killed and wounded. These figures mounted as they searched the fighting grounds for the fallen in the following days, until the final count reached a total of five hundred dead and eleven hundred wounded.

In the scale of these affairs the British report of one hundred and seventy-one killed and wounded was better news for Major-General Grant at his headquarters in the house of the island's Governor, the Chevalier de Micoud. Regimental losses were not specified in the battalion returns, but of the grenadier battalion, the expeditionary force had lost . . . 'three men killed and five officers . . . one of them Lieutenant

Thomas Williams of the 35th, two sergeants, two drummers, and seventy-two rank and file wounded: of the light infantry battalion, seven rank and file killed, one officer and forty-seven rank and file wounded . . .'

Frustrated by land, d'Estaing took his men off and lay sullenly offshore for ten days, as if to threaten another attack. He was joined 'hourly' by new vessels – French and American privateers, hoping for pickings: but since Barrington progressively improved his situation by concentrating his ships and by establishing new batteries to cover the approaches, and because there no longer seemed to be any hope of useful support ashore, d'Estaing finally admitted defeat and, on the 29th, made sail. His departing fleet could still be seen from St Lucia on the following day when the Chevalier de Micoud, representing his anxious leading citizens, formally capitulated to Major-General Grant.

Among the victors, James Cockburn.

This Cursed Country

Cockburn was to remain on St Lucia for two years, variously at the Cul-de-Sac and on the hill of Morne Fortune: but save for the now silent guns, he was to find little peace there. In the aftermath of the campaign there was work enough on the island for a few hundred soldiers but for the bulk of Grant's huge army there were more pressing requirements elsewhere.

All but three of the expedition's regiments were therefore dispersed to the British islands most urgently demanding reinforcement: the 15th, 28th and 55th Regiments under Brigadier General Robert Prescott to St Kitts – from where he would also oversee Antigua, garrisoned by the 40th lately commanded by Lieutenant-Colonel Thomas Musgrave. The unlucky 4th, 5th and 46th (no favouritism here: this was Vaughan's own regiment) were to serve at sea aboard Byron's men-of-war and the 27th, 35th and 49th Regiments to garrison St Lucia under the temporary command of Brigadier General Sir Henry Calder.

Brigadier General Anthony St Leger succeeded to this command in May, 1780. Vaughan's further disposition for his Brigadiers put Anthony Tottenham into the command at Barbados and Gabriel Christie, at Antigua. It will avoid confusion if it is noted that Christie afterward moved to Barbados to take over the command of the army on Vaughan's return to England in August 1781. The Brigadier's subsequent correspondence with Lieutenant-Colonel Cockburn will prove to be of great interest.

On St Lucia, there was little peace and, initially, work enough. The island secured, the dead hurriedly buried, the wounded patched or given to the surgeons and military order imposed on a population which scarcely veiled its hostility, it was urgent to find quarters for the officers and men of the three regiments. Although the reasons were not fully understood and another century would elapse before the lethal role of the fever-carrying mosquito would be identified, dreadful experience had taught that in such climes, soldiers should not remain exposed at night.

The galling problem of shelter had long haunted the British Army in the West Indies, wherever they had established themselves. Expressions of goodwill towards the Army were not always forthcoming from island assemblies oppressed by war, by poor crops, reduced revenue and inflated risks: given all this, it was futile to press them for money towards the cost of housing the troops. The message, even from the most well-disposed of the legislatures, was that in this regard as in so many others, the Army must look after itself.

The 35th alone mustered 603 men and St Lucia owned very few suitable buildings. In the course of the Seven Years' War the French had built two barrack blocks on Morne Fortune, a house for the Governor, a hospital and magazines for powder and provisions. Now the barracks were required to serve as hospitals, leaving the soldiers to construct ramshackle hovels for themselves out of reeds and thatch, which offered no protection whatsoever against the rains . . . Such desperate measures goaded General Lucius Carey, on Tobago, to protest that the plantation negroes were better housed . . .

Cockburn himself made use of a tent while at the Cul-de-Sac (although there are later references to 'his room') but it was not until Vaughan arrived at St Lucia in April, when the garrison had endured these conditions for some sixteen months, that any truly determined effort to relieve them was initiated. On Vaughan's personal order, supported by funds advanced by the officers of the garrison, work was begun on the building of sheds and on the construction of a new barracks to house 300 men. In uncompromising terms which His Majesty's Ministers could only concede, Vaughan conveyed this news to Germain along with the engineer's estimate of the cost – two thousand five hundred pounds – and with it, a memorial from the officers who had financed the building of their own shelters and who now asked for repayment. Vaughan also pressed for more barracks to be built and for timber to be supplied from England for this work.

To all of this Germain agreed, but for all the goodwill no such practical aid came from Britain or indeed from other potential sources in America. Matters of scarcity, other priorities and lack of transport or suitable convoys are cited as reasons. These were familiar replies to pleas for medical staff, medicines and wine for the fast weakening troops, but in the single respect of shelter the effect was to perpetuate the hardships of military life on St Lucia and greatly to contribute to the later disorders of the garrison and its progressive undermining by sickness.

For the enemy now was disease and St Lucia a ferment of yellow fever, malaria and blackwater fever. More potent than any human adversary and as devastating as any cannonade, the wastage was evident daily in the unfortunates who remained prostrated and sweating in their shelters or who stumbled to the hospital, or were carried there by fearful bearers. For Cockburn, these scenes were all too familiar. Here was the experience of the Floridas recreated and all of his misgivings in New York now vindicated, for the fever swept the West Indies, felling men in such numbers that regiments were halved, made less than half or even – as happened to the 91st Foot at Barbados – near destroyed. There, wrote Tottenham to Vaughan on 17 May, the troops were '. . . to a man unfit for duty . . . a violent fever rages amongst them which is, I am afraid, epidemic . . .'

As a precautionary measure, Tottenham ordered the burning of their bedding and blankets. He would additionally have consigned the troops' poor rags of clothing to the flames, save that there was nothing else to cover them.

The appalling companionship of disease during the campaign is summed in the regimental returns for 1780 but once again it is a personal view implicit with emotion and despair which better conveys the reality. Here is St Leger's grim letter to Vaughan dated 5 September, wherein he reported that:

> . . . the deaths of this garrison (St Lucia) do not decrease, nor do I believe it is in the power of man to prevent them till the sickly season is over . . . The 89th, 90th and 91st Regiments are only nominal and of very little use. The 89th (at Barbados) are not able to bury their dead . . . Our Physical people fall ill and when that is the case, are not sufficient for the number of sick. The two principal posts where the 89th and 91st are could not withstand the attack of a company of grenadiers . . .

*   *   *

In the spring of 1780, the army in the West Indies totalled little more than 6000 effectives but by the time Vaughan sailed for home in August, 1781, disease had taken more than 2500 of these men and of that number, more than 1300 had died at St Lucia in the second half of 1780.

How distressing, then for the General that in December of that year, the dedicated John Stewart, Inspector of the hospital at Barbados should appeal to him requesting the urgent transfer of one of his few 'physical people' . . .:

Sir – Should His Excellency the Commander-in-Chief think it Compatible with the service – I beg leave to request that Mr A – Surgeon now at St Lucia, may be Ordered for the Hospital Duty at Barbados: As I have now A Hundred and Thirteen Physical and Surgical Patients & but one Mate to Assist me just removed from Sickness . . . Besides My Attending on Several Officers All of Whom Cannot be done justice to, with my best Inclinations . . . I am etc . . .

The army also bled from another artery. Throughout the period, Vaughan was repeatedly tried and disappointed by the numerous pleas of officers seeking leave to depart that malign environment, to delay their return from America or England, or worse yet, not to come out to the West Indies at all. Lord Chewton wrote from New York on 9 November, 1780, and included a further frustration for Vaughan with his own submission; the General should not await the return of yet another officer:

Having been very ill during the closing part of the time I was in the West Indies, I have applied to Sir George Rodney for leave to stay here, as I am afraid if I was to return to the West Indies at present, I might have a return of the same disorder . . .
. . . Having experienced your kindness to me on many occasions, I trust, Sir, that you will not disapprove of the step I have taken. My intentions are to go to Lord Cornwallis in the Carolinas and to remain with him the winter. In case you should think it necessary I should join my Regiment sooner, be assured Sir, that the first notice I have of it I shall take the earliest opportunity of returning to the West Indies . . .'
I am sorry that Lord Winchelsea is in a very bad way and it seems to be the opinion of the Doctors here that he should return to England for the recovery of his health. What his intentions are . . . I do not know . . .

Other men were less inclined to depend on Vaughan's indulgence in this matter and therefore brought overpowering weight to bear: Lieutenant-Colonel Haslam, for example, who solicited the aid of Lord Amherst . . .

Whitehall, 24th March 1780 –

Lt-Colonel Haslam, Captain of a Company in the 5th Regiment of Foot, having represented to me that his health will not admit of his joining his Regiment in the West Indies, and he, having produced to me a Certificate thereof which I have laid before the King, I have the honour to acquaint you that His Majesty has been pleased to give Lt-Colonel Haslam leave to remain in England for the recovery of his health . . .

It was a rare white person, soldier or sailor, who was left unmarked by the searing experience of the Caribbean. Perhaps Captain Thomas, of the *Ulysses* (44), voiced the fears of every man for themselves when he wished Vaughan good health '. . . while you continue in this Cursed Country . . .'

* * *

Drewe

The early months of 1780 brought much more to trouble the generals and all the British-garrisoned islands were affected. All commodities were scarce and inevitably, such staples as rum, fresh meat and vegetables, firewood and candles became the objects of opportunistic and relentless profiteering by merchants and residents alike. In the nature of their calling, the troops employed stealth and cheek to achieve some small balance: but there was now little or nothing in hand, as Vaughan reported to Germain in April, for further expenditure and to meet the commissary's debts. The deputy commissary at Antigua indeed risked imprisonment on this score while, given no other recourse, Christie pledged his own credit for over £800 to ensure a supply of fresh food for the sick and convalescent. But increasingly, the blunt demands for cash and the refusal of further supplies until it was forthcoming meant that the army's credit had reached its limit.

Money had drained from the war chest for pay and provisions, for the most vital needs of the sick and the hospital, for materials and labour for the barracks and sheds and in particular, for that killing task, begun by Calder in the Autumn of '79, of hauling cannon and supplies to the top of Morne Fortune. The British, vociferous on the rights of the individual at home found no difficulty in making use of slaves elsewhere. However, at hostile St Lucia they were especially obstructed in the purchase or hire of slaves from their reluctant owners. St Leger pressed negroes where he could, but in this respect St Lucia's planters remained defiantly unhelpful: one of them, the Chevalier d'Agron, to the point of incurring banishment for his obduracy.

90

The army was now at least as concerned for its very subsistence as for any prospect of renewed battle with the French. Letters of appeal flowed from Vaughan to Germain and from the commanders of the islands to Vaughan or to his secretary, Captain Alexander Bradshaw, or to Major Joseph Ferguson, Deputy Adjutant-General, all of this a harassment for Vaughan and his brigadiers and a weighty distraction from their purpose. Underlying all, too, was the continuing feud for authority over the military waged by Governor Burt at Antigua. It would be ended only by Burt's death in January of 1781: but meanwhile it was yet another annoyance for Vaughan to take into account.

All these issues exercised the generals but at regimental level, Cockburn was concerned with his own failure and frustration. Entrapped as they now were in the heat and boredom of St Lucia, the 35th were far from the model regiment he had promised to Campbell and it was not something for which he could blame his soldiers. There was work enough to keep the men occupied and while on guard, or other duties or on their twice-daily parade on the hill of Morne Fortune, their opportunities for mischief were notionally limited. There was, in addition, the rough commonsense of the NCO's and if that needed reinforcement, their ever-ready rattan canes.

But much more serious and threatening to Cockburn's peace of mind was the insubordination and insupportable behaviour of a number of his officers which reached its peak early in 1780. One of these he had already brought to a court martial for misconduct and another for responding to his commanding officer's rebuke by challenging him to a duel. Yet another had sent in his resignation rather than face a court martial for an imprudence – unstated – for which he was shunned by his fellow sub-alterns. And two others who had earned approbrium had escaped it by dying: '. . . happily for them' observed Cockburn sourly.

Since all of this was necessarily within the domain of Brigadier General Calder and ultimately, of Vaughan, as well as having become common knowledge among the garrison, it is likely that Cockburn considered himself sufficiently embarrassed in their eyes. He could not, therefore, have welcomed the prospect of yet another clash and this time with the 35th's field officer, Major Edward Drewe.

*   *   *

Cockburn was to make plain that he detested Drewe for his pretensions and his vainglory. If this were not enough – and it was in painful contrast with Cockburn's own hard road and more than possibly contributed to his aversion for his subordinate, Drewe was also ostentatiously wealthy and encouraged by that fact to be entirely irresponsible in his approach to regimental duties – a failing early detected by Cockburn when Drewe had served, first as Ensign and then as Lieutenant in his company.

Now, more than ten years of an association punctuated by misbehaviour and admonition had honed Cockburn's dislike and it had been returned by Drewe in his own inimitably insolent fashion. Their feud, however, had not come to a head since at sporadic intervals their duties had fortunately separated them. However, when the notoriously wayward Drewe had boarded Cockburn's transport as it lay at New York and announced himself to be now 'major to the 35th' – having paid the extraordinary sum of four thousand guineas for the privilege – Cockburn had received the news with astonishment and anger. He was extremely concerned, he told Drewe, on two counts, first, for the good of the regiment and second, for Drewe's own sake: 'You would have done better in a strange regiment' Cockburn affirmed, 'a regiment you were not known in.'

Having little option in the urgency of embarkation Cockburn could only accept Drewe's assurances of future good intent. These could have been other than barely credible at the time. Any belief in these promises was soon abandoned as both men found new causes for friction. Given the long history of conflict between them and the manner in which their relations reached a climax at St Lucia, a final confrontation became inevitable.

Having simmered enough, Cockburn chose to vent his spleen by humiliating his major before the regiment. Knowing that Drewe was incapable of carrying out the order since he had made no effort to learn the drill movements, Cockburn had required him to 'put the regiment through the manual' . . . and had had the grim pleasure of hearing the startled major's public confession of inadequacy. The effect on those officers within earshot and those others to be informed thereafter is to be imagined: but Drewe's response had been to absent himself from further parades and, in the course of a rapid descent downhill, to choose to carouse with 'undesirable' companions i.e., disgraced officers, to leave the island without permission, albeit inadvertently (he had chosen a bad moment for an unauthorized visit to friends aboard a man of war and while he was aboard, the vessel had slipped its cable in order to cruise off Fort Royal) and otherwise to let the regiment go to the devil, even while Cockburn lay fevered in his tent at the Cul-de-Sac.

Provocation enough for Cockburn. It is something of a surprise to find him attempting to dissuade Vaughan from ordering a court martial but this moderation probably owed less to charity than to prudence. There could be no credit for him in the dismal turnover of the 35th's officers. Drewe possessed a quick wit and a sharp tongue and there was no telling what damaging barbs might be hurled at his commanding officer. Cockburn had therefore suggested to General Vaughan on two occasions that the troublesome Drewe should sell out or be removed to another corps. He had also forwarded Drewe's own request for transfer to the Commander-in-Chief with his own request that this should be granted. But with many more serious matters at hand, the tally of charges against Drewe was clearly more than Vaughan was prepared to overlook and accordingly, a court martial was convened for Wednesday, 24 May. Drewe's defence, although delivered with a fine sense of theatre – '. . . is it a crime to die?' he asked the Court, referring to Cockburn's bitter comment on the two officers who had cheated him in this manner – nevertheless boiled down to no more than injured dignity. Measured against his indiscipline and the needs of a regiment on campaign it could only seem trivial. The decision of the Court, announced on Friday, 2 June, was that Drewe should be cashiered.

The record shows Cockburn in a difficult situation, openly mocked by the prisoner – for whom he made his contempt plain, describing Drewe as 'a Major in his cups only' – and deeply disappointed by the failure of some respected fellow-officers to support him. The minutiae of the exchanges between Drewe and his prosecutor and of the witnesses called on their behalf belong elsewhere, but amidst the week-long recital of accusation, complaint and self-justification can be found the core of the dispute. It was offered, for example, that in 1777 Drewe, although most eligible by seniority, had been passed over by Cockburn in favour of Hugh Massey for the command of the Grenadier company following the murder of Captain Phillips '. . . by some of the country people . . .' This clearly rankled with him but Drewe spoke of an earlier origin for Cockburn's malevolence. Because of its implications of shabbiness and perhaps also, because it touched on sensitive ground, his allegation could not have been comfortable hearing for anyone in attendance.

Drewe had led his light infantry company bravely at Bunker Hill and had seen it cut down from its original strength of 38 to six privates. He had on that day received '. . . three wounds, two contusions and had my shoulder dislocated . . .' and had languished '. . . near eighteen weeks of these and the disorders of the climate . . .' But he had protested from his sick-bed – and so incurred this lasting enmity – when Captain Cockburn had laid claim to the effects of those men Drewe had 'led to the slaughter.'

Cockburn refrained from comment. The members of the court were equally tactful in regarding the matter as irrelevant but the Lieutenant-Colonel's image was to suffer again as a result of a striking outburst in the course of his evidence. Scornfully dismissive of Drewe's wounds, he claimed them to be 'no mark of the merit of an officer' (Massey may have received this badly: as one of Drewe's company, he had taken his own

93

wounds on that day along with twenty-four NCO's and men. Fortunately he would not be present when Cockburn proudly mentioned his own wounds before another court in the future). It was Cockburn's next sentence however, which shows us the demon behind the hostility and which perhaps told the court rather more than he had intended:

> . . . ever since that day it has been rung in our ears, the military achievements and exploits of that Captain Drewe . . . all founded on those accidental wounds he received . . .

*   *   *

It was good to be rid of Drewe – who was shipped home at length to write and publish his own exculpatory account of the court martial, in 1782 – but the lesson remained for Cockburn that he stood very much alone. His most worthy officers – notably Massey, Smelt, Lamb, Wheeler, Fitzgerald and Campbell – were by now wary of his choler. They continued to behave correctly towards him but respect for his rank and severe temperament was neither regard nor friendship. Too many of them appeared to have supported Drewe as a 'good and diligent officer' while the much respected Massey, in particular, had been courageous enough to describe Cockburn's manner during that mortifying parade as 'haughty, imperious and overbearing . . .'

These were not words and opinions to be easily forgotten.

*   *   *

It was thankfully necessary – even a relief – to turn again to the work of guarding and fortifying the island, of building those desperately needed huts and of trying to do these things in the face of the sickness which would kill another 600 soldiers during June, July and August. The terrible circumstances created their own urgencies but now all effort was spurred by the threat of an even greater crisis. The hurricane season was upon them and while it lasted, its dangers would make even war and sickness matters of secondary importance.

HURRICANE

In the afternoon of 3, October, 1780 the first cyclone rushed on Jamaica from the south. Its mighty wind and enormous waves battered the little port of Savannah-le-Mer and laid waste the country, the parishes and the plantations and cane beyond. Those who were exposed to this force died

94

in their hundreds: scores of others were buried under the ruins of houses and other buildings in which they had cowered for shelter.

'About ten,' reported the Annual Register . . . 'the waters began to abate and at that time a smart shock of an earthquake was felt. All the small vessels in the bay were driven on shore and dashed to pieces. The ships *Princess Royal*, . . . *Henry*, and *Austin-Hall* . . . were forced from their anchors and carried so far into the morass that they will never be got off. The earthquake lifted the *Princess Royal* (a vessel of 90 guns) from her beam ends, righted her and fixed her in a firm bed: this circumstance has been of great use to the surviving inhabitants, for whose accommodation she now serves as a house . . .'

On the morning of the 10th the tempest of rain and wind brought similar calamity to Barbados. By noon, many ships were hard ashore: by four the frigate *Albemarle* had lost its anchors and, accompanied by all other vessels capable of making sail, had fled to the less certain destiny of the open sea.

For all its terrors, the sea was preferable to the stricken island. The wind had levelled almost every building: soldiers abandoned their falling barracks while, in the hospital, the sick lay piteously under the rain of debris as roofs and walls disintegrated about them. Those evacuated remained mired and sodden wherever they had been carried.

The early collapse of Vaughan's own house killed seven and left his Secretary, Captain Bradshaw, to lie helpless with a broken thigh and shortly after, to die. Vaughan himself escaped much bruised, but lost all his papers – and indeed, all his clothes and other possessions – buried among the rubble. Where, as at Government House, walls three feet thick failed to protect the Governor's family and all who sought refuge with them – the wind '. . . forcing its way into every part and tearing off most of the roof . . .' and '. . . the water rising within four feet deep and the ruins falling from all quarters . . .' the unfortunates fled, risking the dash into the open to throw themselves under the carriage of the cannon and to pray that they might not be crushed should the gun be dismounted by the gale – like the twelve-pounder which was '. . . carried from the south to the north battery, a distance of 140 yards . . .'

Reporting the catastrophe to Germain at the end of the month, Vaughan estimated that the casualties might total 'four thousand whites and slaves' and losses of livestock of all kinds, nine thousand. In addition, the force of wind and flood had destroyed a huge proportion of the crops for future provisioning. Despairing of the inadequacy of words and imagination, Vaughan wrote of the 'indescribable misery' of a scene (already enacted at Jamaica and now re-enacted at Barbados) – where relatives searched among the bodies of the dead and dying and families . . 'wandered among the ruins seeking for food and shelter.'

Other countryside wanderers were footloose slaves with an eye on what accounts called 'plunder' but was more likely to be anything to keep themselves alive. And likewise dazed by their unexpected liberation but a source of further trepidation for the islanders, were some 800 prisoners-of-war whose prisons had been so magically demolished. But by the 12th, Vaughan had been able to organise them, under the policing of his troops, for salvage and restoration. So grateful for this vigorous help were the merchants and senior residents – who had also organised their own committees for burials and to provide food and relief – that at Bridgetown, '. . . They voted their thanks to General Vaughan and the troops: to whom they proposed as a reward for their service in protecting their property, a sixpence per diem, to which Mr Shirley, purveyor to the navy, promised another sixpence.'

* * *

The storm spared Antigua but raged through the Windwards, hammering Martinique and the French islands, driving ships ashore at St Christopher and descending on Statia – as described by Curson and Gouverneur in their letter of 6 November. Their letter, however, was short on detail for on the 10th the gale had driven seven ships ashore at the North-Point of the island and wrecked them with the loss of every life: nineteen vessels had fought their way out to sea, only one limping back afterward . . . 'in a most dismal condition' . . . houses had fallen and only the 'old and new Fort, the States barracks and hospital and the churches left standing. The destruction of people on this melancholy event is reputed (whites and blacks) to be between 4 and 5000 . . .'

In its turn, St Lucia, leaving for its bewildered inhabitants, after thirty hours of violence, the same desolation of uprooted or stripped trees, fallen homes and despoiled land and provisions. The barracks on Morne Fortune, the hospital, those huts on which so much effort had been invested and the fortifications so painfully strengthened . . . all these were now in ruins or so damaged as to require months to restore to usefulness. As to the state of the sick, as at Barbados, it was impossible to increase the misery of their conditions, and almost, beyond resource and endeavour to alleviate them.

Hotham's report to Vaughan on 13 October, written aboard *Vengeance* at the Carénage, spelled out the cost to the navy:

> The *Ajax, Egmont, Montague* and *Amazon* that were moored across the Entrance of the Carénage were forced out to sea in the early part of the storm. The *Vengeance* in the Harbour parted her cable and struck on the rocks, which rendered it necessary to cut away her Masts . . .'

Fortunately she was saved but: 'The transports, Victuallers etc. have suffered greatly.' Hotham had seen nothing of the other vessels and 'feared much for their safety as well as for the *Deal Castle* and *Cameleon* (sic) that were forced out of Gros Islet Bay. The *Beaver's Prize* I am also fearful may not have reached Barbados before the Storm came . . .

Lost with one of the foundered vessels was Lieutenant-Colonel Mitchell, nominated by Vaughan to replace the sick Musgrave as Quartermaster-General. The news of his shipwreck sparked a wistful aspiration from the disgraced Edward Drewe, whose letter to Vaughan could barely have merited an impatient glance. But in the next months of counting the grave misfortunes of the fleet – which at Barbados now included Rodney's ships, returned from New York in December, but badly storm-damaged en route – of re-establishing the army, of piecing together the means for shelter and supplies throughout the islands, of appealing through Germain for relief – money, medicines and supplies would arrive in January with the ships of Sir Samuel Hood – Vaughan, writing on 2 December, was at pains to ask Germain to remember his late Secretary, '. . . one of the number that suffered in my house on the night of the Hurricane, as he has left a Wife with little to support her. . . . I could wish if your Lordship could show her some mark of Favour in a Situation so truly unfortunate . . . he has been Aid-de-Camp to Lord Adam Gordon who can give your Lordship any information respecting her . . .' Vaughan also took the necessary time to repair two urgent vacancies. On 24 November he appointed John Gillan, currently at Antigua, to the majority of the 35th. Scanning the field of officers who might now fill Musgrave's post, the General settled on that embittered and bileful soldier on Morne Fortune, Lieutenant-Colonel James Cockburn: to whom the summons came as a sudden beam of sunlight and who could not soon enough shake off St Lucia's dust.

'I have this moment received the honour of your appointing me QMG . . .' wrote Cockburn on 23 December: 'accept the Tribute of a grateful heart, not only for the appointment, but for the kind manner of conveying it. . . . I shall repair to Barbados as soon as possible and beg leave to assure you that I shall seek every opportunity of convincing you that I am, etc. etc . . .'

LOYAL CAPTAIN YOUNG

For all their sorry state they were still an army and the ships, no matter how mauled by wind and sea, still men of war. The terror of the hurricane was past: it was time for Rodney and Vaughan to return to their purpose and to decide where they could most damage the French. This was an intent wholeheartedly welcomed by both men but Vaughan especially was spurred by a personal urgency.

His association with Rodney was at best uneasy: at worst, it was an embarrassment of which he was only too conscious. At the age of sixty-one, gout-ridden, testy and in worsening health, the admiral remained a hugely imposing figure. His record was replete with solid service and victories, from Finisterre in '47, the destruction of the French invasion boats in '59, Martinique in '62 and this year, that tremendous return to action which had begun with Gibraltar, destroyed Admiral Langara in the Moonlight Battle, and contained the French naval challenge in the West Indies.

For all his competence Vaughan's light could only be dimmed beside Rodney's achievements. If Vaughan was not actually dwarfed by the other man's stature and personality he proved himself, as future events showed, to be calamitously intimidated by him.

In painful contrast, Vaughan himself, near eleven months in the West Indies, had so far achieved nothing of strategic significance. The problems of military administration in the British-held islands, of doing what he could for his stricken soldiers, of pleading desperately for reinforcements and of struggling to assert his authority and that of his generals over civil governors – of whom none could be more obstructive than the man he described to Germain as 'that turtle-catcher from Bermuda', Governor Burt – had more than filled his time. It had all been necessary, wearisome and unrewarding: but he could only be aware that it was not at all the progress they looked for in Whitehall.

Sorely, the need was for action against the enemy and better still, for a substantial success. The ultimate prize, of course, was Martinique and such a coup would have been sweet triumph indeed for its former conqueror. The French had only four sail of the line at Port Royal and they were greatly outnumbered by the ships under Rodney, Graves and Hotham, but the time was not yet ripe: Martinique was no fitting target for a depleted army and even for a lesser expedition, Vaughan must scrape the barrel for men fit enough to be useful. Within easier reach and, it seemed, more realisable with the forces available, was St Vincent, reported to have been devastated by the hurricane, its defences and garrison supposedly weakened and its population in no condition to oppose a British landing.

On 12 December, 1780, therefore, Rodney, aboard *Sandwich* at Gros Islet Bay, informed Philip Stephens, Secretary of the Admiralty that '. . . notwithstanding the reduced state of His Majesty's Ships and the Troops on this Station, General Vaughan and myself are determined to undertake an Enterprize which we flatter ourselves will be attended with success . . . an Account of which I hope I shall send to their Lordships in a few days . . . Four Sail of the Enemy's Line of Battle Ships from the

Squadron at St Domingo are in these Seas: I shall do my best endeavours to take or destroy them before the very great force the Enemy hourly expects arrives . . .'

*   *   *

It is best to let Rodney speak for the fiasco of this Enterprize [sic]. There is silence on the part of Vaughan and no help for the curious in Trimen's History, since this episode too, is lost in that single line noting that the 35th Regiment were '. . . still quartered in the West Indies'. Cockburn, of course, could have been more specific: it was, in fact, Brigadier General St Leger, at St Lucia who was called on to provide the bulk of the soldiery. Flank companies of the garrison were among the three hundred troops, the grenadiers and artillery embarked for the assault on 9 and 10 December: fifteen sail completed the armada.

It was at this point that the preparations were abruptly halted. Rodney's flag captain, Walter Young had previously displayed a disconcerting readiness to relay his admiral's alleged deficiencies to the Comptroller of the Navy, Sir Charles Middleton. True to form – (or perhaps to his instructions, suggests Spinney), Young wrote of this occasion on 26 December that '. . . an unsteady fit seized the admiral and the whole was put a stop to . . .'

It might have been due to second thoughts about the promised walk over or merely to difficulties which arose during the embarkation – a later generation of soldiers coined the word snafu – i.e. situation normal all fouled up – to describe the military's inexplicable delays – but the hiatus of two days before the resumption of preparations attested by Rodney's letter to Stephens on 12th had given St Lucia's properly vindictive French ample time to alert de Bouillé. At once, St Vincent was provisioned with powder and flour from Martinique and its regular troops, militia and reliable Caribs stood to their arms.

The result probably gratified the British troops, if not the Commanders-in-Chief. Arriving at St Vincent on the 16th, the ships of the fleet duly took up their stations: St Leger landed the force on the beach of Warrowarow Bay and marched them some way inland, unopposed. Soon after, Vaughan followed and led his men forward, halting them before St Vincent's main defensive position.

It became clear that all was not as they had supposed. Here was no storm-cowed island and garrison to be easily reduced: merely the sight of the bristling cannon, muskets and bayonets on the mountain citadel protecting Kingston was enough indication that they had disastrously under-estimated their task. Not their paltry few hundreds but something like two thousand troops would be required for an attack, making

99

Vaughan's next decision, however ignominious it was to seem, inevitable. The troops were turned about – the tale of the Grand Old Duke of York comes irresistibly although perhaps unfairly to mind – and marched back to the shore.

Two of Rodney's letters sum this episode, the first to Vaughan, written aboard *Sandwich* in Warrawarow Bay on 17 December:

> The Admiral's compliments to General Vaughan and sends him the enclosed information which he had from an Inhabitant last Night, the Enemy are too well prepared for a Coup de Main, having received Intelligence from the traiterous [sic] Inhabitants of St Lucia, and a supply of Powder from Martinique.
>
> Ever since . . . they have had a great number of Negroes at work on the fortifications upon the Mountain which fortification the Admiral has been informed has a ditch round it . . . if the General is of the Opinion that an Attack would not answer the intended purpose all the Boats at Day light shall be ready to receive the Troops . . .

The second letter, written from '*Sandwich* at Sea, 18th December' was addressed to Commodore Sir Chaloner Ogle.

> I must inform you that we arrived with the Squadron and the Troops in Warrawarow Bay on the 16th Inst . . . the landing was made good and the General with the Troops advanc'd to the Mountain on which the Enemy had made their principle Fortification, but so far from finding it in a ruinous State, as we were made to believe, it was in perfect repair, and so well supplied with Troops, Cannon and Ammunition that an attack on it was impracticable, and if made must have ended in the destruction of the Troops. We therefore reimbarked [sic] them Yesterday morning and though the Enemy from their Mountain diverted themselves by Cannonading and Bombarding the Ships, no damage ensued . . . I am now on my way to join you at Gros Islet Bay . . .'

But it was not all farce at St Vincent. The need to concentrate the defence on the mountain had left the plantations exposed to the murderous Caribs of the interior, who ranged and killed at will. Ever alert for default and culpability promptly to be reported to Middleton, Captain Young furnished the Admiralty with his own acid views. Earlier, writing in October from New York, he had incriminated both Admiral Arbuthnot and his secretary, Green, in that quarter, writing that:

> Mr Arbuthnot is so led by Mr Green that he is directly or indirectly in possession of every place under the navy – victualling, sick and hurt, and

every other branch where the public money can be got at. Indeed, there is no method that has not been put in practice – such as forgery in pilots' bills, serving the condemned provisions to the French and American prisoners, and charging the government with serviceable, and every other species of villainy. I would therefore recommend it to the public offices in general to pay none of his accounts until they have applied to those gentlemen whose names may be affixed to his bills, to know of them whether they did attest them or not; and proof likewise in every other circumstance where the said Mr Green or Admiral Arbuthnot have been concerned respecting the market prices . . .

And without granting his reader the respite of a new paragraph . . . 'The abuses of the hospital are beyond description . . .'

On 15 November Young informed the Comptroller of:

. . . 'the immense neglects of the Woolwich Yard in the lading of storeships for New York' and more of the villainous peculations of Admiral Arbuthnot's secretary 'supplied with fresh beef at 10d. York currency per pound and charges the public 1s. sterling per pound; consequently he clears 5d sterling, or near it, on every pound supplied' . . . and 'he has supplied the squadron ever since our arrival [at Gardner's Bay], on the same principle as at Sandy Hook.'

But there was, of course, an Admiral at closer range, lately returned to St Lucia from St Vincent. The tireless Young again unsheathed his stiletto:

Sandwich: Gros Islet. 26th December, 1780 . . .

We have been on an expedition to St Vincent, and shall refer you to Sir George's letter for an account of it. Never was there such a scene of confusion as at the embarkation of the troops; the Caribs had begun their slaughter and devastation the instant they saw the troops begin their retreat, when down came to the beach the planters, with their wives, children and negroes. Many of them were taken on board, and the whole shore lined with those that could not be taken off. We were obliged to quit the bay in consequence of their bombarding us with two mortars, the shells of which fell very close to us; they had got our length and would have in a little time done execution.'

The plight of the embarked negroes presented the admiral with the problem of their care. Responding to Captain Philip Affleck of the *Triumph* (74), who was 'getting a Description of the unhappy negroes I have on board and shall be happy to have them out of the ship as soon as possible . . .', Rodney instructed him that '. . . as for the unhappy Negroes you will please Order them to be landed at the Carénage. Brigadier General St Leger will appoint proper Persons to receive them. You will please to give Directions that each has a Days Provisions . . . we must do our best endeavours to put your Mast in proper Order . . .'

No great enquiry followed and it would seem from that last line that Sir George had attempted to lay the matter of the 'Enterprize' to rest. His massive reputation could easily absorb such a minor reverse: not so for Vaughan, of course, whose best efforts had still brought him nothing but crushing disappointment. And not so for Young, who on the same day dashed off a second letter to Middleton:

> – I am sorry to be obliged to contradict my admiral's account of the fail-
> ure of our expedition to St Vincent; his delineation of the expedition is very
> plausible, and although I detest detraction, yet I think it my duty to give
> you information of it, both as my friend, and a friend of our country, that
> we may not be imposed on by such plausible and pompous accounts . . .

It was in this letter that Young reported the 'unsteady fit' said to afflict Rodney. The description of events is otherwise unexceptionable but Captain Young regained his form for the closing paragraph:

> I have many other matters to relate to you of inconsistency &c., &c., but
> shall suppress it on purpose to avoid giving uneasiness. I assure you I exert
> myself to the utmost of my power to keep our matters in order; at times
> they will get a little outré, but in this I am obliged to you great men at home
> for, who have so poisoned my admiral that he really and *ipso facto* thinks
> and believes himself to be the very man you have represented him. God help
> us, how much mistaken you and he are.'

❖ ❖ ❖

Thus Captain Walter Young, of Rodney: the dismissive wisdom born of a close and continuous relationship with the admiral since Young had become his flag captain in October 1779. It is a kindness to Young to remind ourselves that no man is a hero to his valet: but one finds in the man a special talent for vindictiveness, although some of his targets were plainly deserving. Rascally contractors, he told Middleton, were '. . . get-ting at the masters of the navy victuallers' and had even attempted to bribe Captain Young to permit the use of these vessels for their own devious transactions. Governor Paterson of St John's (Prince Edward Island) had offered a bribe for a similar indulgence: Wilkinson, the con-tractor for transports, was a scheming opportunist: Arbuthnot and his secretary were thieves . . . Admiral Parker was criminally incompetent . . .

Yet there is a strange ambivalence in Young's relationship with Rodney towards whom, he claimed, he had '. . . discharged the duty of a son to the admiral, as well as that of his captain and shall continue to do so, both for his advantage and that of my king and country . . .' Entirely admirable sentiments, these, albeit they had not deterred Young from his assiduous diminishing of Rodney or from claiming to be the author of the admiral's most important decisions at sea, or – as at the action fought off Cape St Vincent on 16 January, 1780, – the superior tactician thwarted by '. . . the admiral's ill state of health and his natural irresolution (which) occasioned our shortening sail frequently, which prevented me from bringing the *Sandwich* so early into battle as I could have wished: and it was with difficulty that I succeeded at last, as he attempted several times to have the ships called off from the chase . . .'

SUBDUE THEIR POSSESSIONS

We have come to know something of Walter Young. We might now look a little more closely at the object of his disparagement.

Rodney's background has been encapsulated in an earlier chapter: here there is an opportunity to see the admiral at work as he considers and dictates his letters during the rest of December and all through January. There is nothing to be found therein of the 'unsteadiness' implied by Young – only the sense of ready decision, of a vigilant eye on great and small affairs and of a total authority. Above all, this is the witness of a man very much in command of himself. This last is important for in a very few weeks it will no longer be true.

But in these two months, the pace of Sir George's correspondence with his Admirals, Commodores, Captains, the Navy Board, and with Matthew Burt is unabated and secretary Pagett scratches busily away at letters which, as always, are terse and all-encompassing. Rodney's Letter Books and Order Books are voluminous and their content astonishing in its variety. The few letters selected below typify only some of the demands on him in a single week.

On 3 December, 1780, Rodney informs Laforey, Commissioner for the Navy (at Antigua), that: '*Boreas* having sprung her Main Mast and other damages . . . I have thought it necessary to send her directly to English Harbour, in order to her having a new one got in and her being properly refitted . . . which you will please to Order to be effected as expeditiously as possible . . .'

Boreas is to remain there for further orders: Laforey is to send a frigate to Rodney at Barbados, with all news of 'Occurrences' since the admiral's departure from there and he is also '. . . to have the Fire Ships and Bombs in Constant readiness to join me whenever His Majesty's Service may make it necessary, so for me to send them Orders for that purpose . . .'

He acknowledges letters and Admiralty dispatches sent to him by Hotham. 'Without loss of time' – and how this phrase appears and re-appears in that century's naval affairs – Rodney has sent away the *Alcemene* and *Sylph* cutter to tell Hotham of his arrival at Barbados with '. . . *Sandwich, Triumph, Terrible, Intrepid* and *Cyclops* . . . this morning Commodore Sir Challoner Ogle and Drake are arrived with *Resolution, Russel, Alcide* and *Centaur*: we shall sail . . . to join you at St Lucia . . . it gives me the sincerest pleasure to hear you have enjoyed your health during the very sickly Season etc . . .

In a postscript, Rodney refers to the 'Gale of Wind that took us the very Night after we left Sandy Hook . . . I fear some of the Frigates have perished. The *Torbay* and *Shrewsbury* are missing . . .'

In preparation for the expedition to St Vincent, he tells Major-General Cunningham, Governor of Barbados [letter of 7 December], to continue the Embargo he has placed on all non-naval vessels there, so as not to risk forewarning the French. (That laudable move, as we know, was countered by information from St Lucia.)

The 7th is a busy day for Pagett. There are two further letters from Rodney to Cunningham on that date: hard put to it to man his ships by reason of sickness and desertion, the admiral knows that '. . . there are a great number (of seamen) at present secreted in the island of Barbados . . . I must request your Excellency will be so obliging as to Consult your Council in what manner the said seamen may be procured for the Public Service . . . as I should be extremely unwilling to Impress them without the Assistance of the Civil Power . . .' Not trusting entirely in patriotism and anticipating a famous epitaph*, Rodney added: '. . . the Civil Officer . . . employed on this service will be allow'd 40 shillings for every seaman besides the expence of bringing them to Bridge Town . . .'

There is an embarrassment of Prisoners of War. Rodney agrees with Cunningham that the island is utterly unfit for their reception but '. . . as I have order'd those belonging to the French to be sent as expeditiously as possible to Old France, the Spanish to Port Rice [sic for Porto Rico] and the Americans to be sent immediately on board the *Russel* to be carried to St Lucia, it will not be necessary for the Commissary either to find or provide for that purpose . . .'

The business of the fleet is conducted without pause and the admiral must find answers for its endless problems. Dr John Crawford, Surgeon at Barbados, informs him that '. . . there are now One Hundred and fifty-five men in the ruins of the hospital . . . they are without covering or the

*'. . . Patriotism is not enough': Edith Cavell, 12 October, 1915.

smallest shelter from the inclemency of the Weather . . .' Captain Charles Thompson, *Alcide*, begs to go ashore to recover his health, Cunningham gives news of the arrival of a Flag of Truce with the prisoners, recommends the bearer of his letter to Rodney as a reliable 'man of business' and, having condemned a 'Spanish Launch', asks for 'some Carpenters from the Navy to fit her up'.

He is polite and firm with de Bouillé on the matter of the exchange of prisoners: specific with the Agent for Prisoners of War at Barbados . . . 'I desire that you will give Orders that One Hundred French Prisoners are sent on board His Majesty's Ship *Cyclops* by day break tomorrow, taking care that you send none but those that are healthy . . .'

Rear Admiral Francis Drake is informed that the *Gibraltar* and *Princess* are to be placed under Drake's command . . . Hotham that *Alcemene* should join Rodney at Barbados with all dispatch, and Drake again, on the parlous state of *Intrepid*'s foremast . . . '. . . if you cannot, by taking off the Cheek and putting on a new one make the Mast serviceable, you will find the Main mast for a 64 gun Ship at the Carénage that is faulty about 18 feet from the head and by reducing it to the length of the *Intrepid*'s Foremast (which will take away 12 feet from the head) I apprehend it may make a Mast . . .' And to Cunningham again . . . 'Enclosed I have the honour to send your Excellency the Letter found in the Dutch *Boston Man* that arrived this morning, whose vessel I have seized as it is an American, the Master being a Boston Man and of Course a Traitor . . .'

* * *

In the middle of December, Rodney ran out of patience with Admiral Sir Peter Parker, commanding at Port Royal, Jamaica. We find Sir George appealing angrily for the release of his frigate, *Alert*, which had taken dispatches to Jamaica and also for Parker's co-operation in returning any ships of Hotham's Squadron which may have arrived at Jamaica after the hurricane . . . 'all of whom were dismasted and render'd useless as neither Masts or Rigging are in the Stores, or any to be purchased . . .' In addition, he told Parker of the loss of eight ships of war with their officers and men and of the possible arrival of an Enemy Squadron '. . . superior to my own . . .'

Rodney listed the elements of this force in a letter to Philip Stephens, urging that the Admiralty should help to stir Parker '. . . from Brest under De la Touche, the Squadron from Cape François (Haiti), under M Montrial [sic for Monteil] . . . exclusive of M Ternay's Squadron from America and a strong Reinforcement of Line of Battle Ships which the French expect from Cadiz . . .'

He asked for Parker's own *Thunderer* and *Berwick* 'and whatever Line of Battle Ships could possibly be spared to join me as Jamaica could not be in danger while I commanded a strong Squadron to Windward . . .'

Preoccupied by the problems of his own battered domain, Parker remained unmoved by the Admiral and their Lordships alike, but the disappointment is submerged in December's later flurry of letters and events. St Vincent must be shrugged off. There were other targets to be considered, an activity much encouraged by Hood's arrival at Barbados on 7 January, 1781, followed over the next few days by his great convoy – his 120 sail mysteriously lacking twelve of his merchantmen, of which more will be heard in the next chapter – bringing welcome reinforcements for the Army of some 2000 troops of the 1st, 13th and 69th Regiments, substantial quantities of supplies and, most welcome of all to Rodney, the essential masts and stores to enable him to refit his badly damaged ships. Hood's seven sail of the line, consisting of *Gibraltar* (80), *Invincible* (74), *Princessa* (70), *Panther* (50) and *Sybil* (28) provided a massive addition to the fleet. With such relief, new ventures, with every prospect of success, had become possible for Rodney and Vaughan.

*　　*　　*

Let us briefly leave them in conference in order to pick out a single soldier on the packed deck of one of those newly arrived transports. By now these thoroughly seaweary passengers have been aboard since 14 November: unfortunately for them, however, tide and wind ensured that the vessels of this convoy would remain heaving and rolling at their moorings in the Downs, at Spithead and the Motherbank, unable truly to sail until the 29th. They have since been forty days on passage and the troops would welcome the feel of land under their feet: but they will remain aboard – indeed, there is nowhere else to house them – until their masters have pondered their next move, whether it should be Grenada, as Vaughan desires, or Martinique or Guadeloupe, favoured by Rodney.

Unknowing and uncaring, save that there should be action and honour is the young Ensign, William Rogerson, whose red coat displays the dead-leaf yellow facings of the 13th Regiment of Foot. Mark this novice soldier embarked on his first campaign as he gazes from the ship at Carlisle Bay and the houses of Bridgetown beyond. At this moment he is at the bottom of the commissioned officers' ladder and even to the merest subaltern he is no more than a smartly-uniformed errand boy. Rogerson's lowly presence duly registered, however, we may thrust him back into limbo for a few months. When we meet him again he will be making his own mark on military history.

Lieutenant-Colonel James Cockburn, now arrived in Barbados from St Lucia, has already reported for duty. As for their weighty decisions in gestation, all such problems were resolved for Rodney and Vaughan on

27 January. On that day, the sloop *Childers*, bearing their Lordships'
instructions to the Commanders-in-Chief, signalled her arrival at
Barbados and hastened her dispatches away for Sir George's exulting
eyes. Great Britain, he learned, had now been at war with the Dutch for
thirty-eight days and as yet, he was the only person in the Caribbean to
know this. Few orders could have pleased him more than that he should
'attack and subdue the Possessions of the States General within your
command': and nothing more satisfying than the thought of descending
first on those irritating havens and comforters of the enemy, St Eustatius
and St Martin. On that subject, Rodney's expressed bitterness was
boundless: the enemy had indeed 'derived great advantages from those
Islands' and history may legitimately be embellished with an emphatic
nodding of the admiral's head at these words.

He would lose no time in summoning Vaughan and with him, put
immediate measures in hand to make ready an expedition to seize the
two islands.

– 5 –

ST EUSTATIUS

There had been no fatal delay in getting that expedition away from St Lucia. In three crowded days since *Childers'* arrival, the Commanders-in-Chief had immediately imposed an embargo prohibiting departures from the islands under their control, concerted their plans and seen to the reorganization and readiness of their ships and soldiers. Meanwhile, Sir George dictated and Secretary Pagett's obedient pen flew: there is a single sentence in the admiral's correspondence at this time which might pass for light relief but thereafter it is all business. Thus, to Laforey . . . 'I am happy to find His Majesty's Sloop *Rover* is retaken and that she was commanded by that Officer who behaved so extremely Ill to Captain Savage by demanding his Purse out of his Pocket . . . it is necessary such behaviour should be known' . . . And because the French '. . . are in the greatest want of Men . . . no exchange [of prisoners] shall be made in these Seas without my approbation . . .'

Again on 30th, to St Leger . . . 'I have been favoured with your Letter late last Night. General Vaughan is with me, we are going instantly upon an Expedition of some Consequence. Rear Admiral Drake with his Squadron, who will be left here, will have Orders not only to annoy the enemy but to give you every assistance . . .'

To Hotham at Antigua: '. . . I must desire you will give directions (to all ships) . . . to hold themselves in momentary readiness to join me, as you may expect in a few hours to receive particular Orders from me . . .'

Cunningham was informed of the plan. He might lift the Embargo at Barbados '. . . as the General and myself purpose Sailing this afternoon on the intended Expedition . . .' But to William Matthew Burt, on 31st, the request was for an immediate embargo at Antigua, so perilously close to their target: '. . . I am now on my way with His Majesty's Fleet under my Command to attack the Dutch islands of Eustatius and St Martins . . . I am sure I have no occasion to point out to your Excellency the necessity of this being a most profound secret and how highly proper it will be the Enemy may obtain no knowledge of our design . . . As the Embargo will only be for a few days it can be of no detriment to His Majesty's trading Subjects . . . You will oblige me very much if you can procure any Persons acquainted with the present situation of Eustatia, its Forts, Forces and some good Pilots . . .' – who would be required for Rodney's ships. But in other respects such as fire-power and numbers of men, nothing was lacking. The navy's standard armament for these ships consisted of 32-pounders on the lowest gun-tier and, on the upper decks, 24-pounders, eighteens, twelves and nines, or perhaps the recently intro-duced carronades. The admiral's own force represented more than six hundred such guns, the ninety-gun *Sandwich* being accompanied by five seventy-fours – *Terrible*, *Torbay*, *Shrewsbury*, *Resolution* and *Belliqueux*. With these vessels were *Princessa*, of seventy guns, the *Prince William* (64) and the *Convert* (32) plus the Fireships and Bomb vessels expedited by Laforey. Shortly, Rodney would add Sir Samuel's six ships – *Barfleur* (90), the four 74's *Alfred*, *Alcide*, *Invincible* and *Monarch* and the *Sybil* (28). But until these ships were required, Hood was ordered to station them . . . 'between Monteserratt and Nevis, in such a manner as may appear to you most conducive to the Public Service, stopping and detaining every Vessel of what Nation soever, that may attempt to pass towards Eustatia . . . and agreeable to the enclosed Order make Prizes of all Dutch Ships whatever . . .'

The most modest estimate suggests a minimum of ten thousand seamen crewing the British ships but in all probability their numbers were con-siderably greater. Each vessel of any consequence also carried its detachment of Marines: with Vaughan's reinforced army now in the order of three thousand soldiers, the Commanders-in-Chief needed to fear only the possibility of intervention by the French. The puerile state of the defences and militia on St Eustatius was no secret to anyone and justified their Lordships' confident supposition that little would avail against '. . . such a Land and Sea Force as you can send against them, if the Attack be suddenly made . . .'

In that confidence, in the afternoon of the 30th, buoyant in a mission so clearly a long-overdue reckoning and so grandly a release for Rodney's own anger and contempt for the Statians, the war fleet sailed for that most desirable objective, St Eustatius. As we know, this destination was guarded, if that is the word, by those of its twenty-five cannon actually mounted or trusted and by that fifty or so of 'the very worst men in the West India Company' – and perhaps, if they were still occupying their chosen emplacement at Fort de Windt, by that unlikely gun-crew observed by de Jongh – the constable, the small boy and the black maid.

The above comparison of relative strengths must be capped by Brigadier General Christie's comment to Germain written four days after the British landing. It is, of course, the vision of hindsight, and somewhat unfair – not at all in character: but St Eustatius, he wrote, could have been taken at any time by no more than a single man-of-war and a company of Foot.

If that had actually had been the case, how different this history and how much the better for all concerned – except, no doubt, for Sergeant William Gordon of the 35th: but having made that essential reservation, Gordon might join that other soldier, Ensign Rogerson in awaiting his own turn to reappear.

* * *

The Fleet sailed northward. A mere two hundred and forty sea-miles lay ahead, requiring little more than two days of easy sailing, but first:

> . . . To prevent the enemy penetrating our Design, the whole Fleet appeared before Fort-Royal and St Pierre's Martinique, which Island we greatly alarmed: and having left Rear-Admiral Drake with Six Sail of the Line and Two Frigates to watch the Motions of the Four Sail of the Line and Two Frigates then in the bay of Fort-Royal, late in the Evening of the same Day we proceeded for the Dutch Island of St Eustatius . . . and dispatched Rear-Admiral Sir Samuel Hood, with his Squadron, to environ the Bay of St Eustatius and prevent the Escape of any Dutch Ships of War, or Merchant Ships that might be at an Anchor there: he most effectually performed that Service . . .

'THE GLORIOUS CAPTURE'

Rodney's Letters dealing with the capture of St Eustatius note that '. . . on the 3rd Instant the General and myself with the Remainder of the Fleet and Troops arrived in the Bay. The Men of War being stationed against the Batteries and the Troops ready to disembark, the General and myself, in order to save the Effusion of human Blood, thought it necessary to send the Dutch Governor the Summons I have the Honour to include . . .'

For the manner of its delivery and the immediate aftermath for Statia's residents we have Governor de Graaff's solemn truth, as reported at Amsterdam on 3 December, 1781, to the Honourable and Worshipful Gentlemen Representatives and Directors of the General Chartered Dutch West Indian Company . . . and repeated in the *Nieuwe Nederlandsche Jaerboeken* dated April, 1782. His words are quoted below in their context.

At ten o'clock in the morning of Saturday 3 February, 1781, Rodney's

St Eustatius. A contemporary drawing (*Reproduced by courtesy of the Vereeniging Nederlands Historisch Scheepvaart Museum, Amsterdam*)

Admiral Lord Rodney. Painted in the style of Sir Joshua Reynolds (1723-92) (*National Maritime Museum*)

Major-General The Hon. John Vaughan (*Reproduced by courtesy of the William L Clements Library, University of Michigan*)

Rear Admiral Lord Hood. Painted
in the style of Sir Joshua Reynolds
(1723-92) (*National Maritime
Museum*)

Johannes De Graaff. AL
Brookman, Pinxt, February 1843,
Surinam (*Copy of the portrait in
State House, Concorde, New
Hampshire. Photograph : Bill
Finney*)

ships appeared before the island, coming to anchor at their stations at eleven o'clock. When this presence became widely known through the town – not at once, for ashore the island was intent on its business and the antennae of the Jews, normally so sensitive to the faintest vibrations of danger were necessarily retracted on the Sabbath – it brought a collective alarm to Statia and, among some of those present, a special fear of arrest. The British descent on the Piratical Rebel ships, safe, as they had assumed themselves to be in the harbour of St Martin, was fresh in memory: now – and again wrongly – it was assumed that it was the turn of the five armed American ships in Statia's roadstead. With their crews and merchant passengers, this chilling visitation threatened two thousand men: but no less a frisson would have been shared by the captains and the crews of those twelve English merchant vessels which had so artfully made use of Hood's protection before disappearing from the convoy at a convenient moment. To these opportunists, in particular, interrupted thus as they unloaded their cargoes at Statia's warehouses, Rodney's dramatic appearance was indeed the very 'thunderclap' he claimed it to be. It could not have been far from their thoughts that the seizure of their own vessels and impressment into His Majesty's navy would follow in short order.

An uneasy hour elapsed before a boat was seen to put off from the flagship, and its small complement of two officers and four soldiers – one a drummer and another with a white flag affixed to his bayonet – was set ashore. One of these officers whether soldier or sailor, remains anonymous. The second however, confident and proud in his new appointment was the latest member of Vaughan's staff, Lieutenant-Colonel James Cockburn, on his first mission for the Commanders-in-Chief. We can see him perhaps kicking Statia's sand from his shoes as the escort forms up, and striding stern and masterful among them as the little party begins its march from the strand and uphill, to the Upper Town and the house of Governor de Graaff.

*　*　*

An indulgence here for the author, who finds a hiatus in the matter of Cockburn's march to confront de Graaff. We simply do not know whether anyone managed to find a horse for Cockburn: but if not, we should spare a thought for him – and certainly for his fellow officer and the four men in their red coats and stocks and full marching order as they trudged, sweating and panting in the heat, up that steep and infinitely punishing Bay Path. How those uniforms, those packs and muskets, must have irked them: how difficult to maintain some fierce dignity with each laboured breath . . .

The island of St Eustatius was in reality a fief, but to Johannes de Graaff, it had been his very own kingdom: and it came to an end at one o'clock that day when Cockburn, unannounced, splendid in scarlet and orange and backed by his stolid retinue, entered his house, presented the surprised Governor with a sealed letter and stood impassively as it was opened and read.

Headed *Sandwich, St Eustatius, 3rd February 1781* and over the signatures of Rodney and Vaughan, His Excellency and Governor was therein Summoned to take heed that:

> We the General Officers, commanding in Chief his Britannic Majesty's Fleet and Army in the West Indies, do, in His Royal Name, demand an instant surrender of the Island of St Eustatius and its Dependencies, with every Thing in and belonging thereto, for the use of his said Majesty. We give you One Hour, from the Delivery of this Message, to decide – If any Resistance is made, you must abide by the Consequences.

*　*　*

We can feel for de Graaff, too, at that moment, for his surprise was now become total shock and his emotion, 'extreme' . . . '. . . it appeared to me as a dream' he said in his report, but one he was forced by the circumstances to accept as reality: '. . . I asked James Cockburn if war had indeed been declared between Holland and England: to which he replied . . . "Yes Sir, and I carry the manifesto in my pocket . . ."'

But it was impossible, protested de Graaff, for him to make a decision on such an important matter within the given hour. It was not solely for him to decide: he needed the advice of the island Council. Perhaps they could have more time in which to assemble a deputation to the Commanders-in-Chief so that they could come to some agreement . . . ?

'You have one hour,' said Cockburn firmly. 'We shall wait for one hour and then return to our ship: And if we are obstructed,' he added, . . . 'there will be consequences.'

What was meant by that word 'consequences' was appallingly plain to the three gentlemen – Olive Oyen, Jacobus Seys and Hendrik Pandt, and the island Secretary, Alexander LeJeune – who were the only Council members who could be found by de Graaff at such short notice: apprized of 'the great and awesome power directed against the island' and knowing of their nakedness before it, albeit with baffled anger, there could only be one reply:

Governor de Graaff not having it in his Power to make any defense against the Britisch Forces which have invested the Island of St Eustatia, Surrenders the same & all its Dependencis to St George Bridges Rodney & General Vaughan — Well Knowing the honor & Humanity of these two commanders in Chieff, the governor recommand the Town en its inhabitants to their Clemency & Mercy —

St Eustatia the 3d February 1781

The Document of Surrender, given at St Eustatius, 3 February, 1781
(Crown copyright, PRO 30/20/22/9. Reproduced by courtesy of the Controller, Her Majesty's Stationery Office)

Governor de Graaff not having it in his Power to make any defence against the British Forces which have invested the Island of St Eustatia, Surrendered the Same & all its Dependencies to Sir George Bridges [sic] Rodney & General Vaughan, Well knowing the Honour & Humanity of these two Commanders-in-Chief, the Governor recommends the Town and its inhabitants to their Clemency and Mercy . . .

Signed by the Governor and the three Council members, this document was carried back to Rodney and Vaughan: and with this exchange St Eustatius ended its days of luminescence as the Golden Rock. For its people, the ordeal of military occupation lay ahead and they would survive it as best they could. It would, in addition, bring disgrace to the Commanders-in-Chief and tragedy to their willing instrument Lieutenant-Colonel James Cockburn.

* * *

Few victories are complete without gunfire and it remained to deal with the sole guardian of Statia's harbour, Count van Byland, in the frigate *Mars*, who had observed the silent arrival of the British men of war with concern. He may have trusted in the assurances of peace which he had brought for the islanders only two days previously, but it was impossible for this sailor to mistake the purpose for which the British stationed themselves to bar the roadstead, the efficient laying of springs to cables to bring guns to bear on the Fort and the town and the ominous absence of any courteous salute. And as if these indications of menace were not enough, each deck was bright with its red-coated array.

Much troubled, for this was merely one year since that humiliating encounter with Commodore Fielding off the Isle of Wight and the memory of that was fresh – and even more so the insult of the British descent on St Martin in August – Van Byland despatched one of his officers, Lieutenant Van Stuivezand '. . . with a sloop to the Admiral, to welcome him and to ask if I could be of service to his fleet . . .'

Before Van Byland's apprehensive eyes, sloop, crew and the unfortunate lieutenant were at once seized and their craft manned by armed men, although still flying the colours of the Republic – an astonishing provocation this must have seemed to Van Byland, to which he reacted by ordering that the stolen vessel should be fired on. It was as well for the Count and for the crew of *Mars* that this order was frustrated as the sloop ran under the lee of another British man of war. Shortly, however, he was made aware of the true state of affairs by one of *Resolution's* officers who came aboard and demanded the surrender of the frigate

'. . . in the name of the King of England who supposedly had declared war on the Republic.'

The disconsolate Van Byland was to relate this catastrophe in a letter to the Prince Stadtholder written on 6 February in the bleakness of imprisonment aboard *Sandwich*. What wretchedness for Rodney's agonised guest as he bites this bullet for the second time in an honourable naval career . . .

Illustrious Sovereign,

. . . It is not but with great grief that I see myself forced to acquaint Your Highness with the sad event of the taking of the frigate *Mars* as well as the surrender of the island of St Eustatius to the English Fleet on the 3rd of this month . . .

He had met the situation with dignity: like de Graaff, he was unaware of any such declaration by the English King. He therefore informed his visitor that he would await the outbreak of hostilities – which, no sooner had the emissary departed, came at once, although with the inevitable conflict as to who was the first to fire. According to *Monarch*'s captain '. . . at half past two the [Dutch] frigate began firing at our ships – the *Resolution, Prince William, Gibraltar & Princessa* fired at ditto . . .' . . . but without Rodney's order and igniting his scarlet fury against the over-eager captains. It was not the moment, but he would find time to make them answer for those shots.

No smoke without confusion: Van Byland's account therefore differed in two respects:

Forthwith, three ships of the line, one of 80, one of 74 and one of 64 guns commenced to fire on the frigate, which compelled me – after having replied with both broadsides, to lower the flag, for it was impossible to resist such a superior force. There were no people killed or wounded, for most shots were aimed at the rigging . . .

'I do not doubt,' finished Van Byland sorrowfully, 'that Your Highness will learn from investigation that it was impossible to do more . . .'

* * *

Mars was promptly commissioned and manned as a British ship of war and although this brisk action was not regarded by Sir George as being yet wholly complete, other matters claimed his attention and that of his officers that day. The surrender safely in hand there was a matter of spoil, for example: for no aspect of their profession could have been more dear to their hearts than the transfer of riches from the enemy to themselves. This prospect, now shining with such unimaginable brilliance before them was so memorably to condition all that follows that we should pause for a moment to examine it.

Avid prize-takers all, many of them had previously benefited from these captures, ungraciously termed thefts by the deprived victims. But the practice was licensed and enshrined in maritime – and particularly, in naval – culture and success in this underwrote many an envied sea-officer's dignified and affluent retirement. Rodney himself, as captain of the *Eagle* in 1747 had taken six ships of the French convoy out of St Domingo and had collected more than eight thousand pounds as his quarter share of its value – and this net of the eighth due to his Admiral. Eighth shares were allotted to the three separate classes of the ships' officers and warrant officers while a quarter share went to the crew. Their greater number ensured only modest benefits compared with those enjoyed by the officers but all of them dreamed hungrily of the next prize – a Spanish treasure ship, perhaps, like the fabled *Hermione* captured in '62 by the frigates *Active* and *Favourite* and subsequently valued by the Prize Court at more than half a million pounds. Those shares brought each of the captains £65,000, £13,000 each for their Lieutenants and the dizzy bonanza of £485 to every seaman. This was indeed extraordinary. Reward was usually on a more modest, but still welcome, scale. The treasure of the *Havannah* had yielded three million sterling, in '62, all distributed as prize money: each private soldier gained four pounds, one shilling and eightpence: presumably seamen received something similar but Trimen's Regimental History does not deign to mention them.

But there was always the next capture and the vision of prize money in uncountable amounts therefore served the Navy as a chimera in which they passionately believed. It helped, also, to divert minds from dwelling entirely on the bloody and possibly fatal process of obtaining it.

* * *

The spectacle now before the Fleet in Statia's road, of one hundred and fifty valuable merchantmen ripe for seizure and no longer with even the pretence of protection – they were not all enemy vessels and thus legitimate prizes but the arguments would come too late to save them – was every sailors' dream realized. Eagerly, the prize crews swarmed aboard the trapped vessels in their hundreds, under the impotent lowering of the dispossessed and the guns of the British men of war.

Statia's neighbours, Saba and St Martin were as peremptorily dealt with: but holding out the promise of even greater enrichment – for although the wealth ashore was yet to be counted it was manifestly there for the taking – was the challenge of the Dutch convoy which had left Statia under the care of Rear-Admiral Krul. These vessels had had a 36-hour start on any pursuit from St Eustatius but they were, of course, no more than merchant vessels, their Captains – and Krul himself – sharing the general ignorance of imminent peril from the British. There was every hope that they could be overtaken by hard-driven naval vessels and Rodney therefore detached Captain Reynolds with the *Monarch*, accompanied by *Panther* and *Sybil* with instructions to 'pursue as far as the Latitude of Bermudas, should Reynolds not intercept them before he got that Length . . .'

* * *

At 3 o'clock Vaughan began to disembark his soldiers: the officers and men would later quarter themselves in every house and building, the unlucky, thereafter, wherever there was space to lie. But the first task – and it would require only a company or so – was to empty Fort Oranje of its hangdog garrison: these men were marched out without ceremony and within the next few days, shipped to St Kitts. The Fort was now re-named Fort George and the British flag raised above it – but soon after, at Rodney's order, the Dutch flag was restored in order to entice enemy merchant vessels into Statia's roadstead. His cruisers would see to it that they did not leave.

The soldiers threw a cordon about the town and sealed off the entries between the Lower and Upper Towns. They were too late to prevent the temporary escape of very many of the Americans who had abandoned their initial thoughts of resistance and fled to the mountains, most of them to the area of The Quill, but the hopeless nature of this flight was confirmed by the Admiral in one dismissive sentence: '. . . Hunger will compel them to surrender at discretion . . .'

Hunger would soon enough threaten all of Statia's residents: as the full realization of the invasion dawned, the traders in the market did what they could to safeguard their goods – how pathetic were those efforts to seem – before abandoning stalls and shops and making for their homes. By order, the shops were to remain closed: in describing his own rough treatment at Rodney's hands later, Richard Downing Jennings noted that this edict harmed civilian and soldier alike:

I shall not enlarge upon the particular severities which were exercised upon the inhabitants, the military parade which was observed and the withholding of every necessity of life for the space of twenty-seven days before the retail shops were permitted to be opened . . . in consequence of which, although the place abounded with sugar, wine and other refreshments, the more soldiers died for want of nourishment . . .

Each street was patrolled and guards were disposed at all significant buildings and sites and to cover the shore. They were set over the piled hogsheads of sugar and tobacco and bales of merchandise alongside the filled warehouses, some revealing among their contents the coveted naval stores: but all of these buildings were immediately locked against their owners. The soldiery meanwhile looked knowingly at one another and took note of other means of access for themselves, when time and circumstance allowed.

Other soldiers were sent to the top of Signal Hill, to watch all approaches to the island and still others, to occupy the coastal batteries. These operations occupied them all for the rest of that day and, as they made their progress, so rumour grew with each new discovery of the unbelievable wealth of St Eustatius; and in all of the victors' minds, from the Admiral to the lowliest seaman and from the General to the lowliest private, dawned the delirious knowledge that in due degree, it was now all theirs to share.

*   *   *

On the morrow, on Sunday the 4th, Sir George prepared a brief account for Germain and a rather longer letter for Philip Stephens. 'It is a vast Capture' he told Germain: '. . . the whole I have seized for the King and the State, and I hope will go to the public revenue of my Country . . . I don't look upon myself intitled [sic] to one Sixpence: nor do I desire it . . . My Happiness is having been the Instrument of my Country in bringing this Nest of Villains to condign Punishment: They deserve scourging, and they shall be scourged . . .'

There is no doubt of the sincerity of Rodney's anger against this enemy, but if it existed at all, his professed indifference to financial reward – it was not quite a rejection – was short-lived and was not repeated in that day's letter to Stephens. So early, the Admiral could not yet have been fully aware that in specie and goods this capture might be worth between three and five millions of pounds: but that Statia was incredibly wealthy was no longer conjecture but lay self-evident before him. It lay, too, before the Fleet and the Army, among whom such disdain for the spoils of war was not a notorious characteristic.

At this tremendous moment of opportunity for Rodney, some contrasts are in order. We now enter the murky realms of the Admiral's conduct at St Eustatius and one factor must strongly have influenced those controversial activities. He would not have been able to reconcile the bitter memories of his years of harassment by debt, of the humiliating flight to France in '74 as a fugitive from his creditors and the four years of threadbare exile in Paris which followed. He would long for the relief of solvency, and like most mortals, for more: in his own mind, for the comfort, dignity and rank which only money could provide. It would have been strange if he had not already considered what salvation from this source was now in his grasp.

*   *   *

To Stephens:

> . . . the Surprise and Astonishment of the Governor and Inhabitants is scarce to be conceived . . . the *Mars*, a Dutch man of war . . . having arrived at St Eustatius on the 1st Instant, had allayed their Fears of Hostilities.
>
> I most sincerely congratulate their Lordships on the severe Blow the Dutch West India Company and the perfidious Magistrates of Amsterdam have sustained by the Capture of this Island. Upwards of One Hundred and Fifty Sail of all Denominations are taken in the Bay . . .

Sir George informed Stephens of the capture of Van Byland's frigate and the five American vessels of war: he wrote of the ships he had sent in pursuit of the Dutch convoy, of the filled warehouses and the crowded beach and of his plans for the booty . . . 'all of which shall be shipped on board the Vessels now in the Bay (if they are sufficient to contain the Quantity), and sent under a proper Convoy to Great Britain to abide his Majesty's Pleasure . . .

The Islands of St Martin and Saba have surrendered: no Terms whatever having been allowed them . . .

*   *   *

It had been an excellent day's work. With the island stabilized by the troops, Sir George prepared to join Vaughan ashore. The Commanders-in-Chief had so far spoken in common accord and with one voice: it would still be one voice from this day but it would be that of Admiral Sir George Brydges Rodney. He did not leave the ship, however, without closing that matter which had so displeased him, namely, the unforgivable transgressions of his captains during the taking of Van Byland's frigate. There may have been embarrassment for all of the culprits – Spinney notes that Rodney sent to put the captains under arrest – but the

Letterbook tells us that the lash of Rodney's wrath fell solely on Captain Stair Douglas of *Prince William*:

I have received your Letter relative to your Ships firing yesterday without my Orders or Signal for that purpose. It might have been easily perceived by the whole Fleet that the *Resolution* was anchored in such a manner, as not only to force the said Frigate to surrender, but likewise, if she was obliged by the obstinacy of the Dutch Captain to fire, the few shot she might by compelled to expend would not hurt any of His Majesty's Ships . . . Your, and the other ships in shore, were anchored to batter the place, had there been occasion, and I had made a Signal for that purpose . . .

Your ship firing as she did, not only endangered the Lives of the Men on board other of His Majesty's Ships, but was an Insult to all order and Discipline . . .

There is more in this vein but Rodney allowed his burning Captain a perhaps unworthy refuge . . .

. . . however, you may be assured that I have great pleasure to hear you was not concerned in such a breach of Discipline, but that it was owing to the disobedience of your Men . . . These Delinquents, Rodney required of Douglas, should be detected, punished and Lectured on Silence and on '. . . paying implicit obedience to your Orders . . . Two essential Articles almost forgot by the Inferior Officers and Men . . . It must be restored, or the British Navy will be without Discipline . . .'

You may easily imagine Sir what I must have felt at the time the firing commenced, and how much it must have hurt me to observe in the Sight of the Fleet, Army (and an Island which a few moments before had submitted to His Majesty's Arms) . . . such a wanton display of the Slackness of Discipline in a British Fleet . . . Trust it will never happen again . . . etc . . .

*   *   *

This letter of 4 February, 1781, is the only reference to the capture of St Eustatius in Rodney's letter-book, yet we have seen how detailed and prolific Rodney invariably was. It is the more disconcerting to find that entries in the letter-book are not resumed until 10 December, 1781: thus there is a gap of eleven months in that record which encompasses the period of the British occupation of the island and remains unblessed by any contemporary comment by Sir George.

An important collection of relevant Letters attempting to repair this discontinuity was published by Rodney in 1783 following public criticism of his conduct at St Eustatius . . . 'as the best Mode of convincing the World that those Censures are malicious and unjust . . .' but these late contributions like the version published with additions in 1789, and that of his son-in-law, Basil Mundy – later still, in 1830 – are designed specifically to justify Rodney's activities, whether in deploying his ships or in carrying out their Lordships' wishes in legitimately neutralizing the source of contraband trade. These afterthoughts tell us nothing – determinedly so – about what those crucial months meant to the Statians and on that subject, Rodney, Mundy and Vaughan himself are reticent.

Fortunately, there are other witnesses.

It is possible that Sir George had by now heard something of the rigours of the Bay Path.

Sandwich, Sunday 4th February . . . noon

'Dear Vaughan –

– If you will send down a horse at 5 o'clock I will come ashore. I propose sending the *Renard* [sic] to Antigua tomorrow if you have any commands. I have wrote to the commissary of Prisoners at St Kitts and Antigua to prepare accommodation for your Governor and his family at either of those Islands and when you choose they should go, a Ship of War shall carry them – adieu.

Yours Sincerely,

G B Rodney

. . . LAST OF DE RUITER'S STRAIN . . .

On the latitude of 18 degrees 46 minutes North and separating the most northerly of the Leeward Islands from the Virgin Islands to the west, is the forty-mile wide gate between the Caribbean Sea and the Atlantic Ocean. This channel is called the Anegada Passage and its eastern and western gateposts are marked by the two islets of Anegada and Sombrero, the latter being something less than seventy sea miles northwest of Statia. It was to this point, making no more than two or three knots, that Krul's convoy (see page 117) had laboured by daybreak on 4 February and it was then that the sails of their pursuers, *Monarch*, *Panther* and *Sybil* were sighted.

Sybil . . . 'at 7 A.M. made a Signal for seeing a fleet in the NW, made sail and gave Chace [sic] and came up with the fleet which proved to be . . . Dutch Merchantmen under Convoy of a 64-gun Ship. The *Monarch* run down to the Dutch Admiral and Engaged him about 10 minutes when she struck as did the whole Convoy . . .'

Oddly enough, like the unhappy Van Byland's frigate captured at St Eustatius, Admiral Krul's ship too was called *Mars*. '. . . we kept away towards them' noted Reynolds: '*Panther* and *Sybil* signalled to look, positioned themselves 2 points on the Starboard bow, at 10 came alongside the Dutch Man of War & ordered them to strike . . .'

Panther's log is equally laconic although the *Mars* is described therein as a '50-gun Ship' . . . 'the Dutch Man of War exchanged 2 broadsides with HM Ship *Monarch* and struck her colours as did the Merchantmen also . . .'

Brief they may be, but these contemporary reports are in agreement as to the course of events. There is a different viewpoint from the cannon's mouth and the more detailed and dramatic account provided by Lieutenant Cornelius de Jong aboard *Mars* leaves some problems for students of naval tactics to ponder. It may be relevant however, that his memoir was published in 1807, some twenty-six years afterward.

It is, for example, perplexing to reconcile Dutch and British versions of such matters as the duration of the action and the position of the British ships: and if *Panther* opened fire, as de Jong writes, her Captain has not mentioned that fact in his log. But de Jong's description of the terrible ordeal on the deck of a ship under fire is all too convincing and his place in Statia's story requires that we see these events through his eyes.

*   *   *

The three ships of war were watched uneasily as they closed the convoy: and while there was as yet no alarm, it was an elementary precaution that the loose formation of merchantmen should be signalled by their escort to close up and not to fall to leeward. Krul, called on deck, appeared in his slippers, a cloak drawn hastily about his night attire. He was in time to see the British colours rise to the mastheads of his visitors as the two larger vessels took station to threaten his own 64-gun *Mars*: from the lee side by the *Monarch* with its 74 cannon and to windward, by the 64 guns of *Panther*. *Sybil* meanwhile positioned herself to menace the convoy.

Ordering *Mars'* crew to their own battle stations, Krul left the deck to dress, reappearing in his richly ornamented uniform – 'to hearten his men,' wrote de Jong, but possibly, to enable the Admiral to hearten himself. It would be human to wish to face this moment of crisis in something more dignified than a nightshirt but – like another Admiral after him – he would pay dearly for that prominence in gold lace.

The interval had apparently seen *Monarch* and *Panther* exchange positions: de Jong says that '. . . the English approached from the leeward: we opened the gun-ports on that side and this caused the *Monarch* to keep close to our stern on the windward side . . .' and thus, out of reach of *Mars*' guns: At the same time he gave [*Panther*] the opportunity to fire at us from the place he had left . . .'

Monarch closed within only 'half a pistol-shot' and a confused shouting between the ships followed as Reynolds ordered Krul to strike his flag and heave to. There was no possibility that Krul would do so, but a little time was bought in a pantomime of misunderstanding. Krul had little knowledge of English and although Reynold's tones and gestures made his wishes clear enough he was made to repeat his words several times before he received Krul's emphatic negative. Reynold's response was immediate: the ships were close enough for the Dutch to hear his order to fire. A storm of shot felled men on the deck of *Mars*, to be answered in kind as the battle opened. '. . . at this range' said de Jong, . . . 'every weapon was used: cannon, muskets, pistols, grenades . . .'

de Jong is specific that the major attack came from the leeward position and that the strong wind pressed *Mars* so far over that the lower tier of guns on that side could not be used. '. . . as soon as a port was opened sea-water came in with such force that it required all of (the men's) strength to close it again . . .'

Without those guns and because of the advantageous position of *Monarch*, Krul's men could only operate some '12 or 14 pieces' against their assailants. '. . . ball and grapeshot seemed to shower our deck' . . . of which, said de Jong, '. . . the first ran through the ship. Of my command at the two aftermost divisions of the upper battery, two men had already fallen and several others were injured: of the first two men, one was cut in two by a cannonball while he was in the act of loading and the other was hit in the chest by a musket ball as I aimed the piece . . . Therefore he fell upon me and I caught him, but just as we laid him on the deck, breath and life were lost. This good soul was laid aside, and the other was thrown overboard . . .'

de Jong then went aft to see if the guns in the cabin could be of more use and saw:

. . . at the same moment, the commander of the soldiers, a French officer, Monsieur De Bonne de Regnevalle coming down from the quarter-deck and, helped by some men, carrying the mortally wounded Admiral Krul in

123

his arms . . . to say that I was aghast and terrified is only the truth. I was filled with the most intense emotion when I saw my courageous superior in this sad situation – how his once brave head was hanging, how weak and impotent were his once-strong limbs. His hair, already grey and white with age was now coloured red with blood: no less than three minutes before, that deathly pale mouth had encouraged me at my post and ordered me not to fire too quickly but to be calm and sure . . .

The Admiral was carried to the surgeons but soon that faint pulse ceased: de Jong describes the consternation felt by every man as news of Krul's death spread through the ship, inspiring a vengeful attempt to fight on: but '. . . meanwhile the water in the ship was rising and everything on the lee side was afloat, while [the level] had climbed to 38 inches at the pumps. The rigging, which seemed to interest the enemy very much was already so much battered that no sail could be hoisted and no yard could be braced . . .'

Fifteen minutes after the fall of the Admiral, said de Jong, and almost three-quarters of an hour from the commencement of the battle, *Mars'* captain, Van der Halm, gave the order to strike the colours:

> . . . Now we held our fire, but since the flag did not go down at once, the enemy continued to fire, and on the quarter-deck, to which I had moved, the whistling of musket balls and clattering of canister-shots went on fiercely. Before me, the first steersman collapsed, deadly wounded and begging for help: the sailor Langenbach whose right leg had been shot away moaned in pain: a cannon ball had torn soldier Beugers' body and smashed his gun. He lay, soiled by his own bowels and burning because of a grenade which had also struck him and set fire to his clothes . . . I cannot speak of these others injured: the quarter-deck was slippery with blood: this was the real battlefield.

But at last, at long last, the flag was lowered and the slaughter ended. Captain Fitzgerald '. . . fired a Great Number of Guns to bring the Convoy to & make them Strike their Colours . . .' and it was then, when *Sybil* sent her master and thirty men aboard *Mars* to take possession, that the Dutch learned that their respective countries were now enemies: that St Eustatius, from whence they had sailed so innocently for home such a short time before, was now in the hands of the British: that their ships had become prizes: and that they were now, all of them, prisoners of war.

In a bitter afterthought, de Jong mentioned the behaviour of the unsuspecting convoy captains who '. . . took the first cannonade for a mutual salute, from which dream the shots going through their own sails awakened them: they did nothing for their own safety and remained hove to: if they had scattered to the east, west and south the English, occupied with *Mars*, could not have taken half of them . . .'

He learned later however, that one of the captive ships, the *Johannes*, had managed to escape from its grim shepherds during their slow return to Statia. Captain Pieter Visman and his men somehow overpowered the prize crew – it is claimed that they were encouraged to drink until they were helpless – and had sailed as far as the North of England before being retaken '. . . by an armed whaler and taken to Ireland . . .'

An unforgettable vignette is left to us: macabre and pathetic, it sums the price of such engagements. de Jong records that the enemy had also suffered and '. . . if my information is correct, sustained three dead and several wounded . . . among the last, one of his officers, of whom part of a blue-sleeved arm with white trim was seen floating in the sea . . .'

ON SHORE

The imposing house in the Upper Town which belonged to the Dutch merchant and planter Simon Doncker is traditionally noted as Rodney's Headquarters. Seaward-facing, this pleasant two-storey building with its railed balcony, was augmented in this century with a deeply shaded porch fronted by a row of steps. It is now Statia's Museum.

It is not clear from his correspondence how long Rodney actually stayed there since his letters during the period at Statia are headed . . . '*Sandwich, Saint Eustatius*' and others, sometimes of the same date, merely with '. . . *Saint Eustatius* etc . . .' Certainly both Jennings and de Jong claimed that Rodney enjoyed the hospitality of a '. . . bountiful Dutchman . . .' whose private feelings are not mentioned. Vaughan, who headed his own letters from Statia '*Fort George, St Eustatius*' presumably occupied the commander's house in the Fort.

Discharged 'on shore' from *Sandwich* on the 3rd, along with Vaughan, the Commissary General Matthew Forster and the hitherto insignificant Sergeant William Gordon, Cockburn becomes 'Colonel Coulbourne' in the Muster Book. He was to quarter Forster and himself in the residence of the principal French merchant, Jacques Texier: a populous household, this, for in addition to Madame Texier and the family slaves – four men, six women and their four children, the house was also shared by an Irish merchant, Mr Neagle, later to act as caretaker in Texier's absence. There was perhaps more to Mr Neagle than is suggested by this mundane role. He became '. . . a confidential friend of Lieutenant-Colonel Cockburn . . .' and was able, apparently, to leave Statia to visit the enemy island of Martinique, undeterred by such small impediments as the British military occupation and their naval blockade.

When at length called on to testify to Neagle's character, Matthew Forster considered him to be '. . . a loyal good subject . . .' – but we are not encouraged to depend too heavily on that recommendation after all we shall eventually learn of Forster.

With the occupation of the Fort, now garrisoned by the Royals and by five companies of the 13th Regiment, the troops deployed throughout the island, the residents petrified by shock and the seaboard secure, the purpose of the expedition could be further advanced. All that had gone before was a necessary beginning for the mission outlined by their Lordships and so happily embraced by the Commanders-in-Chief: they were to sever this artery of supply to the Americans and they had duly taken the first step in that operation. Rodney's unalloyed delight and excitement at this time are evident in his letters to Stephens, Germain, Parker, and Cunningham wherein is massive satisfaction in the success of the operation and at the scale of the capture. But in evidence, too, is a sustained rage against St Eustatius and all its works – a malevolence bordering on the paranoic and going far beyond the routine hostility for the enemy expressed by other officers. In these examples, none of the letters from the Admiral is without its blast of vituperation directed at the traitorous islanders and their Dutch masters.

Germain has already been told of '. . . this Nest of Villains . . .' On the same day, Stephens is asked to congratulate their Lordships '. . . on the severe Blow the Dutch West India Company and the perfidious Magistrates of Amsterdam have sustained by the Capture of this Island . . .' There is a joyful account for Sir Peter Parker, perhaps to occasion him some envious speculation: '. . . we took upwards of 150 Sail of Ships and Vessels of all Sorts in the road of St Eustatius, with a Dutch Frigate of War of 38 Guns and a Number of American Armed Vessels. A Dutch Convoy . . . was pursued, the whole taken and the Dutch Admiral Killed in the Action . . .'

This news might have been sufficient for Parker, but he too, was not to be spared. It was '. . . A severe Blow upon the Dutch, French, Americans and those British Merchants who, for Lucre of Gain, have supported the cause of their Country's Enemy, and just Punishment upon the insolent Citizens of Amsterdam . . .'

And in similar vein to Cunningham: '. . . the English Merchants, who forgetting the Duty they owe their King and Country, were base enough from lucrative Motives to support the Enemies of their Country, will, for their Treason, justly merit their own Ruin . . .'

There are but faint echoes of this in Vaughan's letters. Weak reflections of Rodney's aggressive style, his comments on the enemy lack the admiral's venom and seem to be merely dutiful noises. Harassed and Caribbean-weary, Sir John is equally happy at this belated success, but preoccupied always with the problems of his army, his correspondence shows us a less lustrous but more balanced and sober personality.

* * *

Historically, accounts of life under martial law are plentiful: what was to distinguish this episode was the manner in which the acquisition and ultimate destiny of the wealth expropriated from the civilian community was to influence military and naval life, and arguably, the fate of Cornwallis at Yorktown, since it has been suggested that Sir George Rodney's 'dalliance' at St Eustatius contributed significantly to that final defeat. Less debatable – certainly in the minds of victims and critics – was the belief that at every level, from the Commanders-in-Chief down, the rule of the British at St Eustatius was tenaciously devoted to no other cause but that of robbery under arms. Because of its central importance in Statia's story we must now concern ourselves with that which ultimately mocked the great strategies of the expedition, namely, money.

* * *

The earliest victim of record is Johannes De Graaff. On Sunday the 4th, Cockburn again appeared at De Graaff's house, accompanied by 'other English officers' and required the Governor to hand over all the books, papers, charters and money of the Dutch West India Company. LeJeune – again summoned at short notice '. . . and this on the Lord's Day . . .' reported De Graaff, further affronted – was enlisted to draw up a final balance of this money – a nervous business, with the British officers gathered about him, his every line scrutinised and LeJeune himself questioned, threatened throughout the process and compelled to swear on oath to the total of 46155, 2, 4, 1/2 pesos:* 'a few days later' said De Graaff, '. . . all of this, the books and the money, the papers and charters, were taken out of my house in the presence of General Vaughan and carried away . . .'

It is impossible to audit the true wealth of St Eustatius or the totals of the monies which were exploded into so many ready hands after the seizure of the island. This phenomenon obsessed so many, whether as profiteers, as envious non-sharers or like Hood, as stern critics of the proceedings – could they be just a little envious too? – that the actual sums are lost in the resulting clamour. It will be seen that cash, commodities and ships all enriched the captors. Lower down the scale, large numbers

*The basic silver coinage of the Spanish empire, known in the Americas as 'pieces of eight' and equivalent to the US silver dollar.

profited from burglary, theft, adroit transfers and shipments between the islands. Much of this remains impenetrable: we can however, inspect the recorded estimates of the money found by the captors and the intentions of the Commanders-in-Chief, as expressed by Vaughan, in his reports to Germain.

Thus, on 7 February, following Cockburn's removal of the Dutch West-India Company's money, the General wrote that: '. . . the Specie found here belonging to the Publick Company amounting to about £15,000 I have placed on board the *Sandwich* . . . I shall give the Dutch property every Security I can until His Majesty has signified his pleasure . . .'

A second letter of the same date informed Germain that: '. . . the Consternation that reigns here at present is, My Lord, inconceivable . . . it was a Stroke they so little expected that they could scarce believe Lieut Colonel Cockburne [sic] who I sent with the Summons: but while Their High Mightinesses were eating their Soup we took possession of at least three Millions of Money: and what gives me particular pleasure to find is that Amsterdam will bear the chief weight of the Loss . . .

'The Fort called Fort Orange, I now have the Honour to call Fort George . . . etc.'

Whether the gentlemen of the Treasury were entirely satisfied with that loose rounding-off '. . . at least three Millions of Money . . .' is not known, but Vaughan's final estimate came at the end of March. In the absence of other information it is to be assumed that the total quoted included the proceeds of yet another visit to the miserable de Graaff on 10th of that month, when:

> . . . by order of Major-General Vaughan, two officers and a clerk came to my house demanding all the cash money then in my possession. Which unjust claim I was obliged to obey . . . I counted the money, in their presence, it being in gold and silver specie an amount of 54654, 2, 3 pesos. This was taken from me, put on a little cart and transported to the headquarters under an armed escort . . .

Where, no doubt, it was added to those other peripatetic riches whose subsequent travels we shall attempt to unravel. But in this communication, Vaughan informed Germain that . . 'the Money sent out last year from England having been expended in paying the subsistence to the Troops and the departments to the twentyfourth of December, a further supply is wanted . . .:

> As there is upwards of Forty Thousand Pounds of Dutch Money here, I wish to submit it to your Lordship whether this money may not be applied towards the payment of the Troops . . .'

Within two days of the landing, the islanders had discovered the conquerors' frightening appetite for their money. It would, in addition, soon engorge their valuables and plate, but the early reaction of at least one of the Statians indicates the level of panic and desperation reported by others. Clearly, here is the foundation for the bizarre ritual described in the first chapter of this book.

Writing to Vaughan on 6 February, Rodney complained that:

> . . . numbers of people are continually coming from St Christopher and our other Islands. Their only view is villainy and transferring as they think Dutch and French property to British subjects . . . for God's sake suffer none of them to come ashore and be so good as to order every seaman who comes into the Town to be taken . . . whenever your letters are ready let us send our Dispatches away as soon as possible – St Martins has submitted, adieu . . .

> 'PS One of my officers will wait upon you, upon a very good affair – a Rascal of a Jew has hid a chest with 5000 Joes* in a cane patch – a Negro will shew the place, upon a promise of Freedom and reward . . . my officer will tell you the whole affair . . .'

The King's pleasure

From his new headquarters at Fort George, Vaughan wrote to his master in Whitehall describing the immediate problems for the Commanders-in-Chief and the course of action they proposed to pursue. This is the letter of 7 February telling Germain of the specie so far discovered: therein Vaughan, like Rodney, 'begged leave to congratulate Your Lordship upon the Surrender etc . . . a blow I think in its Consequence cannot but be most sensibly felt by the Enemy as it has been a Source of most essential Succor to them . . . nothing could have so deeply affected the Americans as this . . .'

Much of Vaughan's rare happiness was justified. Here, at last, was his own success and he could glow in its measure – in the knowledge that the Dutch had paid the price for aiding the rebels and that supplies of war material would no longer flow to them from this place. It spelled hardship, in addition, for the French colonies, as heavily dependent on St Eustatius and the Dutch islands for a very great deal of their food: the war at sea had long deterred French merchant ships from entering these

---

*'Joes' (Johannes) Portugese gold coin known in American Colonies and West Indies. Contemporary value circa 1780, some four pounds sterling.

waters and Statia had thus become the mart for the produce of the colonies and their vital provider.

As for the Statians, Vaughan told Germain that they were '. . . a Collection from all Nations . . . who have a considerable property in it, the French and Americans in particular which I have taken Care to have properly ascertained . . .'

The seeds of trouble were contained in that apparently firm assurance to Germain and in the next proposals:

> . . . the perishable commodities in the French and American Stores . . . the Admiral and myself think most adviseable [sic] to dispose of in the neighbouring Islands, the rest to send to England in the Ships taken here . . .'

With this letter, the General enclosed the Articles of Agreement made between Rodney and himself: excellent aspirations which were soon to plague them both . . .:

> 'First, that we for ourselves and all those under Our Command do covenant and agree as far as in Us lies, that all Ships and Vessels loaden with Merchandize or otherwise, all Publick Stores, Magazines etc. taken at the Surrender of St Eustatius . . . shall be distributed according to the King's pleasure . . .'

This wish was endorsed in Rodney's letter to Stephens on the 10th. The King's pleasure was yet to be known but Sir George included some helpful guidelines for the royal consideration:

> . . . as General Vaughan and myself perfectly agree in Opinion relative to this great Capture, we flatter ourselves, if His Majesty is graciously pleased to bestow any Part of it between the Navy and the Army employed in these Seas, that he will dictate in what Manner his gracious Bounty may be bestowed, that all Altercations and Disagreements may be prevented between His Majesty's Servants serving in his Royal Navy and Army employed in this Part of his Dominions . . .

An early measure was to convene a meeting of the senior military and naval officers who were '. . . to form themselves into a Board to forward His Majesty's Service, prevent Irregularities (how appropriate that capital letter was to be: the Irregularities, in fact, whether furtively undertaken or shamelessly blatant transpired rapidly thereafter) . . . and to Establish Order in the Island of St Eustatius . . .' This document, signed by Sir George but undated, names the members of the Board, for which body Vaughan had chosen three Brigadiers – Ogilvie, Skene and Fraser.

The Army was also represented by two Lieutenant-Colonels: Edhouse of the 13th Foot and Cockburn in his capacity as Quarter-Master General, and by three majors – Craford, Roberts and Nickson. The sole civilian in this group was the Commissary-General, Matthew Forster.

Four Captains represented the navy: Rodney's flag captain, Young, Saxton of the *Invincible*, Gidoin of the *Torbay* and Inglefield of the *Centaur*. With this group were the Reverend Pagett and Hood's own Secretary, Joseph Hunt. Young and Pagett were additionally instructed by Rodney on the 11th that they were to '. . . take Cognizance of everything relative to the Great Conquest of the Island and its dependencies as Agents on his part . . .' and as Agents '. . . for all Vessels and every Species of Merchandize Sold in any of the West India Islands . . .' On the 9th, Rear Admiral Sir Samuel Hood, supported by all the captains of Sir George's Fleet had agreed that this function should be allotted to the Captains and Secretaries already appointed to the Board. Agents would also be required for the captured commodities to be shipped to England: George Jackson of the Admiralty and Messrs Wesbster of Leadenhall Street were therefore appointed on behalf of the captains, officers and seamen who might have a 'concern' in that booty.

The harmony was immediately jolted on the day that document was signed. *Panther* arrived at St Eustatius with the battered Dutch flagship *Mars* in tow and the remainder of the captured convoy crawling miserably after. Much to Rodney's annoyance, his victorious captains, Reynolds, Harvey and Fitzgerald declared that they did not feel themselves to be bound by the agreement between the Commanders-in-Chief and had no intention of including their prizes in the general booty. Appealing to Germain for advice, Sir George was required to bottle his anger until 30 April when he learned that the Secretary of State was no less concerned but . . .

It was true, wrote Germain, that ships of war had an exclusive right to all captures made at sea: '. . . and if Captain Reynolds and the other Officers insist upon their Right their Claim must be allowed . . .' However: by the same rule, if they wished to take advantage of that law, then these captains had no entitlement to the Booty taken on shore and Rodney and Vaughan should see to it that they were excluded from any such distribution.

The Board was to meet 'from Nine till Twelve every day . . . appoint a Secretary and have all proceedings regularly Entered . . .' while it would fall to the Quartermaster General '. . . to appoint a Place for meeting . . .'

Cockburn was to do much more. It is unlikely that he had any knowledge of the protest of the unwilling Nathanael Greene, appointed as Washington's QMG in 1778: '. . . whoever heard of a QuarterMaster in History?' but by virtue of that status and as a member of the Board,

Cockburn, well groomed for the role by his early service in Ireland, was about to personify the occupation in the eyes of the residents and so become an exception to Greene's rule.

In his dealings with the civilian population, Cockburn was to be supported by Forster, and by Daniel Ross of St Eustatius, who was appointed 'Vendue Master or Auctioneer' for the forthcoming sales. The QMG's retinue also included Sergeant William Gordon, as acting Deputy Quartermaster – who was also to provide a special note in Cockburn's career – and another NCO drawn from the 35th, Sergeant Isaac Miller, 'assistant to the Deputy Quartermaster.'

The name of Arietas Akers, agent for the prisoners of war at St Kitts had been put forward to augment this group. The nomination was at first rejected after Captain Young disclosed to Sir George that Akers 'claimed a debt of between £40,000 and £50,000' against Statian merchants. Despite this, Akers was subsequently appointed under circumstances which earned the vexation of Admiral Hood whose own nominees, Inglefield and Hunt, were thereby displaced. Hood's comments on this matter will appear in their proper context.

The Board had much to consider, but their stated plans for the island, approved and clearly laid down by Sir George at this first meeting, were as quoted below:

1. To settle a proper Police and Trade for such people as may be deemed proper to remain in the island.
2. To ascertain all neutral bottoms.
3. To dispose of Americans resident in the island.
4. To dispose of French residents.

5th . . . And the Dutch that may be judged proper to be sent off the island.

6th . . . Jews shipp't off, they being desirous to go to St Thomas's . . . to have fourteen days' Provisions and ships appointed to carry them by the Admiral.

7th . . . All discoveries of Money, Goods, or any articles whatever to be reported every Morning to this Board.

8th . . . Provisions to be allowed the resident Inhabitants as Prisoners of War when applied for. A Consideration for the Board.

and 9th . . . All decisions of this Board to be constantly Reported to the Commanders-in-Chief for their final Judgement and approbation.

With these guidelines the captors began the work of stripping the island.

... TO LEVEL THIS NEST OF THIEVES

It was intended to ruin the merchants by confiscating their goods and personal wealth: that accomplished, most of them would be deported, the French – 'an Agent and many Merchants' – to be embarked in cartel vessels for Guadaloupe and Martinique. They would be permitted to carry with them '... their Household Furniture, Plate, Linen, etc. etc ... and their numerous Household Slaves ...'

With similar concessions, the American traders would be returned to America – save for Rodney's Prisoners of State, Curson and Gouverneur, who would be taken to England in the *Vengeance*. The Dutch 'Amsterdam Merchants' would likewise be allowed cartel ships to carry them, their families and their household furniture ... They can have no Pretence or desire to remain in this island' Rodney affirmed: '... as I hope it will for ever cease being a Place of Commerce.'

That extraordinary violence in Rodney's references to Statia boiled again in a letter to Parker, in April. Sir George's hope became a promise that he would '... take Care this Nest of Thieves shall be levelled with the Earth, as an Example to Perfidious States ...' But from the very first day, even as Vaughan's troops were still being ferried ashore to become files and companies on the beach, and from there, to go on to swamp the little town in a milling sea of red coats, Rodney had set the tone in that triumphant letter to Germain: he would 'bring this Nest of Villains to condign Punishment: they deserve scourging and they shall be scourged.'

And to this end, no more salutary beginning than to arrest the leading 'Villains' on Rodney's list and to hasten the prisoners aboard the King's ships. In this, the Admiral was unflagging: we find him urging Vaughan, on 13 February – a day of reckoning for the Jews, among others – to seize '... Mr Smith at the House of Jones – they cannot be too soon taken care of – they are notorious in the cause of America and France ...'

Among the people who, in Sir George's phrase, were 'taken care of', Samuel Curson and Isaac Gouverneur had been marked by their inclusion in Lauren's intercepted papers: Jacques Texier as the most prominent of the French activists, and now to his cost, informed on and singled out as a Dutch Burgher*: and Pieter Bummels, the seventy year-old Councillor and senior Burgher, described by de Graaff – himself on notice to quit the island – as ailing, 'deprived of help and assistance, parted from his family and robbed. At last, due to constant soliciting ... Bummels was permitted to return to his house where soon after, he died ...' – the only civilian death, it must be said, attributed to the British

---

*An option for those qualified by eighteen months residence in St Eustatius, enabling them to trade advantageously as Dutch citizens.

occupiers. In our own savage Twentieth Century this is a point to be remarked.

There were more rewarding activities, for no stone – literally – was left unturned in the hunt for the residents' money or possessions. It is futile to search for admissions of this in the carefully worded letters of the Commanders-in-Chief to Germain and to the Admiralty although we do indeed have Sir George's reference to that 'rascal of a Jew,' but the testimony of those 'other witnesses' previously mentioned, considerably amplifies our knowledge. A telling record of personal experience is contained in Governor de Graaff's report to his superiors, in the revelations of de Jong and of Richard Downing Jennings, and in the letters and petitions of others attempting, mostly without success, to avert their own ruin. These are presented in later pages. The distress of these people may be better appreciated however, if it is seen in the frame of the series of Proclamations issued by 'the Commander-in-Chief' between 6 February and 24 March. The title refers to Vaughan as the military commander but the announcements clearly carried the weight of the Admiral.

Of the 38 Proclamations, printed in English and in Dutch, posted up in a variety of locations and brought to the notice of the residents by the roll of a drum, eight appear over the signature of J Cockburn, or Coekburn, Quartermaster-General. The Dutch rendering may be that by the island secretary, Alexander LeJeune who, until the time came for his own expulsion, was kept busy by Vaughan and Rodney, notably in drawing up documents offering a census of the residents, their length of residence on St Eustatius, their countries of origin and their status as Burghers where this applied.

All of the Proclamations were concerned with the expropriation of the residents' property, with the deportation of the islanders, with rules of conduct for those permitted to remain and for the policing of the island. It was made plain in the very first of the Proclamations that there would be no nonsense about velvet gloves:

. . . *Headquarters, St Eustatius 6 Feb: 1781*

. . . His Excellency the Commander in Chief, orders that every Inhabitant of this Island (without exception) do forthwith render a full and just account of all his effects to the Quartermaster-General, of every description, viz:

Plantations, Houses, Furniture, Plate, Merchandize, Slaves, Horses, Horndcattle [sic], and all other four footed beasts. This order to be strictly complied, in its fullest sense, on pain of confiscation and banishment. NB All Inventorys are to be written in English . . .

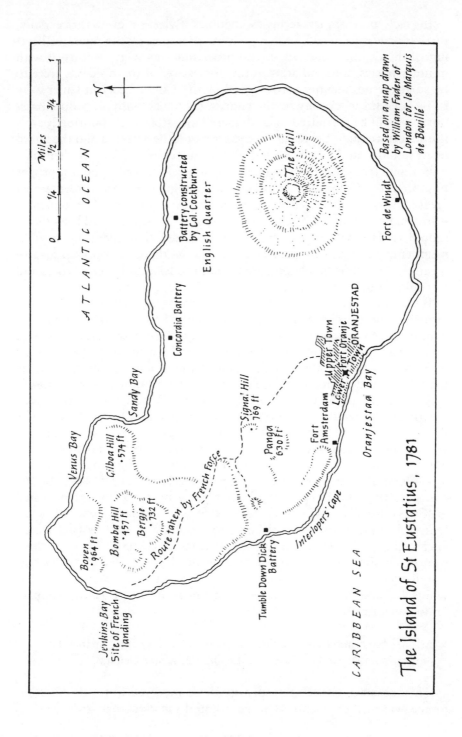

The Island of St Eustatius, 1781

Based on a map drawn
by William Faden of
London for le Marquis
de Bouillé

ATLANTIC OCEAN

Miles
0   1/4   1/2   3/4   1

N

The Quill

Fort de Windt

Battery constructed
by Col. Cockburn

English Quarter

Concordia Battery

Sandy Bay

Venus Bay

Gilboa Hill
•574 ft

Boven
•964 ft

Bomba Hill
•457 ft

Bergje
•732 ft

Route taken by French Force

Signal Hill
•769 ft

Panga
630 ft

Upper Town
Fort Orange
Lower Town ORANJESTAD

Fort
Amsterdam

Jenkins Bay
Site of French
landing

Tumble Down Dick
Battery

Interlopers' Cape

Oranjestaa Bay

CARIBBEAN SEA

135

In such peremptory terms, sometimes twice or even thrice daily, further orders followed, each new blow presaged by the ominous beating of the drum. Some few of the proclamations were concerned with military basics: thus, all arms in the possession of the residents were to be surrendered: identity cards signed by the Commander-in-Chief were to be issued, for scrutiny by the guards: no boats 'without proper passports' would be permitted to land: merchants from neighbouring islands found ashore on St Eustatius thereafter would be arrested and the guard nearest to the landing place 'marked for neglect of duty': no soldier to go half a mile from the Town on any account whatever 'without a proper pass from the Commanding Officer of his regiment – (this order, transgressed, was to raise three lowly soldiers to an undreamt of prominence) – and, in Proclamation No. 4 of 11 February, '. . . since it had been represented to His Majesty's Commander-in-Chief that there are a great number of Strangers in this Island' . . . it was therefore ordered that all Strangers do immediately prepare to quit the Island, till such orders and a regular Police can be established . . .'

But as they were meant to do, the majority of the decrees harassed and punished the merchant community and served to command immediate submission to every confiscation. Only '. . . the few respectable men who owned the Sugar plantations' were exempted, since most were deemed innocent of participation in the contraband trade: but as speedily as Cockburn could bring out the Proclamations, all others were methodically plundered: their negroes to labour for the British, their horses given up for the enjoyment of the officers and their mules for transport. The demands continued: the merchants were to give in returns of all provisions they held to the Commissary-General, Matthew Forster . . . 'at Mr Texier's, specifying quantities and how long they have been imported . . . Flour, Biscuit, Beef, Pork, Oats, Meal, Peas, Butter, Rice, Beans, Vinegar, Rum and Wine . . .' and quickly '. . . by 12 O'clock tomorrow.'

'Coekburn's' Proclamation No. 14 of 22 February, first called on '. . . All Inhabitants of this Island (foreigners and natives [sic] Dutch excepted . . . to deliver to the Quartermaster-General, by 12 o'clock tomorrow, sign'd Certificates of the time they have resided in this Island.' But Rodney's express command is reflected in the next requirement, which – although he could not foresee it – proved to have a crucial impact on his own future.

All Merchants and traders in this Island are forthwith to give up their Books of Correspondence, Letters etc. to the Quartermaster-General.

This measure, intended to identify those involved in traitorous commerce, was further prompted by the Admiral's instinct that at some point, he might need to justify activities which daily brought him a stream of protesting merchants, notably from neighbouring St Kitts. Rodney and Vaughan's 'Glorious Capture', far from earning the applause of British merchants in the West Indies, had left them appalled, angry, and fearful for their own property stored in the Statian warehouses, and for that of their friends and business correspondents in that island.

In a pathetically ineffective endeavour to halt the indiscriminate confiscations now in hand, therefore, they offered strong representations to the Commanders-in-Chief which were unfailingly rejected by Rodney. With Vaughan nodding his meek assent to the Admiral's angry explosions on this subject, Rodney became at first indifferent to appeals by the men of St Kitts – in the persons of their leading citizen, Mr Moore and other members of the committee appointed by their legislature – and finally, as the protests continued in the next weeks, coarsely abusive. Indeed, he told the members of the deputation from St Kitts, he had 'a special place' for their petitions – namely in his quarter-gallery: the Admiral's privy.

Apart from that initial bluster, however, Rodney soon came to accept that Vaughan and himself were indeed at risk from this quarter. He had been delighted, of course, on receiving a letter from Germain, dated 20 March, informing him that His Majesty had relinquished all rights to the booty of St Eustatius in favour of the Captors – 'the said Ships, Vessels, Merchandize, Naval and Military Stores and other effects of the enemy so captured by you, Our said Commanders-in-Chief and Our Land and Sea Forces under your respective Commands (except only the whole of the Provisions and the Ordnance, Arms, Ammunition and other Military Stores provided for the Defence of the said Islands . . .' the rest was graciously granted to the Captors albeit with the instruction that 'the settled inhabitants were to be left with their Lands and Produce thereof, Houses, Slaves, Cattle, Furniture, Utensils and Stock . . .' It was the next paragraph however, which left him exposed to a chill wind, for it specifically forbade the captors to seize 'all such effects as shall prove the Property of British subjects lawfully Exported thither, or which may lawfully be imported into Great Britain from thence.'

This Instruction was to be ignored by the Admiral. It was received by Vaughan at St Lucia on 30 May. Spinney suggests that Rodney, then at Barbados, may not have done so, or may have deliberately anticipated this proviso by instructing Akers to arrange for the sale of the stores belonging to '. . . the people calling themselves British merchants.' Yet the threats of legal action proved to be all too serious, for more than ninety plaintiffs brought suit against Rodney and Vaughan for the recovery of their property or its value. The actions would keep the lawyers for the Commanders-in-Chief busy for a number of years and in fact, until the Admiral's death a decade later. Time would show that Rodney's instinct of looming trouble, expressed in letters to Germain, had been only too well-founded: but for the moment, at St Eustatius, he ruled with all the arrogance of the conqueror, answerable as yet, to no-one but himself. And in this, he was considerably aided by the enthusiasm for the role of despot being so clearly displayed by the Quartermaster-General, Lieutenant-Colonel James Cockburn.

Unmilitary Practices

Cockburn's name had appeared for the first time (as Coekburn), in Proclamation No. 6 of 13 February, wherein he had attended to some unfinished business arising from the immediate flight of the Americans on Rodney's arrival.

> All persons that have any property or cash belonging to any Americans that have either been sent on board Ship or have absconded are forthwith to give up the same to the Quartermaster-General on pain of military execution.

But Cockburn's were not the only ears to prick up at the clink of money, nor was he alone in his determination to track down the source of that sound. Incarcerated aboard their ships as they were, the seamen were largely denied the same opportunities: any resentment at this however, must have been safely damped by the grim spectacle, on 5 March, of six erstwhile mutineers summarily executed aboard ship at Rodney's order. But ashore, others were now feverishly employed in a grand treasure hunt. Only a very few of these men have been identified by the outraged Statians and names misquoted or attributed in the Dutch reports require some careful consideration. But no such confusion surrounds the activities of the leading players.

One of the most evident characteristics of the eighteenth century naval officer appeared to be an enthusiasm for informing on his colleagues, and that to those quarters where the intelligence might do the victim the utmost professional injury. The letters to be quoted herein are prize examples: from Sir Samuel Hood to Jackson at the Admiralty, unequivocally naming Rodney, for all his exalted status, as a mere thief: and that from Commissioner John Laforey at Antigua, to his own friend at the Admiralty, Sir Charles Middleton, Comptroller of the Navy, accusing Rodney of ludicrously inflating the value of the captured naval stores sent to Laforey for the dockyard. 'Barrels of rusty nails' claimed the disgruntled Commissioner, who was in turn suspected by Rodney of having made his own pecuniary arrangements with dockyard staff and suppliers.

* * *

Meanwhile, at St Eustatius, the unrelenting search for cash and valuables to be seized became the major task for officers and men. Where these possessions were not surrendered on demand they would be taken from houses, pockets or purses by force: '. . . many people had their pockets searched when they left their houses, only because these pockets seemed a little full . . .'

But the searches were not limited to pockets and purses. The assignment also gave the soldiers an excellent pretext for much coarse groping of any person crossing their path. The sport continued without official hindrance until indignant reports came to Vaughan and generated Proclamation No. 28, dated 7 March.

> Complaints having been made to the Commander-in-Chief that frequent irregularities have been committed by the Soldiers on, and of [sic] duty upon the Persons of both Sexes, by stopping them in the Streets and searching them in a most Shameful manner, His Excellency takes this Publick method of declaring his utter abhorrence of such unmilitary Practices, and Strictly orders that nothing of the kind be committed in the future, on pain of the most Severe punishment . . .'

Rodney reveals his interest in buried money in his letter of 6 February, wherein a frightened Jew – 'a Rascal', naturally – had '. . . hid a chest with 5000 Joes in a cane patch.' Resort to this desperate expedient, which was to become a staple of Statian legend, was common enough to exercise the Army and Navy. The *Nederlandsche Jaerboeken* reported on some of these earnest burrowers:

> . . . on the 17th, three lieutenants (of the Navy) were sent by Captain Sarter [sic] to the houses of Mr Carrere and Candeau, to search the ground around their houses to see if money was hidden there . . .'

Neither did the Navy neglect Richard Downing Jennings, despite his protests to the Admiral. But Jennings had been long under suspicion and his name was on Rodney's List of villains, and so he too, was to be scourged: and so thoroughly indeed, that he eventually laid a claim against Rodney for seventy thousand pounds on behalf of his associate, George Tucker and himself, in respect of '. . . a very great quantity of merchandize . . .'

This doubtless refers to goods and commodities in the warehouses owned by Jennings and Tucker, but all of their wealth, and that of the other traders, wherever located and in whatever form, was in hazard.

139

Jacob Howel, Master of the schooner *Adonis*, formally testified before Charles Payne Brotherson, Governor of St Martin's, that he had sailed from Curaçao on the 13 February and had arrived at captured St Martin on the 23rd. There he landed the sum of eight thousand dollars at his dwelling, 'shipped by Messrs Thomas Webb and Co merchants of Curaçao for account of Messrs R D Jennings and Co . . .'

In this field, naval intelligence shone: for '. . . on the twenty-eighth of said month, Walter Young, Captain of the *Sandwich* about nine o'clock at night, together with other officers and soldiers, called at his house: and the said Walter Young did by order of Sir George Brydges Rodney demand sixteen bags of money agreeable to an information landed by this deponent at [his] house on the twenty third, between the hours of twelve and one o'clock at night.'

Faced with the confiscation of his own property should he fail to comply, Howel had no choice but to give up '. . . fifteen bags of money, four of which were shipped by Messrs Webb for Jennings' account at St Eustatius, each bag containing one thousand dollars (and) being marked RD1–4. The schooner was then taken to St Eustatius and thence, to St Christopher's where '. . . her loading was labelled . . .' and Howel – examined further and on oath – made to admit that more of Jennings' money was still in the possession of Mr Thomas Richardson and Abraham Howel. Four more bags, indeed, each bag again containing 'one thousand dollars and marked RD-1 No. 5–8: and taken from the said Thomas Richardson and Abraham Howel by Mr –* commander of His Majesty's cutter *Sylph*, by order of Sir George Brydges Rodney, while this deponent was at St Christopher's under libel: and further this deponent saith not.'

* * *

Little could be successfully withheld from the searchers and nothing at all safeguarded from the soldiery set to guard the warehouses. That mile-long avenue of stone, those swollen magazines which had been built to withstand mere hurricane and sea, had challenged the mischievously agile among them at first sight. So too, had their keen eyes – and not only theirs – noted the busy preparation of the convoy that was to carry so much of the booty to England, the fitting out of the ships and the incessant porterage as their cargoes were loaded.

It was common knowledge that everything else, not only captured vessels, goods and merchandize, but also provisions of all kinds, would be sold. In time, the soldiers hoped that they would be included in the general benefit, for the grapevine had told of such enquiries from the commanders of the British islands, ostensibly on behalf of their garrisons.

*The name is illegible. It may not have been that of the *Sylph*'s commander.

These representations were strong enough to cause Vaughan to refer the question to Germain, on 5 March:

> . . . I have received Memorials from the Troops at several Islands claiming a Share in the Seizure of this Place, but as this is new, never having been practiced before, I can only at present advise your Lordship of it . . .

Meanwhile, the soldiers were not content simply with hope and had taken to burgling the locked warehouses. Five years on, Vaughan was to allege that it was necessary to expedite the Sales of the goods in those stores by reason of '. . . the inhabitants Plundering their own Stores (!) and the depredations Committed by the Soldiers and Sailors which could not be Effectually Restrained . . .' Not even by his belated attempt to lock the stable door and to throw the onus on the residents, as in Proclamation No. 25 of 6 March:

> . . . .As depredations are committed in the night at the Stores in the Lower Town, the Commander-in-Chief hereby directs that the Inhabitants do immediately take all means and place such safeguards as shall be proper to preserve all Property, Stores & c . . .

. . . *With regard to the Jews* . . .

On 13 February, the blow fell on the Jews. The men of the community were rounded up, their wives and families being denied news of them or access to them, and assembled in Statia's weigh-house pending deportation. It is not at all clear who conducted this operation, but the *Nederlandsche Jaerboeken* states that 'this eloquent deed was executed by the adjutant of the Commissary-General and a Sergeant (Gordon or Miller?) under the command of "Mr Fenton", Captain of the ship *Invincible*.' *Invincible* was, of course, commanded by Captain Cornish: but whether inflicted by soldiers, sailors or marines, the allegation is that the prisoners were brutally handled and so thoroughly searched for concealed money or valuables that their clothing was ripped apart in the process. It is claimed that some 8000 pieces of money were found in this way.

All were unfortunate, but only Myer Pollock's story has come down to us: this unhappy Loyalist had lost his family during the Americans' attack on Long Island and like Samson Mears who, it will be remembered, had fled to Statia from Norwalk, Connecticut, and who had since become Secretary of the Synagogue, only to find himself cheated of that better fortune he had hoped for, both had sought that refuge in St Eustatius now brought to an abrupt end.

After three days, all but a selected twenty of the Jews were released. These prisoners were then herded aboard the *Shrewsbury* (74) and their names solemnly entered in the ship's Muster Book under the stern eye of the Boatswain, (and immediately below the names of thirty-five captured American seamen). They were then carried, not to St Thomas, as Rodney had directed at the first meeting of the Board – . . . 'The Jews being desirous to go to St Thomas's . . . to have fourteen days' Provisions and Ships appointed to carry them by the Admiral . . .' but to St Kitts, where they were disembarked. But here, where Rodney and Vaughan were not in the least admired, they were among friends and were humanely received: 'The Assembly of that island passed an immediate Act for their present relief and future provision, until they should have time to recover from their calamitous situation.'

On 16 February, an anguished Petition was presented to the Commanders-in-Chief by the Jews of Statia. Humbly, they asked permission to approach Their Excellencies to lay their grievances before them. In elegant and respectful language they pointed out that it was 'with the utmost concern and astonishment' that they had received Their Excellencies' afflicting order and sentence, having given up the keys of their Stores and provided inventories for them, and for their household plate and furniture, they had been warned to prepare to leave the island 'leaving our beloved wives and helpless children behind us, and our property and effects liable to seizure and confiscation . . .' But they had now discovered that the deportation order had already been carried out: they pleaded therefore, for Their Excellencies 'lenity and humanity . . .'

Authors have treated Rodney and Vaughan badly in this matter, since they have claimed that the Petition went unheeded. Yet there is indubitably a second Petition dated 10 April, little more than seven weeks afterwards, in which the same elegant language is employed and by the same people: David Abendonone, Warden, and the elders: David De Leon, Benjamin Wellcome, Solomon Levy and Joseph Abendonone. In this Petition, however, the tone is joyous and grateful. The Commanders-in-Chief have rescinded the deportation order and we know from the evidence subsequently offered (in the General Case against Rodney and Vaughan) that the Jewish deportees were indeed back on St Eustatius at that date and repossessed of the keys to their warehouses. Unfortunately, these too, had been pillaged.

Reports of their especially rough treatment by the Captors were later to give Burke further ammunition for his brilliant performances in the House, and while the members on the Government side had long been possessed of an essential thick skin for Burke's tongue, enabling them to weather his scorn and attempts to shame them with practised indifference, it is clear that on the matter of St Eustatius – despite a vote of 160

Bouillé Gouverneur de la Martinique, Commandant des Troupes de Terre, à la reprise de l'Ile de St Eustache en Amerique.

...chez Bance, Rue St Jacques au coin de celle des Mathurins à l'Image St Genevieve. Il tient Magazin de Papiers en Rouleaux.

A contemporary French engraving of de Bouillé. The French caption reads: M. Bouillé Governor of Martinique. Commander of the ground troops at the recapture of the Island of St Eustatius in America. (*Bibliotheque Nationale, Paris*)

Count de Grasse. (*National Maritime Museum*)

The Dutch Flagship *Mars* under attack by the British warships *Monarch*, *Panther* and *Sybil*, 4 February 1781 (*Nederlands Historisch Scheepvaart Museum, Amsterdam*)

Admiral Willem Krul (*Nederlands Historisch Scheepvaart Museum, Amsterdam*)

Cornelius de Jong (*Vereeniging Nederlands Historisch Scheepvaart Museum, Amsterdam*)

The French landing at Jenkinson's [sic] Bay, St Eustatius, Leeward Islands, 26 November 1781. (*From the Royal Library, Windsor Castle. Reproduced by gracious permission of Her Majesty Queen Elizabeth II*). The French caption reads: View of Jenkinson's Bay and on the point at which M de Bouillé disembarked, although there was a high sea running: with the Dilon [sic], Walsh and Martinique Regiments, at daybreak: several men are carrying torches to guide the longboats to the landing place.

St Eustatius Surprised. Cockburn is captured (on his horse, centre). Note also the French troops firing across the half-opened drawbridge. (*Reproduced by permission of the Trustees of the Royal Sussex Regimental Museum*)

The surprise of St Eustatius by M. le Marquise de Bouillé. Dumoulin, 1785. (*Private collection, Vevey*)

to 86 on 14 May 1781 rejecting his motion for an enquiry into the conduct of the Captors – he made his points to good effect. The Members of the House were uncomfortably aware that the voice of that masterly orator was accompanied by the angry chorus from the West India interest: all of which further ensured that there would be no unqualified support in this important quarter for Rodney and Vaughan on their return. Both men, in fact, would find it difficult to muster any support at all when it was needed, except from their hired – and privately cynical – advisers. So effectively had Burke and his supporters sown disquiet, in fact, that a chastened House was later to grant the petition of Samuel Hoheb, an elder of Statia's Jewish community who, despite his age and infirmity, appeared in person to present it. So impoverished had he been rendered by the banditry of Rodney and Vaughan, Hoheb stated, that he had been left 'without a shilling' to pay for the action he wished to bring against them. He therefore requested the aid of the House in this: and to their credit, they agreed that the Attorney-General should proceed on Hoheb's behalf.

Other writers touching on this episode, notably Barbara Tuchman in her book '*The First Salute*' and the Emmanuels' in their '*History of the Jews in the Antilles*' have attributed the maltreatment and arbitrary eviction of the Statian Jews to Rodney's alleged anti-Semitism but there is no evidence for this in Rodney's background. Save for a suggestion that when, as the young captain who had so enjoyed the pleasures of London fifteen years earlier, he had been acquainted with a Jewish 'actress' Eleanor Ambrose of Drury Lane, there is no mention by any serious biographer that Rodney had ever met any other member of that faith. Only one remark of relevance is on record, when Rodney considered approaching the Jews of St Domingo for intelligence: 'They will do anything for money' said our paragon.

Rodney probably possessed the innate prejudices grafted on by Christian dogma and his own social grouping, but the event cannot be explained in this way. There are however, two particularly strange factors in this story. One of these implies an early concession to the Jews, namely Rodney's choice of words in the document drawn up at the first meeting of the Board: 'The Jews being desirous to go to St Thomas's . . .' – where there was a long-established Jewish community. And there is also Rodney's comment in his extenuatory 'Plain State of Facts relating to the Capture of St Eustatius' published in 1787, and it is weightily supported by his response to appeals for their reinstatement at the time. 'With regard to the Jews' wrote the Admiral, '. . . this was a mistake, and as soon as I was acquainted with the news I ordered their return.'

Bounty Paid	Nº	Entry.	Year	Appearance.	Whence and Whether Prest or not.	Place and County where Born.		Nº and Letter of Ticket	MENS NAMES.	Quality	D. D.D. or R.	Time of Discharge	Year	Whither or for what Reason	Straggling	Front of Ledger	Marine Deduct.	
	201	15 Feb 81	Feb		St Eustatia Independant B. American Prize				Pat. Ephrini	D	0							
									Geo Robinson	D								
									Chas Smart	D								
									Thos Griffithsbeck	D								
	5								Elisha May	D								
									Jnº Oliver	D								
									Jnº Tracey	D								
									Thos Dwire	R	21 Feb 81 Lancashire Present Vc in the Adml Burbury							
									Ezekiel Lather	D								
	10								Wm Hodges	D								
									Thos Gurner	D								
									Jnº Brewer	D								
									Simon Attwood	D								
									Thos Williams	D								
	15								Thos Brannin	D								
	11	"	"	"	St Eustatia Jews				Saml Hoheb	D								
									Solomon Levy	D								
									Levy Abraham	D	15 Feb 81 St Kitts						
									Jacob Robeleys	D								
	220								Lyon Mann	D								
										11								

Extract from the Muster Book of HMS *Shrewsbury*, listing captured American seamen and Jewish residents of St Eustatius. The name of Samuel Hoheb heads the list of Jews.

144

Bounty Paid	Nº	Entry	Year	Appearance	Whence and Whether Prest or not	Place and County where Born	Age at Time of Entry	Nº and Letter of Tickets	MENS NAMES	Quality	D. D.D. or R.	Time of Discharge	Year	Whither or for what Reason	Stragling	Front of Ledger	Marine Deduct: Necer Secu rie
	221	13 Feb	81 Feb 13	St Eustatia Jews					Jacob Almida		D						
									Nathn Samuel		D						
									Elias Henna		D						
									Eleazah Abn Levy		D						
	5								Jacob Levy		D						
									Ben Cortieos		D						
									Mr D. Hokeb		D						
									Gomez Waz		D	14 Feb 81 St Kitts				
									Dan Levy		D						
	10								Abm Demazza		D						
									Barnet Levy		D						
									Bn Benjamin		D						
									Davd Porto		D						
									Ben Meirs		D					*	
	335								J. J. Courlanda		D						

... *Nothing but Cash* ...

The hapless traders were not to be left with much but Cockburn rightly suspected many of them attempting to cling to what they could. His ultimatum to them, stark with the threat of destitution, came in Proclamation No. 18 of 24 February.

> ... Whereas it appears, by the Inventory of Effects given in by the Merchants and Inhabitants of this place, that most of them have neglected to make a return of Cash and Plate that they stood posses'd of at the Surrender of the Island.

> It is hereby ordered, that they do forthwith give in to the Quartermaster-General an exact account of all monies and plate now in their possession as well as belonging to themselves as other people, for which they are to be responsible when required.

> And if any future discoveries shall be made of monies or plate, concealed after this return is given in, it will be deemed the property of no particular individual.

On 7 March, Cockburn published the orders and arrangements for the sale of the massive stocks of goods in the warehouses. Much had already been seized for loading aboard the prize convoy which would sail for England under Hotham two weeks hence, and which, Rodney had warned Philip Stephens in a letter of 12 February, was '... extremely valuable: more so, I believe, than ever sailed to Great Britain, considering its Number of Ships – I shall give a positive Order to the Commanding Officer of the Convoy to gain the latitude of the Lizard, at least 200 leagues West from it: that if their Lordships think it necessary to send an additional Squadron for its Protection, they may be acquainted with the Track they are to take.'

Meanwhile there were the forthcoming Sales and Cockburn's arrangements showed an impressive grasp of commercial practice. Thus, the Statians were informed that the Sales would commence on Thursday the 15th of that month, and that they would be continued 'from day to day until the whole be sold ...'

> Nothing but Cash will be received in payment.

> All persons coming to this Island for the purpose of purchasing goods at the Sales will be permitted to pass freely to and from the Islands, without let or molestation.

All sums of Money brought to this Island for the purpose of purchasing goods, to be secured effectually and bona fide to the Owners.

All goods, purchased at the Sales will be permitted to be shipp'd off on to English or Neutral bottoms, for the purpose of conveying them to any of the English or Neutral Islands.

No persons whose goods have been confiscated to be allowed to become purchasers at the Sales.'

And

. . . to begin the sales at the windwardmost Store (warehouse) on the Bay, and to go from Store to Store (s) progressively, care being taken to distinguish Stores by Americans, Dutch, French etc., the English Stores to be left untouched with a label on each by way of discrimination.

This striking notice was to be widely reproduced in American, French and Caribbean newspapers and generated much scathing comment. The *St Christopher Gazette* of 9 March voiced the outrage of the St Kitts merchants in an open letter to Sir George over the highly appropriate signature of 'Cato.' Not unnaturally, this prophetic remonstrance was reprinted in the *Newport Mercury* of 26 May for the edification of American readers.

'I have refrained from writing you for the last month' declared this correspondent:

. . . in hopes that the uncivilized confiscations would not have been put into execution. I had formed great expectations from the generous sentiments and noble soul that in England you have been supposed to possess – I thought you had more of the true British blood in your veins and spurned at all that bore the least appearance of rapine. I must now, from my old esteem for you, give a few words of advice.

A sale is advertised for the 15th instant and I suppose it is the intention of the General and you, that the monies arising shall be deposited in trust till the King's pleasure is known. Surely you do not suppose that the lawful proprietors will be satisfied with such loss! It is notorious in all the islands that commodities will not, at such a sale, bring one tenth their value. People are afraid to go among you – sufferers cannot get access, particularly from this island; and suffered, we know better how to take care of the money we have spared us, than to trust it in the hands of the QM and his crew. This letter is intended as a friendly hint. I tell you the sentiments of the people at large, who are able and determined to prosecute you. They

147

must for the present submit to oppressions and abuse – but there will be a day of settlement in England.

* * *

French traders from the other islands were officially prohibited from attending the sale by De Bouillé: but since there appeared to have been no serious attempt to monitor their movements or to prevent them from setting forth for this unspecified but obvious venue, even from Martinique itself, the decree was to be observed in the breach only. They appeared therefore, at St Eustatius for the occasion, and in sufficient numbers to produce some scandalized witnesses on Statia and furious and cynical observations elsewhere. Nor, in London, was it a matter to be missed by that Parliamentary thorn in the side of the government, Edmund Burke, who berated an embarrassed House to an effect which greatly mortified Rodney and Vaughan on their later appearance in that place.

One week later, on the 15th, Cockburn proclaimed that the sales would begin at 10 o'clock that forenoon, at Mr Jennings' Store, and continue every day, Sundays excepted. It is to the vastly aggrieved Richard Downing Jennings that we owe the most graphic description of the proceedings. Regrettably, it is beyond any mere historian to uncover the full extent of the jamborce of misappropriation, deceit and sheer gall which typified this phase of the occupation: there are enough examples, however, to show that it was in one or another of these side-lines that too many officers serving with the 'Enterprize' of Rodney and Vaughan – to say nothing of the assortment of civilian beneficiaries – contrived to distinguish themselves.

Jennings' account, which he entitled *The Case of an English Subject* was presented in 1784 to declare both his unstained patriotism and his entitlement to reparation. (Jennings had by then, after great effort, recovered the sum of £567 and 4 shillings from the Lords of the Admiralty for his secret intelligence gathering service for Rodney in 1780, but this was to be offset against his still pending claim, on behalf of himself and his partner at St Eustatius, George Tucker, for £70,000.) The narration of events, allegations and justifications runs to fourteen pages of manuscript and includes a lengthy Appendix: all of this providing a valuable indicator of the atmosphere of furious commercial activity which, even before the appointed Auctioneer had begun his work – and who else should this have been but Arietas Akers – now preoccupied the Captors. And apart from a mistaken claim that the Sales had been proclaimed as beginning on 18 March and yet his own property – for which, of course, he was not permitted to bid – had been prematurely sold on the 15th –

(in fact, that proclamation had actually announced that all was to be seized for His Majesty the King, and that it was intended that the said goods, property and merchandise were to be sold. No date was specified.) . . . Jennings' testimony contains a great deal of damaging detail, and in particular, on that obliging traffic with the French.

* * *

'The professed object of the expedition' wrote Jennings, '. . . had been to prevent a supply of provisions and naval stores to the enemies of this country, and Lord Rodney (claims) that he had assiduously adopted the views of those who planned.' For the most cogent reason he had caused Admiral Hood to blockade Martinique with his squadron and thereafter had ordered that no naval or military stores should be included in the general sales.

Open derision for this edict was not in order, but given the acumen of the trading community and a universal eye for resaleable goods, it had no chance at all of being obeyed. As noted, blockade or no, that notice to potential purchasers that they might be 'permitted to pass freely to and from the Islands without let or molestation' was sufficient assurance to bring large numbers of French buyers and their vessels to Statia's shores. The acquisition of such forbidden goods was high on their lists of requirements. Jennings is caustic here:

> . . . To promote the Sales – and of course for the good of the Service – vessels of every description were permitted to sail for the enemy's ports and for Martinique in particular. The number of these cannot be ascertained but might be guessed at from the circumstance of twenty five (vessels) having sailed in one fleet with full cargoes for Martinique. These were furnished with permits authorised by Rodney . . .
>
> More French vessels were seen at St Eustatius, with French colours always displayed, for the three months that Lord Rodney and General Vaughan remained there, than had ever been seen in the Bay at any time before, while it was a free port and open to all nations.

Here Jennings addressed those at the Admiralty and in Whitehall who had been restive at the prolonged stay at St Eustatius and at the immobilization there of ships of war required more urgently in other theatres.

'The *Sandwich* lay there the whole time, and two Captains of His Majesty's Navy (these were Young and Inglefield) . . . were actually left on shore at St Eustatius, to attend the appraisal and Sales of the Stores. The resort of the French vessels to the grand military fair at last became so notoriously flagrant, that the regular question put by the acting duty officer aboard the *Sandwich*, under whose stern they necessarily passed before they anchored, was not: "From whence came you?" but: "Have you money on board?" And if they answered in the negative, they were ordered away.'

There was something equally displeasing for Sir Samuel Hood and his Captains who had spent so much of their endeavour in patrolling off Martinique. The sea traffic generated by the sales had had some effects which were to prove positively disastrous for the British:

> The blockade, since it had not prevented a daily intercourse between Martinique and St Eustatius, the French commanders were regularly informed of what was passing and knew, perhaps better than Lord Hood, when he was to expect the reinforcement of these ships and Captains and the effect which the Sales at St Eustatius had upon the politics of Europe.

It is to be remarked also, that thanks to that gracious invitation by the Commander-in-Chief, the French informers were present at the opening of the Sales, five days before Hotham sailed with the convoy for England on 20 March, and therefore, while the preparations of lading went forward in broad daylight. But of course, Sir George had taken his precautions, as we know, when he had advised Stephens that an escort should be provided for that immense wealth which would shortly benefit the Crown.

The Sales accordingly began on the appointed day of 15 March, attended by the incoming buyers and by such of Statia's own trading community who had so far escaped deportation or arrest. Those utterly dispossessed watched glumly – or if they had succeeded in finding a proxy to bid for their own goods for them, with nail-biting anxiety – as negroes hefted their property from the stacked warehouses under the direction of the Auctioneer: the West Indian and American produce, the pipes and barrels of rum, wine, sugar, coffee and tobacco: the casked provisions of beef and pork and biscuits, and the bales and boxes of European imports of tea, silks, linens, and clothing and hardware. All of this yielded to bids which bore no relation to the true value of the goods offered: the return, nevertheless, represented a handsome profit for the Captors to add to the £100,529.10s – and fourpence three farthings – which had already been realized by the sale of the first fourteen of the captured ships in Statia's harbour. And meanwhile, the auction also provided a source of fascinated interest for the soldiers and sailors present at the scene.

That hopeful ban on the sale of naval and military stores was short-lived, for when it was made clear that it was depressing the market, it was swiftly countermanded. Daniel Ross, vendue master assisting Akers, later deposed – at St Kitts on 10 July, when, among the rising tide of emerging lawsuits it became necessary to give evidence in the case of the King versus the Snow *Joachim St Anna* – that the goods of Messrs Milner and Crawford, of St Eustatius, were sold by him:

> . . . on or about the 27th March. In the Store of J D Piest, purchased by Comund Proudfoot of Grenada, was a considerable quantity of raven's duck and Russia drab [sailcloth] which was, by the consent of Matthew Forster and Arietas Akers, esquires, Agents, sold together with the other goods in the said Store to the said Proudfoot . . . the deponent further sayeth that when the Sales of the stores first began and for eight or ten days after, all the canvas and raven's duck was excepted from sale in all the Stores, but that afterwards, by particular desire of the Agents, this deponent, in order to raise the value of the stores, assured the purchasers . . . that all the raven's duck that might be found in them, they, the purchasers were entitled to . . .

Ross also noted that the goods and merchandise of Mr J D Piest, purchased by Comund Proudfoot had given the Grenada merchant reason to be very pleased with his deal. Loaded aboard a Portuguese snow, the cargo had earlier been sold to John Dunlop, of St Croix: but probably because Dunlop had failed to find the money, Akers had set the purchase aside 'to ease the said Dunlop' and had put the goods and merchandise up for sale for the second time. In order to raise the price, Akers had then offered all the goods in the Store without the customary reserve on bids and Proudfoot had obtained 'in particular, a parcel of raven's duck and Russia drab packed up together and being about one hundred and forty or fifty pieces.'

※　※　※

By the end of March, the operation was clearly a huge commercial success. As Hood had acidly recorded, very much money had been brought aboard the *Sandwich* 'but no one acknowledges to know what the sum is'* and he would put no trust into what he had termed Rodney's 'Flemish' accounting. But not all of the money had found its way aboard since there were many obscure way stations, or was necessarily from the Sales: Akers departed for St Kitts and from there, on 30 June, replied to a communication from Sir George, dated 13 June, giving him news of His Majesty's gracious pleasure in bestowing the booty on the Captors, and on Rodney's directions for the ordering of the money arising from the disposal of stores which had formerly:

> . . . belonged to people calling themselves British merchants.

*All quotations herein may be found in the *Letters of Sir Samuel Hood*, ed. David Hannay, (Navy Record Society, London, 1895).

> . . . till the time that you should call for the Money to make such Division, the Agents appointed by you and the General should hold themselves responsible for the receipts of whatever the Sales should amount to . . .

'In obedience to these Orders, I immediately went down to St Eustatius and communicated the Contents of them to Colonel Cockburn and Mr Forster, two of the Joint Agents who seemed not a little surprised that they had received no Orders from General Vaughan.' The next wording of Akers' letter implies that the Sales had originally been planned for April: '. . . They joined me however in taking the necessary steps to execute your Commands, by making preparations for the Sales which shall commence on Monday, the 9th of that month . . .'

But here we find Akers acting as Rodney's advertising agent as well as giving us a sudden glimpse of the desolation now lying heavy on Statia: for . . . 'we thought it best to defer the Sales until that time to give Notice in the different Islands [including those of the French?!] . . . for the encouragement of purchasers coming down to St Eustatius, at this time being almost deserted by all such people as would probably become purchasers . . .'

Akers also ingratiated himself further. Sir George had not forgotten the matter of those British merchant captains who paid informal and profitable visits to Statia, and had deputed Akers to make 'strict enquiries.' What could Akers find out for him, he asked, of English ships ostensibly bound for other islands but which touched at St Eustatius '. . . sometimes without even suspected in London to have landed their Cargoes at St Eustatius . . . and particularly after a part of Sir Samuel Hood's Convoy which Slip't him and which was strongly suspected to have no Orders.'

Akers had 'very great reasons' he told Sir George, to believe these suspicions to be well founded and assured the Admiral that he would use his 'utmost endeavour to make a fresh Discovery.' His intent was to examine the entries at the different Customs Houses and to take other steps . . . Only his attention to the business of St Eustatius had prevented that person who had the Honour to be Sir George's Obliged and Most Obedient Humble Servant, Arietas Akers, from attending to this earlier. But he would embrace the first opportunity, etc. etc . . .

– 6 –

AFTERMATH

To his own disappointment, Hood remained off Port Royal with his squadron as Sir George had ordered. Resolutely barred by Rodney from taking the windward station from which Hood pleaded he would better intercept whatever fleet the French might send from Europe, there was no possibility that he would nurse his frustration in silence. Nor, he was to make plain, would he pretend ignorance of his Commander's activities on the island.

THE ADMIRAL'S DEAR FRIEND . . .

It would be asking much to accept the complete disinterestedness noted by the historian, Hannay, but Hood himself wrote that he cared nothing for the spoils of the capture. But the smell of easily acquired wealth was sensed by every other officer and man of the Fleet and the Army, and Hannay's portrait of Hood, contrasting that officer's character with Rodney's 'rapacity' implies an unusual degree of indifference to prize money. It might however, have been harder to bear the thought that others were so busily enriching themselves: coupled with his unhappiness at the deployment of *Barfleur* and the squadron, it is possible that this lent an extra edge when Hood wrote to Sir George on 9 April concerning the high-handed affront to himself and his officers of which he had now been informed.

In a blunt reply to a query from Rodney, after both men had heard from Captain Young, the Commander-in-Chief found himself taken to task by his second-in-command. Hood's letter began with a formal courtesy but made no further concessions to Sir George's feelings:

> I am most exceedingly obliged and thankful for the very affectionate letter you did me the honour to write me on the 2nd and think it highly incumbent on me to explain to you the motives that occasioned my writing to Captain Young which you have seen and cannot conceive the meaning of . . .

The purport of Young's letter had been so clear to Hood that he had written sharply to Young and now spelled out that officer's meaning for his apparently less perceptive superior. In one of two particularly disturbing paragraphs, Rodney learned, Young had made use of the following words: and the better to impress them, Sir Samuel underlined every word in the offending sentence:

'Peculation has taken place.'

'. . . and I can assure you, my Dear Sir George,' continued Hood, 'he is the only person from whom I have heard a syllable tending to even a suspicion of the kind.'

If the accusation struck home, Sir George considered it in silence. But it will be seen that by June Hood had heard a great deal more of the business and, for pressing reasons of his own, began eagerly to undermine what virtue Rodney still possessed at the Admiralty. Meanwhile, there was the unwelcome issue of the appointment of the previously unacceptable Akers as Sole Agent and the churlish elbowing aside of his own nominees, Captain Inglefield and Secretary Hunt.

Pointing out that it had only been at Rodney's request that he had offered any opinion on matters at the capture of St Eustatius, and after Young had revealed Akers' personal interest in the assets of the Statian merchants, Sir Samuel went on:

You was pleased to send for me into another room and to say, that from what had appeared, you thought Mr Akers an improper person to have anything to do with our concerns as an Agent. I concur'd in that opinion: when you proposed naming Captain Young and Mr Pagett, desired me to name my Captain and Secretary, and authorised me to assemble the Captains to explain matters to them, and to express your wish that they would appoint two from amongst themselves, to look to, and manage everything as Agents, together with an equal number of Gentlemen, whom General Vaughan would name on the part of the Army.

All had been agreed in February, Hood insisted, and firmly settled as far as the signatories to that agreement were concerned. It was not something of which Sir George needed reminding, but relentlessly, Hood bore down: had Rodney asked, he asserted, 'even after what had passed', he would have consented to this appointment in deference to Sir George's wishes. But it was insupportable that he should renege now, and 'without a syllable' to Hood in explanation as to why the 'general determination' had been cast aside and 'Mr Akers made a principal in the receipt of monies arising from the sales, to the exclusion of those nominated by me, who are not only denied a participation, but are told they are no Agents, and even refused to be a witness to the account of stores taken . . . (this) gives me great uneasiness.'

Which was as far as Hood chose to go in that letter on that sensitive matter of accountancy. Yet with much to inspire him, he would attend more closely to Rodney's financial administration – as well as to his professional judgement – in a letter a few weeks later. For the moment it was enough to declare his own feelings:

> 'Whether the King retains to his own use, or gives to the Captors the effects of St Eustatius, makes neither one way or the other: I admit your power in the fullest extent. But I trust, my Dear Sir George, upon turning seriously in your mind all that has passed, you will not hesitate to think that my Captain and Secretary should have been placed in the same situation with yours since they are on shore by your desire. There, I feel, and there Captain Inglefield and Mr Hunt feel also, their present situation is humiliating.'

*   *   *

By June the resentful Hood was more fully informed and had other matters on his mind. Much had happened. On 30 April he had at last met the French reinforcement, 'in sight of Fort Royal' – the Fleet and convoy under the Count De Grasse. Notwithstanding Hood's own bland version of this affair, he had quite clearly been outmanoeuvred and bested during the encounter. De Grasse had brought his charges safely into Port Royal while Hood had nothing to show for the engagement except the death of Captain Nott of the *Centaur* and considerable damage to some half dozen of his squadron. The failure goes far to account for Hood's concentration on Rodney's deficiencies – he 'knew of no omission on his own part' – in the letter which Sir Samuel despatched to his friend Jackson, second Secretary to the Admiralty, on the 24th. Tobago had been recaptured by de Bouillé on 23 May and here again, Sir George, faced with the prospect of leaving the approaches to Barbados unprotected, had been unable to prevent it. This was an excellent opportunity for some professional knifework and Hood set about it with a will. We learn much from this important letter, of relevance to the story of Rodney at St Eustatius, by now increasingly assailed by ill-health – gout and a cruel stricture – incautiously revealed to Hood, who begins by endorsing Young's description of Rodney's 'unsteady fit.'

> It is quite impossible from the unsteadiness of the Commander-in-Chief to know what he means three days together: one hour he says his complaints are of such a nature that he cannot possibly remain in this country, and is

determined to leave the command with me: the next he says he has no thought of going home. The truth is I believe he is guided by his feelings on the moment he is speaking, and that his mind is not at present at all at ease, thinking that if he quits the command he will get to England at a time that many mouths perhaps may be opened against him on the top of Tobago, and his not fighting the French fleet off that island after the public declarations he made to everyone of his determined resolution to do it: and again, if he stays much longer, his laurels may be subject to wither . . .'

There was not much, it seemed, that Sir George could do to improve the situation. Jackson was treated to an analysis in which Rodney was variously irresolute, boastful and inept:

What a wonderful happy turn would have been given to the King's affairs in this country had Sir George Rodney gone with all his force to Tobago as soon as he might, and in my humble opinion, ought to have done! I have laboured much to effect it, but all in vain and fully stated my reasons in writing so soon as the intelligence came. The island in that case would not only have been preserved, but a severe blow given to the French flag . . .

For good measure, Vaughan too, became a target. It had been assumed by the General that an assault on Curaçao would follow the seizure of Statia and that the project had been frustrated by Captain Linzee's erroneous report that the enemy fleet was at sea, and bound for Martinique. In the interests of harming both Commanders-in-Chief, Sir Samuel gave Jackson chapter and verse.

You reckon without your host, my dear Jackson, in imagining an attack on Curaçao was prevented by the intelligence sent by Captain J Linzee. I will give you proof to the contrary, by the following anecdote. Upon my going on board the *Sandwich*, when we dropped anchor in St Eustatius Road, General Vaughan took me aside and pressed me strongly to speak to Sir George Rodney about going to Curaçao. I replied I did not know how far Sir George's instructions went, but I would sound him on the subject. I accordingly did, and was listened to with attention. The next day, Sir George asked me if I wished to go to Curaçao. I answered most readily. 'Well' says he, 'You shall have five sail of the line and some frigates.' I replied that the force was in my opinion sufficient . . . I immediately wrote a note to the General to say I had succeeded with Sir George respecting Curaçao, desired he would get what information he could of the place, and use his best diligence by means of the people ashore to look out for good pilots, as no time was to be lost.

I received no answer from him, and when I next saw him, repeated the subject of my note, to which he shortly answered that he had no men.

'This is very surprising, General,' said I, 'for when you urged me so pressingly to speak to Sir George upon this business, you did not know but you might meet with resistance here and have your force diminished: but now you have got possession without the loss of a man, you fly from your own proposition, which is what I could not have expected from General Vaughan.' He made no reply, but turned away and addressed himself to some one else.

It was at this point that Hood threw a light on the activities of the Commanders-in-Chief ashore for which historians, frequently bemused by partisan circumventions or lack of specific information on this episode, may be eternally grateful. In criminal terminology, Hood was about to blow the gaff: discounting the obvious acrimony, the detail is such that he is at the very least, a source to be taken seriously.
'The truth is,' he told his doubtless fascinated reader:

> I believe he could not bear the thoughts of leaving St Eustatius, where he fancied there were three millions of riches, as his letter to Lord G Germain expressed: and I dare say he would have been there to this hour had not the arrival of De Grasse obliged him to decamp . . . A pretty large sum was levied upon the inhabitants, and some of the Captains asked the Commissary-General what the sum really was. He answered that he could not say exactly, but something more than 70,000 pounds or 80,000 pounds, he knew not which: and yet there is now, I am told, but 20,000 pounds brought to account.

Instead of preoccupying himself with 'The Lares of St Eustatius' which Hood inadvertently admitted were 'not to be withstood by flesh and blood,' Rodney should have been with his fleet and to windward when De Grasse approached. But having disposed of that, Hood returned to his observations on the probity of the Commanders-in-Chief:

> With respect to the concerns of St Eustatius, I am totally ignorant, not having seen any one account, or had a syllable said to me upon the subject. The irregularity and confusion is beyond conception: a quantity of money was brought from the island in the *Sandwich*, but not a single soul acknowledges to know what the sum is, and a most Flemish account will I am sure be produced. The Admiral and the General have a great deal to answer for, which I told them long ago: and they now begin to be in a squeeze, as many of their actions will not well bear the daylight . . .

Here that rankling wound was exposed for Jackson:

> . . . had they abided by the first plan settled before I left them, and not have
> interfered, but left the management to the land and sea folks appointed for
> that purpose, all would have gone smooth and easy, and to the perfect satis-
> faction of the two corps: but I now foresee much mischief may arise . . .

Sir Samuel at last brought his acid mixture to the boil:

> The money brought from St Eustatius was put on shore upon the island so
> soon as we arrived: and the very day before we sailed (on the 1st instant)
> with a determined resolution to fight the French fleet, it was all re-embarked
> and put on board two of the most crazy ships in the fleet (the *Sandwich* and
> *Boreas*), that almost a single shot in either under water would have sent
> them down. But the Commanders-in-Chief could not bear the thought of
> leaving the money behind them and notwithstanding they talk aloud of their
> disregard of money, they will find it very difficult to convince the world
> that they have not proved themselves wickedly rapacious . . .

And in a final word on the matter, something within Hood's breast sur-
faced to overcome his own indifference to prize money:

> . . . and upon what principle do they act in holding out by their conduct
> that the money is all their own, and no one else has any concern with it?

*   *   *

There we leave Rodney's 'dear friend', Rear-Admiral Sir Samuel Hood,
penning his bitter letter from Barbados. He has given us his account of
events as they appeared to him. He has much more to do in these seas
but he would still depend on Sir George's whim: until late in July, in fact,
when the onset of the hurricane season once more dictated that French
and British alike should make a prudent withdrawal to North America.
Only then, with the fleet now given over to Hood's responsibility, did the
ailing Rodney prepare himself for a return to England, urgently to seek
treatment for that condition so mocked by Young and Hood and less
urgently, but inescapably, to face the embarrassment awaiting the
Commanders-in-Chief at home. Not least was that fermenting in the
House of Commons. Justification for their conduct was yet to be put to
the test but unenviably, the status of Rodney and Vaughan as MPs would
ensure that they would receive the accusations and rebuke in person.

DE GRAAFF

Accounts of their experience as prisoners of Sir George Rodney were written by the young Lieutenant of the *Mars*, Cornelius de Jong, and by Governor Johannes de Graaff – '. . . former Commander over the Islands of St Eustatius, Saba and St Martin, insofar as he remembers the most important business (and) put down as the solemn truth.' Which Report he had the honour to present to the Honourable Worshipful Gentlemen Representatives and Directors of the General Chartered Dutch West India Company on 3 December 1781.

De Graaff has already given us his description of the arrival of the British fleet on 3 February and of Cockburn's appearance with his soldiers: we know the circumstances of the surrender and of the expropriations of the Dutch West India Company's money and of his personal cash – 'in gold and silver specie an amount of 54654,2,3 pesos . . . taken from me, put on a little cart and transported to the headquarters under an armed escort.' But after that, this so suddenly reduced and shaken man gathered the courage of desperation and went the short distance from his house to the Fort, there to make an appeal to Vaughan for some kind of restitution in order that he might support his family and himself.

The General thereupon spared de Graaff 897 golden Dutch ducats from the sequestered money and told him that he must make do with this sum. 'This,' said the Governor sorrowfully, was '. . . the only money I have ever since then received.'

He was next visited yet again by Cockburn, who brought the Governor notice from the Commander-in-Chief that de Graaff was to leave the island shortly, that he was to be sent to England, but that he might still keep and use his silverware (he had already yielded his 'side-gun', matchlock and pistols in the general seizure of the residents' arms demanded by the Proclamation of 11 February). But of the silverware, de Graaff complained that 'what happened to it afterwards is unknown to me.'

In this connection we might note that the Rodney Papers include an inventory of Sir George's furniture and personal effects as they were transferred from the no longer sea-worthy *Sandwich*, in the last days of July, 1781, to the *Gibraltar*, in which he would make his voyage home. This inventory is quoted by Spinney thus: '. . . one large and one small mahogany bedstead, two cots and a field bedstead, two mahogany dining tables, four escritoirs, two sophas, a mahogany dressing glass and a set of curtains for the large bed with mosquito nettings: his plate included as many as thirty silver table spoons . . .'

Which last might, of course, be merely an unfortunate coincidence.

De Graaff saw the arrest of his compatriots, who, in addition to the old man, the member of the island Council, Pieter Bummels, included the Judge Advocate of St Eustatius and Saba, Johannes Lambertus ter Hoeven. This criminal by association was bundled aboard ship without explanation or charge and held for some weeks before being permitted to return to his family ashore. In the interim, de Graaff received three letters from Rodney, dated 10 March and 10 and 21 April – which he included in an Annex to his Report – announcing that a transport was shortly expected from Antigua in which vessel, under convoy, de Graaff was to be taken to England. The deposed Governor was to prepare himself and his family accordingly: furthermore, he was to warn all officers and servants of the States General and the Dutch West India Company to be ready to depart for England in the same ship. He should also take note that His Majesty King George intended to provide only salt beef and water for de Graaff's and their voyage.

De Graaff's baggage and provisions were therefore sent to the transport which, it was proposed, would sail on 19 March. He was to embark at three o'clock but two hours beforehand, a Lieutenant called at the Governor's house with Rodney's postponement of de Graaff's departure and the information that he must obtain a permit from 'Secretary Brooks' in order to recover his baggage. De Graaff made an exasperated protest to his visitor – who confessed himself to be not party to the Admiral's plans and greatly unconcerned by this inconvenience to the Governor – but perforce, complied: and afterwards was obliged to twiddle his thumbs until he received a further order to embark on 30 April, only to be delayed again by the mysterious demands of the Service: which in this case were connected with the assembly of the West India merchant ships forming the convoy.

On 27 April, Sir George again warned Stephens of an impending sailing and repeated his plea for a rendezvous at sea:

> . . . I take the Opportunity by the Swift Pacquet, which sails this day for England, to desire you will please to acquaint their Lordships that the Trade of Barbados and His Majesty's Leeward Islands, will sail for Great Britain, agreeable to their Commands, on the 30th April, or as soon after as possible. This Convoy will be commanded by Captain Affleck, in the *Triumph*, with the *Vigilant*, Sir George Home; the *Boreas*, Lord Charles Fitzgerald, and the *Vesuvius Bomb*, Captain Otway . . .

But two days after the date of this letter, Count de Grasse had appeared off Martinique, seen his 150 merchantmen into Fort Royal, and with his twenty-four men of war, had severely mauled Hood's ships. Captains Affleck and Otway were therefore immediately recalled from their convoy duties and that command left with Sir George Home. However, Rodney's recommendation of the 27th continued:

As Captain Affleck proposes to proceed with the said Convoy into the high Latitude of 49 Deg 49 Min at least Two Hundred Leagues West of the Lizard, I thought it my Duty to signify the same to their Lordships, and to enclose the Signals by which the Convoy may be ascertained, and of knowing any Squadron of Ships that their Lordships might think it necessary to send for the Protection of the said Convoy.

But it was not until 4 May, at six o'clock in the morning, that Governor de Graaff was relieved of his suspense, if not of his anxiety, and escorted down to the crowded shore: from where he assessed the number of West India vessels gathered for the voyage to be 'about a hundred' . . . and among these his own vessel, the transport *Prospect*, Captain Joseph Lawson.

De Graaff was to be accompanied by Johannes Lambertus ter Hoeven and his wife, Mr S G C Seelig, Michiel Raatjes, Gilbert Holl, John Walters and the wife and daughter of Mr Jan Anthony Glindtkamp, the Lutheran minister of Rio Berbice: a lady who had unwittingly chosen this most unfortunate time for her visit to St Eustatius. The island's former secretary, Alexander LeJeune, and his family were soon to follow, but they were given the privilege of passage in a cartel which would take them to Holland.

And so at 11 o'clock that morning, the convoy sailed, the merchant captains grumbled at by their escort until their ships were nudged into the loose cohesion of a common north-westerly course.

*   *   *

De Graaff's ship anchored at Spithead on 23 June: but being forbidden to disembark by the Port Admiral, pending the receipt of orders concerning the deportees which were expected from London, he remained aboard until 3 July. With the Judge Advocate ter Hoeven and his wife, he was then despatched to Gosport, where they were greeted by the Agent for prisoners of war and informed that this was unquestionably their status.

They were to give their parole. Their orders were to travel to Northampton at their own expense and to leave Gosport on 7 July: duly they arrived in Northampton, weary and stiff, at eight o'clock the following evening and found a blessed ease in the Peacock Inn: whose proprietor, William Mills, and indeed 'many respectable persons from surrounding places' earned Northampton de Graaff's tribute for the 'decency, esteem and many politenesses' he enjoyed during his stay there.

On 13 August, the Dutch prisoners were permitted to leave on parole, for Holland. The little company landed at Ostend and from there, de Graaff hurried to Amsterdam. He arrived on the 26th and spent a further day in collecting himself before appearing on the 28th before the Worshipful Gentlemen Directors of the Dutch West India Company, to whom he made all known.

THE YOUNG DAVID

With a Guard of Honour for the deceased provided by the British, Lieutenant de Jong and his captured companions paid their last respects to Admiral Krul in the graveyard of Statia's Dutch Reformed Church. It was not the only act of grace on the part of their captors since the *Mars'* officers had previously been invited to visit Sir George at Simon Doncker's house, where they were offered refreshment, and even some 'good madeira which he served us.' They were also permitted to spend the night ashore if they so wished: de Jong eagerly accepted the offer and took lodgings '. . . with a Mrs Tentoor, widow of one of the members of [the] Council of Justice.'

(It may be that the young Lieutenant impressed the household: for in May, a Miss Tentoor, chaperoned by the wife of Alexander LeJeune, volunteered to sail in de Jong's homeward bound vessel for no other recorded reason, we are told by de Jong, than to enjoy '. . . a trip to Europe.')

But no such politeness prevented de Jong from observing the ruined state of the island, even at that early date of the occupation. For, the next day, he walked through the town and on down to the Bay, there to visit friends and look sorrowfully at the *Mars*, alive now with the British navy's repair parties. De Jong had seen St Eustatius in its heyday, its hectic bargaining, its busy shops and commerce and its Lower and Upper Town crowded with people: but what he saw now was a stricken place of closed shops and apprehensive residents and the streets cleared and dominated instead by the soldiery and their menacing drum.

Lieutenant de Jong took note of all of this. He saw the ensnaring Dutch flag still fluttering over the Fort and the British guns trained to cover unsuspecting arrivals: and he heard the resentful accounts – of personal jewellery and other valuables given up under duress, of the arrests and prohibitions so far visited on the Statians and on the crews of the captured merchantmen. In addition, he was told of the intent of the Commanders-in-Chief to evict the whole of the merchants and traders, of the curfew which had been imposed on the residents, of the lewd searches of their persons and of the manhandling of the Jews and of their peremptory banishment to St Kitts.

The officers and men of the *Mars* soon experienced their own inquisition. De Jong returned to his ship to find that all their personal possessions were to be searched and all their papers, books and navigational instruments confiscated. De Jong believed this to be a further attempt to discover the hiding place of any money belonging to the West India Company: but he was, he says, able to save his own personal papers because the English officer in command of the search party was his namesake, Captain Young.

*   *   *

Soon afterward, de Jong, with the captured French and Dutch officers and their servants were also sent to St Christopher's, where they remained at Basseterre for seven weeks until a cartel could be obtained for them for their return to Holland. This, they were told by Arietas Akers, acting now in his capacity as Agent for the prisoners-of-war, was timely at some date approaching the end of April. There are many references in de Jong's story which would clearly reward further enquiry but none so intriguing as the Lieutenant's statement that, following Akers' message, the prisoners packed their belongings that same afternoon, and made their farewells to all their friends at Basseterre, '. . . including,' de Jong said, '. . . the so important Betsy, who I shall probably never see again.'

Early the following morning, they appeared before the Governor who required them to swear on their honour, and with a Bible on their heads, that none of them would take up arms against His Majesty King George until a proper exchange had taken place. 'With the Bible on my head,' remarked de Jong dryly, '. . . I also had to sign for poor Boeseken, as there seemed to be some fear that, although blind, he might still do some harm to the British Empire.'

Within the day they had been shipped to Statia and marooned on their vessel in the Road, surrounded by the numerous vessels of the convoy, for a very uncomfortable night. But late the next day, they were transferred to one of Rodney's prizes, *The Young David*, which they were to sail home: 103 souls, counted de Jong, '33 from the *Mars*, six men from the *Grave van Byland*, 14 merchant captains and 50 seamen and boys.' It was to be in this vessel that Miss Tentoor and the LeJeune family would also travel, but for the Dutch sailors, their own subsistence and discipline became the first matters to trouble them all.

Sir George had allowed them rations of bread, meat and water 'and once in a while, madeira wine,' but de Jong thought little of this consideration. 'The bread was chewed through by worms' he wrote: '. . . the meat decayed by saltpetre, the water most of the time stinking and the bacon, which we have for a change, has large yellow sides.' De Jong also mourned that the British had the unheard of impertinence to treat the officers in the same way as the common seamen.

As the senior officer and in spite of his reluctance, he had been obliged to take command of the vessel. His reluctance was justified. The ship was in such poor condition as to need such basics as rigging and sails, not to mention an endless requirement of effort and equipment before she could be ready for sea. *The Young David*, it seemed, was in addition not especially stable and it was necessary to load the cases and heavy goods of the passengers with the greatest of care, to reduce the risk of capsizing.

Her bottom, too, was foul, and de Jong found himself pleading for assistance in improving this '. . . from an irritated enemy contemptuous of his youth.' He was also discomfited by the fact that his junior officers were even younger than himself and that they stood in authority – often clumsily exercised and thus, certain to create the maximum of ill-feeling – over older and seasoned men whose knowledge of seamanship was far superior to their own. For a while indeed, chaos reigned aboard, the essential work of preparation being suspended in favour of drinking and fighting: bowing before this impossible situation, de Jong took the safe step of securing agreement from his officers and asking the merchant captains to appoint three nominees who would share the command with him. As they were content for him to make his own choice from among them, he selected the captains, De Bruin, Pauw and Michielsen, 'as they seemed to me the most competent, capable and honourable of them all.'

This decision, made known to the assembled complement of the ship, brought order to the vessel and on that score a sense of relief to de Jong. The men, anxious above all things to put Statia behind them appeared to share the feeling, for the work of the ship went forward without undue hindrance from that day. And further cause for relief a few days later: for the new owner of the vessel came aboard in the person of Alexander LeJeune, who brought them wine, fresh meat and vegetables, and also, the information that the Admiral had permitted him to leave with his family for Holland under the flag of truce and he had therefore bought *The Young David* for the voyage.

It had been at his request, the secretary told them, that they had been freed from their detention at St Kitt's. For this, of course, all were grateful: however, LeJeune was less successful in securing permission for them to go ashore for fresh food and to stretch their cramped limbs. Accordingly, de Jong and two others donned civilian clothes and slipped unobtrusively from their ship, answering the challenges of the sentries on shore with the story that they were Danish mariners who had come from a Danish island.

Once more, de Jong surveyed the desolation and again visited his chastened friends. But on this occasion he copied Cockburn's Proclamations for the information of his countrymen: and noted, too, that the British soldiers were now being laid low in great numbers by disease. By that date, at the end of April, the sickness had already killed 200 men: largely confined to the island, it had also brought both Captain Walter Young and the military governor, Brigadier General David Ogilvie, to the point of death. This would come for both of them in May – on the 2nd for Young and on the 31st for Ogilvie – and while the one would be mourned by the Navy, by Middleton in London, as a personal friend, and thence allowed to fade from the memory of all but naval historians, the death of Ogilvie was to leave a more turbulent legacy.

Work on *The Young David* continued: but she was by no means ready for the long haul ahead of her when, at dawn on the morning of 3 May, ships of Hood's squadron, among them a heavily listing seventy-four kept afloat by furious pumping came into Statia's road.

The news brought by these vessels that De Grasse had arrived to reinforce the enemy at Martinique, as well as the dreadful evidence of their encounter, caused immediate alarm and what de Jong described as 'total confusion: Admiral, General and officers and men all feared the arrival of the French and wanted to leave the island.'

Indeed, in the face of the threat and an impending descent on St Lucia by de Bouillé – on the 10th and unsuccessful in the event – Sir George, accompanied by the *Triumph*, sailed to meet Hood without losing a moment. At St Kitts he would acquire three of Hood's repaired ships of war: with his second-in-command's fifteen of the line, Rodney might hope to counter the twenty-four ships of the French and their designs on St Lucia and even Barbados. But thus concerned and occupied as he hunted for the enemy in those seas, the Admiral could do nothing to prevent the French seizure of Tobago, two hundred miles to the south, at the end of the month.

*   *   *

Given the preoccupations of the Admiral and the General at this time we might pass over in patriotic silence de Jong's claim of 'total confusion' at St Eustatius. But urgency there certainly was, for among other considerations, the massed vessels of the West Indies trade – now numbering 150 ships – presented a prime target as they lay in the roadstead. These, and all other vulnerable vessels, such as *The Young David*, must be sent to sea, and with the utmost haste. The trade, of course, would have its naval escort, but those others must fend for themselves by seeking the safer haven of a neutral island.

This message was brought to de Jong by a brusque lieutenant, disinclined to listen to protests. No matter that de Jong's vessel still had insufficient water and provisions for an immediate voyage, no matter that they lacked essentials for the mere sailing of the vessel, no matter that their ship, proposing to sail under a flag of truce, did not even possess such a flag, – they must weigh anchor at once, or be cut loose by British sailors. De Jong must choose: but they absolutely could not remain at Statia.

But at least, the passengers and their effects were aboard. The ladies, Mrs LeJeune and her charge, Miss Tentoor, volunteered to make a Union Jack, which de Jong called a 'spiderhead.' Aided by their personal slaves they worked through most of the night, their materials the red, white and blue bunting which many of the men used for belts.

Meanwhile, the ship prepared for sea. At dawn, came the signal cannon calling the ships to make ready and at eight, the vast fleet began to move, diverging outside the road into two bodies, one bound for Jamaica and the other, for England. But no sooner had they sailed than the Dutch vessel was boarded again by a British officer who delivered their final eviction notice. They must weigh anchor 'instantly' or, he repeated, their ropes would be cut.

'And so,' wrote de Jong, '. . . against our will and with a shattered ship and only a month's provision and water for two weeks, we set sail and headed north west and west north west, for St Thomas' where they hoped to fit their ship for the voyage home.

But despite their makeshift situation, de Jong's account closes on a more cheerful note: 'We watched the English flagship recede behind us and we were all happy to see the last of the offensive Rodney. Our ship, as if outrunning the wishes of the crew, ran swiftly: and soon the great fleets astern were out of sight.'

* * *

The Young David dropped anchor in the harbour of Danish St Thomas on the afternoon of the following day. It would be two weeks before they could resume the voyage, to reach Holland in June. Lieutenant de Jong has no more to tell us at this point, but we shall encounter him once again, and he will have the last word on these events.

PRIZE CONVOY

In mid-March, the prize convoy was fully laden at last and aboard *Vengeance*, Commodore Hotham awaited Sir George's final orders. The

Commodore had already heard from the Admiral on the 4th and in consequence, on that day *Vengeance* had taken aboard two distressed people, Samuel Curson and Isaac Gouverneur. Only Gouverneur would survive what lay ahead: but now they were to be carried to England as Prisoners of State.

> . . . You are to take great Care that a Guard is kept constantly over them, and they by no Means be suffered to go on Shore until they are delivered into the Custody of some of His Majesty's Messengers.

The sailing orders came on the 18th and opened with the information which Rodney had given to Philip Stephens . . . 'whereas the very great value of the Prizes taken in these Seas from the Subjects of the States-General of the United Provinces are of the utmost Importance to the Public in general, and require that the greatest Care and Attention should be taken in conducting them to Great Britain . . .' for which purpose *Vengeance* would be accompanied by the ships of war. *Prince Edward* (62) – formerly Admiral Krul's ship, *Mars* and with the worst of her battle-damage made good – *Alcemene* (32) and the frigate *Mars* (38) taken from van Byland. Captain Douglas, in the *Venus* (36) would sail with them until they had passed the latitude of the Bermudas and then, at Hotham's signal, part company in order to speed Rodney's dispatches to England to His Majesty's Secretaries of State and the Lords Commissioners of the Admiralty, '. . . it being of Importance that they should be delivered to the King's Ministers as soon as the Nature of the public Service will admit . . .'

The instructions were drawn with all of Sir George's typical care and thoroughness: the Commodore was to see the prizes safely into the Downs, and send into them such officers and men as were necessary to carry them safely into the Thames. And once there, the prizes were to be received by the Agents appointed for the Captors. Once there: but now Hotham learned of Rodney's request to the Admiralty and of his own duty to gain the latitude of '49 degrees 45m, at least 200 leagues to the westward of the Lizard and to keep that Latitude until he got abreast of Scilly' . . . where he could meet '. . . the Squadron of His Majesty's ships sent out to cruize in that Latitude for the safety and better protection of the said Convoy.'

Aboard *Venus* was the Chief Justice of St Christopher's, William Payne Georges, who was to carry Sir George's evidence of the island's trade with the enemy – the books and papers surrendered by Statia's merchants under Cockburn's Proclamation, or otherwise seized from those under arrest. These documents were addressed for the urgent attention of Lord George Germain and, as Georges was to confirm, duly reached the

Secretary of State. Following the exit of Lord North's government at the end of the war, however, the boxes containing this evidence were found to have mysteriously disappeared from his Lordship's offices – much to the chagrin of Rodney who required them to support his own and Vaughan's defence of their measures against the islanders. 'No trace of them has been found from that day to this' wrote Spinney: but let us postpone contemporary findings for a later chapter.

Hotham should act accordingly: and he was to give the strictest instructions to all Captains in the event that any might become separated from the convoy by bad weather or accident, that on no account were they to attempt to enter the English Channel until they were absolutely sure that the convoy had done so. Otherwise, they too, must endeavour to rejoin the convoy on the aforementioned latitude and distance from the Lizard . . .

On Monday 19 March, Hotham made the signal for all merchant captains and for the convoy to unmoor and ready themselves for sea. This instruction, variously perceived, interpreted and performed by thirty-three captains, the convoy did not in fact sail from Statia's road until the afternoon of the 20th, the merchantmen doing whatever they could to obey the Commodore's signal to form and come under the flagship's stern. But not enough, in the Commodore's judgement: *Vengeance* worried the flock, urging the hindmost to make more sail, the leeward ships to tack and gain their stations . . .

Loosely united, their guardians *Vengeance*, *Prince Edward*, *Mars*, *Alcemene* and temporarily, *Venus*, the richest ships of the Great Capture, twenty-one merchant ships, seven snows and five brigs, headed into the Atlantic, and began the voyage to England.

LA MOTTE PICQUET

The watchers on Statia's shores had ensured that intelligence of the convoy had long been known to France. It could not have come at a more opportune time since it was also known there that Britain's Grand Fleet had sailed for Gibraltar under Admiral George Darby, to relieve that stronghold from its determined Spanish besiegers. Thus, the way was clear for the bold stroke now in contemplation: on 25 April therefore, the information from their spies was summed in an instruction for a remarkable commander, Toussaint-Guillaume, Comte Picquet de La Motte, known as 'La Motte-Picquet'.

Born at Rennes in 1720, he was thus Rodney's junior by three years but died one year before Sir George, in 1791. It is said of him that few sailors had shown better seamanship and above all, more audacity, for his name had hitherto been coupled with his refusal, in 1745, to surrender the frigate *'la Renommée,* whose badly wounded Captain, Kersaint, was about to strike his colours to a British ship of the line: with his brilliant command of *l'Annibal* (74) whose name became legendary in the history of the French navy, and with his successful rescue of a convoy bound for Martinique, which had been attacked by a British Squadron of sixteen ships and a frigate. La Motte Picquet had first challenged the British alone and kept them busy for two hours until reinforced by two more French vessels. The three had then fought off the British for more than four hours until the convoy reached Port Royal – for which action, a rueful Admiral Parker sent him a letter of congratulation.

It was this sailor who now considered the manner in which he would intercept not only Hotham's convoy but also, the homeward bound ships of the Jamaica trade: and who thereupon wrote to his Minister:

'It is now 7 o'clock. I have just received my orders and I expect to be under sail at noon. We have agreed with Admiral Hector, the commanding officer at Brest, to spread the rumour that I sail to join the Spaniards: you may depend on it that we shall maintain the deepest secrecy . . .'

Thus, La Motte Picquet and his squadron – three ships of the line, his own *l'Invincible* of 110 guns, and two seventy-fours, *le Belle-aimé* and *l'Actif*: three sixty-fours, *l'Alexandre, le Gardi* and *le Lion*: the frigates *la Sybile* and *la Nereide*, and two cutters, *le Chasseur* and *la Levrette*. With the tide on that afternoon of 25 April, this force slipped out of the great port and headed westward to find Sir George Rodney's prizes.

* * *

Thursday 26 April, latitude 49 degrees 45m North, 51 degrees 38m West: the convoy five weeks at sea and the Lizard north by east, 87 leagues . . .

Aboard *Vengeance,* the day's events logged in the journals reflected an uneventful voyage. In light airs the ship spoke to the *Mars*: they saw two strange sail in the north west and although these faded over the horizon, they were encouraged to exercise and clear the great guns. And always, to run up the harrying signals which had by now wearied flock and shepherds alike, for the straggling merchantmen to leeward to tack and gain their stations.

But in the fine weather they ploughed on, watchful but undisturbed, the routine of the Commodore's ship marred only briefly by two deaths. On the 27th, wrote the Master, '. . . departed this life Jn Nichols, Seaman:' and added Nichol's only epitaph: 'Got up spare Sails to Air and Carpenters Caulked the Sail Room.' And similarly clouded by more urgent ship's business, the one line memorial for Sergeant Hawley, Marine '. . . who departed this life on Sunday 29th.'

Nearer to their rendezvous, other sails appeared but these too, either faded from sight or correctly answered the private signal. On the last day of the month however, as the convoy laboured eastward along the 49th parallel in a light breeze, the Lizard only 48 leagues distant and still no sign of the escort Squadron surely sent to meet them but now fruitlessly searching for them well away from their track, the watchful *Mars* made the signal for seven sail in the south east quarter. It was 11 am and the end of their prayerful hopes that they might remain unharmed: and the end too, as Sir George was to learn, of that eager vision of a rich and honoured retirement which, he had so joyfully written to his wife and family, was now made possible by the wonderful spoils of St Eustatius: for where the ships of the Royal Navy had failed, despite that they wearied themselves in the quest for almost two weeks, La Motte Picquet had found them.

Possibly Hotham, with his lumbering charges spread widely over miles of sea and little hope of driving off the wolves now come among them, felt much as Krul must have done in that emptiness off Sombrero: here was that same smell of impending disaster, of death even and of all those other terrors of sea-warfare. But like Krul and so many others in the face of this, Hotham acted with courage. His first endeavour was an attempt, no more successful than any of the others, to keep the merchantmen close under his protection. Yet again the hoists fluttered with the familiar signals to bring the convoy under his stern, for the laggards to make more sail, and, to compact the group, for the headmost ships to shorten sail: meanwhile, and for the next day, Hotham's ships of war were treated to tantalizing glimpses of enemy sails, three to the northwest, a pair in the southeast . . . And at 11 am the signal from the *Mars*, reporting seven strange sail in the southeast. They had yet to show their colours but there could be no doubt of their intentions.

The arrivals remained in sight. *Alcemene*'s captain boarded the flagship for an anxious conference and returned six hours later but no less anxious, to his own ship: the while Hotham prudently signalled the fleet to go on two-thirds allowance of water and provisions: made yet another urgent signal to gather the convoy under his stern and to warn them of the threatening ships: and fired two shots unavailingly at an intrusive French cutter 'to speak him.' Instead, this nimble vessel went on to board a hastening but far astern and fatally lonely merchantman who had parted from the convoy on 29 March.

La Motte Picquet struck soon after four o'clock on the morning of 2 May, rushing on them from the south west. Finding his interrogatory signals ignored, the French colours now hoisted and their ships making all sail towards the convoy – quite undeceived by the Commodore's ploy of raising the Dutch ensign – Hotham signalled his fleet to disperse: and thereafter, as the ships of his convoy wore on to their new and separate courses, became involved in a hopeless attempt to pursue or head off single attackers who had more purposeful and profitable thoughts in mind than to trade shot with him.

Nor could he bar those others beyond his reach, who went briskly about their task of running down and seizing twenty-two of the fleeing merchantmen, effectively unhindered in this by *Alcemene*, *Prince Edward* and *Mars*, to whom nine of the convoy still clung for protection: yet most of the convoy was snapped up on that day, the French ships continuing the chase for three more days, almost until Hotham's shredded company, now ten sail, found their nearest refuge, Beerhaven at the very southerly tip of Ireland. Fate then took another merciless kick at the humiliated Commodore as *Vengeance* came to anchor on the 8th, for the best bower immediately parted at the clinch.

* * *

The enormous haul and the protracted chase caused La Motte Picquet to abandon any further thought of the Jamaica convoy. His squadron therefore turned for home, and in the event, not a moment too soon, for a swift vessel had brought the news to Admiral Darby now returning with the Grand Fleet from Gibraltar. Darby immediately detached a strong force in the hope of intercepting the raiders and as this squadron forged north and west, so La Motte Picquet headed eastward with his prizes for the safety of his own coast. Time and distance were on his side, but only just: he entered Brest on 11 May, leaving Darby's cheated avengers breathless from the pursuit, close on his heels, but empty-handed.

At Beerhaven they found His Majesty's sloop, *Hound* at her mooring: shortly they were joined by a hangdog *Alcemene* with two merchantmen, and a little later, three more, and on the 9th, another two: and on that day, the *Mars* with four, but these were the last they would see, for the *Prince Edward* came in unaccompanied on the 11th.

It could only have been a cheerless haven, for oppressing Hotham in this calamity were the stern phrases of the Admiral who had entrusted him with the mission. It was no comfort to the Commodore that he had been outnumbered and worsted by eight ships and two cutters or even that there had been no rendezvous with the expected escort: but he had been warned of the very great value of the prizes: that they were of the utmost importance to the public in general and that on Hotham's part, they required the greatest Care and Attention in conducting them to Great Britain. How deeply felt was this failure, how much of self reproach, may be imagined. The log of the *Vengeance* from the moment of coming to anchor at Beerhaven and until 29 June when that despondent ship moored at Spithead is all prosaic ships' business: of the people variously employed – but they served mutton to the ship's company on the 12th – of watering, of receiving from the contractors bags of bread, barrels of pork, firkins of butter, fresh beef 'and 22 sheep for the ship's company', of sending boats to help warp *Prince Edward* into a berth . . . there is nothing to indicate Hotham's grief and apprehension.

Alcemene's log presents a very different picture, for hardly had she got her anchors down than out came the lash for Robert McGie, seaman: McGie received twenty-four lashes for neglect of duty and insulting language, but the Captain's satisfaction in this matter at least was to be shortlived. On the following day two more seamen, were triced up and punished, John Collins with thirty-six lashes for neglect of duty and James Arthurly with twenty-four lashes for disobedience. The lesson taken in by their shipmates however, was far from that which the Captain had in mind, for three seamen then ran from the ship.

For more of *Alcemene*'s company considerations of duty had no place beside the attractions of the Irish hinterland: beyond the harbour were those beckoning green slopes and surely, beyond them, some prospect of freedom from this or any other of His Majesty's hateful ships. When, therefore, Hotham signalled, on the 11th, for all boats to be manned to assist the now grounded *Prince Edward*, four more of *Alcemene*'s men made off in the ship's long boat. *Alcemene*'s barge retrieved the abandoned boat, the master-at-arms and five men being detailed to hunt for the deserters. They spent enough time in this to ensure the hopelessness of their errand and returned to their ship, the five seamen now without the master-at-arms, who had decided to make his own bid for a better life ashore.

They were not yet finished with Beerhaven or with a final tragedy to add to the ill-fortune bequeathed to them by the illusory riches of St Eustatius. On Sunday, 13th, four of the American prisoners escaped from *Alcemene* in a shore boat after which event Hotham ordered that seventeen of them – but not his own Prisoners of State, Curson and Gouverneur – should be transferred, in groups, to *Prince Edward*, *Mars* and *Hound*. And on the 21st, as they bore away from Crookhaven, seventeen sail, for they had been joined by the appropriately named HMS *Nemesis*, *Prince Edward* signalled that her Captain had died.

*   *   *

There was nothing illusory about the value of Hotham's convoy brought so triumphantly into Brest. The underwriters in England mourned their loss of six or seven hundred thousand pounds, but the grand total produced by the sale of the ships and cargoes was some four million and seven hundred thousand livres. It will not matter if these are thought of as French pounds since in any currency this represented a staggering amount of money – the greatest of the prizes sold off in Brest, accounting for one third of the total value of booty sold in the port during the whole of the war.

A diplomatic hiccup was not permitted to impede the proceedings of the *Conseil des Prises*, for on 1 May, France and the United Provinces had agreed and signed a Convention whereby all French and Dutch ships recaptured from the Common Enemy would be restored to their respective navies: or in the case of merchantmen, to their owners. This treaty was ratified on the 27th but its existence failed to influence the prize court which firmly ruled that the captures were legitimate and decidedly British. Neither were they influenced by the fact that only one of the eighteen vessels put up for sale, the *Spitwell*, had a British name, the remainder bearing names such as *D'Drie Gesusters*, *Vriend Schap*, *De Jong Frou Rebecca*, *Welbedagt* and the *D'Juffrow Sara*.

On 2 June therefore, La Motte Picquet and his Captains attended the Brest *Conseil de la Marine* for the happy task of examining bids from three business houses. This was a splendid meed of fortune, since they would receive a third of the 4,706,497 livres offered by the successful bidder, Monsieur Borel, who foiled a matching bid by agreeing to take delivery in Brest: another third share went to the War Invalids and a third to the crews of La Motte Picquet's squadron.

Inevitably there were indeed appeals against the decisions of the prize court, but these came before the *Conseil Royal des Finances*, presided over by the King and with the Minister for the Navy and the Colonies, the Maréchal de Castries, as rapporteur. The claims, largely by Swiss or German nationals concerned ships whose names do not appear on the notice of the sale posted at Brest: these appellants held that they were neutrals, and one, successfully, that the ship in question had not been part of the original convoy but had merely joined it for protection. These voices too, must now fade from this story: but La Motte Picquet's coup remains to contribute another of the misfortunes now at hand for Statia's conquerors.

MILITARY GOVERNOR

Always the Army's companion and indifferent to rank, the sickness which had taken Brigadier General Ogilvie had opened an opportunity for his aspiring senior officers. Ogilvie died on 31 May, following which his body was laid to rest close by the grave of Admiral Krul: but the matter of the succession had not waited.

The surgeons' opinion that Ogilvie was sinking and that at most he could not live beyond two or three days caused Cockburn to be visited by the senior officers of the garrison, Lieutenant-Colonels Andrew Edhouse of the 13th, and Joseph Stopford of the 15th. With them came their Majors, Crawford and Roberts.

It was Edhouse who acted as spokesman for the deputation and who proposed that in the event of Ogilvie's death, the command should devolve upon himself: a proposal Cockburn greeted first with angry surprise and then with an emphatic rejection. He was, he asserted, the senior Lieutenant-Colonel by six or seven months and he had no intention of relinquishing the command in favour of an officer of inferior status. His Majesty had thought it proper to give him his commission and he would on no account waive the right to which he was entitled by his seniority.

That was the rule, Edhouse agreed: but it was not fitting that the command should go to one who already held two choice appointments, one as Quartermaster General and another as Agent for the Captors: among whom of course, were the officers of both regiments . . .

Cockburn remained unimpressed. Never far from ill-humour, he lost all patience at Edhouse's next suggestion that they should refer the matter to Major-General Prescott at St Kitts: which brought a final explosion from Cockburn. His own claim was paramount, he insisted, and for all he cared, they might consult Jesus Christ himself. He would not accept a decision from that quarter, either.

So firmly rebuffed, the Colonels could make no further protest: perforce they stifled their resentment, although this must have been felt most deeply by Edhouse. Nevertheless, they returned dutifully to their regiments, leaving Cockburn indifferent to their wounded feelings. He had, after all, had much experience of living with unhappy fellow-officers and these of the 13th and 15th regiments were only discovering for themselves something the officers of the 35th had learned over many painful years. What mattered now was that from 1 June, 1781, James Cockburn could add to his appointments the title of Military Governor of St Eustatius.

NOT TO BE CAUGHT ASLEEP . . .

Cockburn was now comfortably quartered in the house vacated by Jacques Texier, following the Statian's exile to Martinique with his step-son, Charles-André Chabert. This was indeed a striking household, since Cockburn's fellow lodgers were Matthew Forster and an unfathomable Mr Neagle – an Irish merchant of the island currently acting as Texier's steward. Neagle was one of those fortunate residents who had been adjudged to be 'of good character', i.e. loyal to Britain's cause, and had therefore had his property returned to him. But for all of this however, and his cosy proximity to the military governor, it seemed that he was able to visit Martinique on private business: although, not to offend too brazenly, his vessel was cleared for St Lucia . . . and the information confined to Cockburn and Lieutenant George Mackenzie of the 15th Regiment. This officer had previously been the Army's official envoy to de Bouillé in connection with the customary exchanges of prisoners of war and as we shall see, had established a remarkable relationship with the Marquis.

If Cockburn gave any thought to that occasion on which he had asked Major-General Campbell for a free hand with the 'poor old 35th' in 1776, he had no cause to complain on that score now. On hearing of Ogilvie's death, Vaughan had sent Brigadier General Fraser to St Eustatius to succeed in the command, but Fraser had not held it for more than three weeks before leaving for fresh fields. To all intents and purposes, it was Cockburn who now ruled Statia. Later, perhaps, he might find it necessary to account to a more senior officer, but for the time being there was no hint of interference and all authority lay in his hands.

Both the Commanders-in-Chief had left the island early in May. That flurry of activity noted by de Jong may not have been the total confusion which he claimed had followed the arrival of Hood's mauled vessels, but it had sent Rodney to sea at last after three months at Statia and would keep him occupied with the security of Tobago, St Lucia and Barbados: nor would he return to St Eustatius, except for a brief visit in the *Gibraltar* on 30 July, before sailing for England on 1 August. On that day too, Vaughan, disappointed in his own hopes for the Antilles campaign, would sail for home in the 28-gun *Boreas*: but meanwhile the threat from the French would keep him busy at Barbados.

Cockburn then assumed the command at a moment when Vaughan had not yet appointed Brigadier General Gabriel Christie as temporary commander of the Army pending the arrival of his replacement, Major-General Edward Mathew. But until Christie's appointment became effective on 22 July, there was nothing to prevent the new military governor from altering such of Ogilvie's arrangements for the defence of the island as he now saw fit. It will be useful to set his decisions against the military situation at that time, much of which must have been known to Cockburn.

It is a matter of surprise therefore, that his first decision as commander of the island – in fact, on the day after he had taken up this responsibility – was to reduce the guard at the post of Tumble-down Dick, some six miles to the north-west of the town. Ogilvie had conceived this post to be of importance and required its battery of nine guns to be manned by a subaltern, two sergeants, two corporals, a Drummer and twenty privates. For his own reasons Cockburn ordered that this guard should henceforth consist of a corporal and three privates only. Similarly, and again without explanation, he withdrew the outlying picket, quartering the soldiers in the barracks and desiring them to remain dressed and armed and at readiness to turn out at 'a moment's notice.' This was a mixed blessing for the men since the soldiers of the 15th regiment protested in vain that they had no bedding and '. . . only boards to lie on.'

Ogilvie had seen to it that all of the bays accessible from the sea were properly fortified and Cockburn made no changes at those posts, other than to put in hand some repair work, or at the look-out station on Panga, which the British called Signal Hill. In October, however, he received a letter from Mr Ross, of St Eustatius, clerk to the prize Agents, and also, a merchant with extensive associations in many of the islands. This warned of an impending attack on St Eustatius, a landing being projected on the east coast at the bay known as English Quarter.

According to Mackenzie, Cockburn 'damned the information' but nevertheless required Captain Garstin, the senior artillery officer of the garrison, to survey the location and its vicinity and indeed, the whole of the island: for this purpose, Garstin took along his Lieutenant, George Lewis. Their conclusions, reported to Cockburn, were that the island appeared to be adequately furnished with batteries, save at English Quarter, where there was '. . . a very good beach and a possibility of the enemy's landing in two places . . .' although there was a battery at the adjacent Concoran Bay.

Cockburn responded to this with alacrity, telling Garstin – and later, Christie – that he would not be 'catched asleep.' Garstin was therefore requested to act as an Engineer to oversee the construction of a battery of three eighteen pounders at English Quarter, with a guard-house and magazine. This work was not to be completed and the post not yet manned, because – as Captain Garstin said later – '. . . it was not very necessary to have artillery men where there were no guns . . .'

Similarly, the two officers reported early in November that a landing could possibly be attempted at Jenkins' Bay, in the north-west, but that the enemy '. . . would find it very difficult to get up the rock, which was almost perpendicular, near three hundred feet . . . and that a few men posted there would keep off numbers . . .'

It is curious that Cockburn, so attentive to the needs of English Quarter that he ignored his orders not to erect extra works, did nothing about posting a single soldier at Jenkins' Bay, on the opposite side of the island. It was one circumstance among so many others of no less grave implication.

*   *   *

Vaughan had sent two flank companies from St Eustatius for duties in Barbados. Statia was therefore now garrisoned by 335 men of Edhouse's 13th regiment and 261 of Stopford's 15th, with a detachment of twenty-seven artillerymen under Captain Robert Garstin. Apart from the token soldiery at St Martin – two officers and sixty-one rank and file – the nearest British presence was Prescott's garrison at St Kitts, six miles to the southeast. Further to the south east was the naval base at Antigua: and beyond, although too far away to be of immediate help or nuisance to Statia, the headquarters of the Army in the Antilles, at Barbados. Save for contact with St Kitts, therefore, where the garrison awaited a French challenge – this would come in January and they would not be able to withstand it – Cockburn's inheritance was isolated, with not a single British man of war on station to keep a vigil over the approaches: 'not even a canoe . . .' Cockburn was to remark later, in reference to his hour of need: '. . . they did not leave me even a canoe.'

Nevertheless, he appeared to be confident and outwardly unworried despite the events of the early summer. So lasting his confidence, it may be said, that when Christie offered him an additional company of the 15th Regiment, then at Antigua, Cockburn airily waved the proposal aside. He had no high opinion of the troops on Statia '. . . I have vagabonds enough' he told the messenger, Captain McLaurin, of the *Triton*: 'I do not want for more.'

Yet by that month of September he would have heard of de Bouillé's abortive landing on St Lucia, early in May. He would have known of the threat to St Eustatius emphasised by Hood's limping messenger and he would have seen the excitement generated on Statia by its tidings, encapsulated by de Jong in the assertion that 'Admiral, General, officers and men, all feared the French and wanted to leave the island.'

Cockburn would also know that Barbados itself was threatened and he would also come to hear of the surrender of Tobago. There had been enough enemy activity to keep the British in a state of tension and Cockburn in particular, alive to his immediate prospects. These were to take a wholly unexpected course and they were to be shaped, not only by the fortunes of war, but also because Lieutenant-Colonel James Cockburn had something else on his mind.

CONCERNING MONIES . . .

Not a canoe, said Cockburn: but the Commanders-in-Chief had left him with something else of substance at Fort George, even if they had not intended to do so. This was no less than £65,000 'mostly in Dollars' Vaughan noted, derived from the capture and intended for the payment of the Troops in North America. To this end, on the day of Sir George's departure from St Eustatius, Vaughan had instructed Lieutenant-Colonel Cockburn, the Commissary-General Matthew Forster and 'the other Agents' – such of the elected Captains as were then on the island – to send the money aboard His Majesty's Ship, the *Montague*, Captain Bowen, bound for New York. There it was to be delivered to Messrs Hartley and Drummond's Agents and receipts obtained on behalf of the captors.

Before he embarked on *Boreas*, Vaughan had repeated this direction to Cockburn, in the presence of Captain Bowen: but although the ships for America remained at anchor in Statia's road for another day, being delayed by the need to assemble a court martial, no money came aboard the *Montague* and no news of it came to Captain Bowen before he sailed.

But this was only a part of the money now under Cockburn's hand at Fort George. Secured in strong-boxes, this cash, all in gold coin, represented both the product of the sales and the personal wealth of the Dutch merchants, identified as such: but there was no firm knowledge as to how much of it there actually was.

Arietas Akers reported to Rodney that the total amounted to £250,000: but among all the estimates – and since Vaughan had written to Lord George Germain in February that the captors had taken possession of 'at least three millions of money' there is plenty of room for guesswork – there is only one well-supported figure of '2,800,000 livres' – roughly two hundred thousand pounds: and that, as we shall see, was counted out before Cockburn in due course by de Bouillé.

But not before Commissary-General Matthew Forster, who had removed himself to Barbados, had made his own inroads into the loot. As Joint Agent, erstwhile fellow-lodger in Texier's house and temporarily, as keeper of the strong-boxes, it is possible that Cockburn was aware of Forster's activities, although this he strongly denied. But certainly Forster's operations had drawn the attention of Brigadier General Christie, and subsequently, focused it on Cockburn.

Christie required explanations from both men and in the absence of satisfactory replies had warned them of his intention to refer his findings to Germain, to whom he gave a startling résumé on 29 September. These discoveries signalled the first tremor of the ground under Cockburn's own feet which was finally to become an earthquake.

The Brigadier had first become restive on the score of the sale of the Provisions found at St Eustatius, which had been reserved for the use of His Majesty. The Commanders-in-Chief had left him no instructions about this and Christie, seeing it as his duty to look into the matter, had been disturbed to find that a considerable amount of money, namely £17,000 remained in Forster's hands. Christie was even more disturbed to find that the Commissary-General proposed to send this sum to England, to a private Banker, a step which the Brigadier pointed out, '. . . would be attended with manifest advantage to said Commissary-General and greatly diminish the King's money.'

Some part of the Provisions, or money arising therefrom still remained at St Eustatius, and Christie therefore required Forster to account for this and to pay all monies into the hands of the Paymaster-General, until His Majesty's pleasure was made known. To which Forster replied that he had left the money with Cockburn at St Eustatius and that before complying with Christie's instruction, it would be necessary for the Commissary-General to consult and obtain the approval of the other Agents.

Informed of this by Christie in a letter of 16 September, Cockburn replied on the 30th:

> . . . I should not hesitate a moment in complying with that order relative to the money arising from Provisions sold here if I was the least concerned in the matter . . . but I solemnly swear to you, that I know nothing of any transaction of provisions sold, and of course, never was concerned in receiving any money on that account.
>
> I shall go further and tell you upon honour, that from the first Day to this Hour, I never set foot in any Merchant's Store, nor did I ever attend One Sale: that business was entirely conducted by Captain Young, Mr Akers and Mr Forster: the Money received without any interference of mine, for I never handled One Dollar of it.'

The ground underfoot trembled yet again when Christie challenged Forster with this, but the Commissary-General insisted that the money was with Cockburn. Yet he was to be even more hard put to it to explain the further vagaries related to Germain by the Brigadier.

Mentioning his distrust of Forster, Christie added that he had become confirmed in this opinion after learning that Forster had since transmitted large sums of money 'as often as he had opportunity' to St Eustatius. The assumption here is that these sums were the profits of the covert dealings described below: but unfortunately, Forster had shipped the last consignment of 1000 half-Joes (each worth eight dollars) aboard the *Amazon* frigate, Captain Dickerton, who had not after all sailed for Statia but instead, had been obliged to escort a convoy for Demarara. Dickerton, presumably innocent of mischievous intent, had thought it reasonable to return the money to Forster, from St Kitts, care of Captain Christian of *Fortune* (38) . . . and Captain Christian had informed Christie of this traffic.

There was more to come from an angry Captain Saxton, of the *Invincible*, who was, of course, one of the appointed Agents. So angered was he by Forster's devious conduct that he desired Christie to call on him as a witness to prove what he now alleged. His estimate of the value of the 'reserved' Provisions on Statia was 'above £120,000', but 'a great deal was sent off in Shipping by the said Commissary-General, whose Deputy was Collector of the Port . . .' Nobody knew where these shipments were bound, and Forster, safe, as he thought, in the status of his office, refused to give this information to the other Agents.

It seemed however, that the informal transactions of the Commissary-General were destined to come to light from other sources. One of Forster's vessels, clearly heading for Curaçao, was stopped by the *Triton*: but Captain McLaurin, about to declare the trader a prize, was checkmated by its Master who produced a pass signed by the Commissary-General certifying that the vessel was bound for St Lucia with cargo 'for the King's use.'

Reluctantly, McLaurin allowed her to proceed, but: '. . . said vessel never came to St Lucia, nor was any Provision wanted there, nor could it be intended, as said Provision was of much inferior quality to that which is sent from home for the Troops . . .'

*　*　*

There could be no doubt that Germain would act on this information but he would not have received it until October was out: it might then be another six weeks before a vessel carrying the Secretary's instructions could reach Christie. In December therefore; in which month the

Commissary-General would surely find himself in serious trouble and just as surely, would drag in Cockburn, now enmeshed in problems of his own making. It is important that we understand how Cockburn had brought himself to this pass.

His first and fatal decision had been that easy disclaimer to Christie – the assurance that he 'had not handled One Dollar' of the money and that it was in Forster's hands. Yet Cockburn was perfectly well aware of the strong-boxes in the Fort and of where that money had come from, although he chose not to mention any of this to the Brigadier. Nor did he tell Christie that he was still the guardian of the King's chest containing sixty-five thousand pounds, which he had somehow failed to deliver to the *Montague*.

Since, he had had some seven weeks before he next wrote to the Brigadier; seven weeks in which to think better of that dangerous denial and to attempt a retraction or some face-saving amplification. He could have told Christie that very much money was in the Fort but that it was not yet audited – which was true – and therefore, that he did not know what proportion was the 'Provision money' – which may or may not have been true but might pass as an explanation. It would help in this, of course, if he took care to add that the Quartermaster-General would welcome such an inspection to ensure its proper allocation. It was not beyond Cockburn's wit to offer something like this to repair the situation.

Unless he had other plans, and it seemed, from his letter of 24 November that he had, for he then told Christie that '. . . If Mr Forster only wanted my concurrence to Pay in the Money for the Provisions that, I promise you, he should soon have . . . I think he should be happy to get rid of the encumbrance of all Monies not belonging to himself: at least, I would be so.'

As if the matter was no longer of concern to him, Cockburn went on to repeat the information which he claimed to have sent the Brigadier on 12 November, '. . . by a Brig that said she would call at Barbados . . . although uncertain.' This letter too, contains some striking observations, coming as they do from an officer commanding something like 500 effectives and artillery enough for Statia's 15 batteries: an officer hitherto so confident that he could decline the offer of reinforcement because he had vagabonds enough . . .

The purport of my letter (of 12th) was, that from repeated Information of the Preparations making at Martinique, I was resolved not to be catched napping. This Island is such that when a Landing is effected, it must surrender, as there is no place of Arms tenable for an Hour. Therefore I must watch the whole Coast to prevent a Landing, for which purpose I have constructed Batteries in every Bay and Creek that is acceptable and have dispersed some small detachments throughout . . . the last of these Batteries (at English Quarter) is just finished, and I believe they will prove the Cheapest to the Government of any that have been ever made. A few materials and Artificers are the only Expense . . . I impress Negroes to Labour, as well as to do all Drudgeries as much as possible, to save the Soldiers . . .'

I am much Indebted to the Abilities and Application of Captain Garstin, who has very Amply supplied the Place of Engineer . . .'

Cockburn could only be aware that his letter, for all of its diverting information and carefully qualified assurances on Statia's defences would not prevent Christie from pursuing a final reckoning on this matter of money. That reckoning, with all of its too clearly imagined consequences – possibly for Forster, but certainly for himself – must come soon, surely in the Brigadier's next communication. Having Christie's measure, Cockburn knew that only a miracle could avert what lay ahead.

Only a miracle: and at any moment, from this day of 24 November onwards.

A TRAIN OF TORCHES

Martinique was indeed the scene of preparations for an assault on St Eustatius and these were completed by 14 November. The British hold on Statia had challenged de Bouillé from the moment of Rodney's arrival in February, but the presence of Sir George's ships and Hood's patrolling blockaders had so far ensured that the occupiers could enjoy their victory without interference.

But now de Bouillé's opportunity had come. That window had opened when Sir George had ordered Hood to America in July, and had himself sailed for England in August. The two Admirals would soon return to these seas and to Barbados, Hood in January of the new year, and Rodney in February, both having suffered their own humiliations in the interim but eager for the catharsis of new activity.

Hood had returned to the West Indies fresh from that miserable debacle for Admiral Graves and himself at the Chesapeake in September, wherein they had so crucially failed to succour Cornwallis, trapped at Yorktown. Some six weeks later, on 19 October, 1781 Cornwallis paid the price and put Yorktown forever into history. That surrender ended the war on land with the Colonists, but not the conflict at sea: that decisive British triumph would be for Rodney and Hood to achieve in the great battle of The Saints some seven months hence.

Hood would meanwhile do better in the defence of St Kitts in January 1782 although he could not prevent its surrender to the French attackers: but Sir George too, seethed on his own account. A flagship on war service was hardly an appropriate place for a patient fresh from the painful surgery he had undergone in England, but adding to his trials there, he had found himself made the poorer – much poorer – by the loss of Hotham's prize convoy and the accumulation of lawsuits awaiting the Commanders-in-Chief. To compound it all, both he and General Vaughan had suffered their tongue-lashing from Edmund Burke in the House: enough members had countered Burke's censure, true, but that and the accumulated Protests of the West India merchants had left both the Commanders to be surrounded henceforth by an aura of suspicion.

Indeed, Burke's censure was painful to recollect. No-one could be more searing when in full spate and on this occasion, on 4 December, he had rampaged in areas which the Admiral and the General would have preferred to have left unexamined. But Burke had declaimed on the need to rescue the reputation of the country from the disgraceful imputations under which it lay, and reminded the House of what these were: '. . . Abject thefts, atrocious rapine and every species of uncivilized barbarity had been charged in the face of all Europe on British commanders . . .' It was for Great Britain to show that she was '. . . prepared to listen to the complaints of the injured, to punish the authors of violence, and to redress the wrongs committed in her name . . .' All of which were duly revealed: the peremptory deportations, the avid searches, the clothes-ripping 'to come at the few pieces of money . . . concealed by the victims for their present subsistence . . .'

The House had been given further enlightenment on Rodney and Vaughan's Great Capture: 'This island was known to be in a state totally defenceless. A single gun, for saluting arriving ships, remained upon the walls of a neglected, mouldering castle with a garrison of twenty-seven soldiers . . .' And against these were thrown 'fifteen sail of the line, a proportionate number of frigates and near 3000 chosen troops . . . kept upwards of two months in a state of total inaction for the important service of protecting the sales of St Eustatius . . .' And as to those sales, and the incredible business of safe conduct for every purchaser . . . the burning Commanders and an astonished House heard that: 'Seventeen vessels, principally French, were accordingly freighted with stores and other articles purchased fifty per cent under the intrinsic value, for the service of our enemies: and less they should become captures to the British privateers which were hovering round the island, and waiting for the return of the purchasers, they sailed under the convoy of an English ship of war.'

Three months had been spent by the British commanders in disposing of and securing the plunder of St Eustatius, said Burke, concluding that this 'disgraceful cause' had led to the final misfortune: for the Commanders-in-Chief had detained three sail of the line for that same laudable purpose and without those ships, Hood's attempt to prevent the junction of the French fleet and to oppose De Grasse off Martinique had been fatally undermined. More: 'this separation of our naval force, in all human probability, brought on the whole train of calamitous events which followed: the junction of the French fleets, the loss of Tobago and finally, the dreadful disaster in the Chesapeake.'

*   *   *

The Commanders had vigorously defended themselves: 'the perfidious attachment of the Dutch to the enemies of Great Britain' had determined Sir George's conduct and in his opinion, fully justified the confiscation of property, . . . while as for the charge that he had permitted stores and provisions to be transported to the enemy islands, this was the very reverse of the truth. He had given the 'strictest orders' that such should not be sold, but should be sent to His Majesty's dockyard at Antigua. 'So scrupulously exact had he been in this respect that he had not only examined himself the clearance of every ship that went out, but caused them to anchor under his stern, where they were strictly examined by commissioned officers of the Navy . . .' (and possibly, we might wonder, in the manner previously described by Richard Downing Jennings, wherein that examination had consisted of the single question: 'Have you money on board?')

Further: Sir George had remained at St Eustatius 'for three months' only because matters of the utmost importance had made his presence there 'for some time' absolutely necessary. But during that time he had planned to go against Curaçao and Surinam, save that at the last moment he had heard of the arrival of de Grasse, falsely reported to have only twelve sail of the line to Hood's fifteen. Hood had failed, true, and so he himself had sailed to join him. He had alerted St Lucia to the danger of the subsequent and unsuccessful French attack and he would 'doubtless' have intercepted de Grasse himself 'had not his designs been traitorously discovered to the enemy'. The details of the fall of Tobago were already public knowledge and there was no need for Sir George to repeat them: while with regard to the disaster of the Chesapeake, he had advised Parker at Jamaica to send ships to America to reinforce the fleet . . .

Vaughan too, had declared himself to be equally blameless on all counts, assuring the Members that he had had nothing to do with any of

184

the alleged depredations and outrages. Why, even the Jews had sent him an address testifying to his great kindness toward them . . .

Whether these were truths or not, the damage had been done.

* * *

But in this month of November, 1781, the moment was ripe for de Bouillé. In furtherance of his plans, the Marquis also had the benefit of information from two fervent enthusiasts for his project, namely Jacques Texier and Charles-André Chabert – two men fiercely determined to reverse their expulsion from Statia. Their intimate knowledge forearmed de Bouillé with the disposition of the garrison, and on the terrain and the most favourable location for a landing. De Bouillé's own mulatto, Malcolm, born at St Christopher's and familiar with Statia would serve as a guide, in addition to Chabert himself and Chabert's son.

There had been time to create a potent assault force, to gather and organise ships and men. There may not have been 'even a canoe' at Statia, but wisely, de Grasse had not sailed for the Chesapeake without leaving a naval presence at Port Royal: de Bouillé had thus acquired three frigates, the *Medée*, commanded by de Girardin, the *Amazone*, by M de Villages and the *Galatée*, captained by Rochart de St Michel. To these King's ships de Bouillé added four armed vessels of his own – the schooners, *Felicité* and *Charmante* and the sloops, *St Louis* and *Diligent*. The Marquis himself proposed to sail in an eighth armed vessel, the corvette *Aigle*, which completed the squadron.

The complement of troops included drafts from other French islands, giving de Bouillé some 1200 soldiers – 400 from the Regiment of Auxerrois, 320 of the Royal Comtois, 50 grenadiers of Martinique and 24 '*matrosses*' – artillerymen below the rank of gunner. Four hundred of the 'Wild Geese' – soldiers of the Irish Regiments in the service of France, under their Colonels, Dillon and Walsh, brought the force up to strength. Like the British, these soldiers wore red coats and white breeches, but there the similarity ended: for of these 'Jacobites' it was truly sung that they had been driven from Ireland by the dark hand of tyranny and that they had '. . . joined the Brigade in the wars far away . . .'

The vow to return contained in that defiant song was now being honoured: for Dillon and Walsh and for all of their officers and men, this was to be another blow against the English who had dispossessed them since the Boyne.

To divert unwelcome attention, it had been given out that the squadron proposed to meet de Grasse, whose fleet was now returning to these seas. To lend substance to this story, de Bouillé embarked local pilots from the harbour of St Pierre before sailing on the 14th. Alas, de

Bouillé has omitted to tell us of the moment of disillusion for these men as two days of cruising to windward of Martinique to imply an intent for Barbados or Antigua gave way to a beat around the southern coast of Martinique and, on the 22nd, a purposeful course to leeward of the island for St Eustatius: where they arrived, unobserved, off Jenkins' Bay, that cliff-barricaded indentation on Statia's northwest coast, at nine o'clock on the evening of the 25th.

The frigates provided a protective screen for the landing, cruising beyond the length of the island, while *Aigle* would follow in support of the assault force. With difficulty, the sloops anchored in the mouth of the Bay, but for the crowded boats carrying the troops – Count Dillon's long-boat in the lead and in another, de Bouillé himself – the sea, and a disastrously high surf combined to hazard the entire operation. Dillon and his chasseurs succeeded in scrambling ashore on the ludicrously narrow strip of beach but these natural defences, far more dangerous than the sleeping garrison, extended the landing over six hours, hurling boats against the offshore rocks and drowning many of their occupants. De Bouillé's own boat was overturned, although with no loss of life: but even with the providential arrival in the early hours of the morning of three more boatloads and others yet again, it had become plain that in these conditions, there was no hope of landing the rest of the assault force. There would not be 1200 men: if the attack was to be pressed forward – and de Bouillé wasted no time in considering the option of withdrawal – then he would do that with the 400 men who had been able to come ashore. But first they would need to climb the 300 foot high rampart towering before them. Near-vertical, raw rock, shale, stone, scree and tussock, it would be difficult enough for unencumbered men by day. Armed and equipped as they were and in a darkness lit by only wind-blown torches – and still, no hint of vigilance by the British, not a sound from the four soldiers of the battery covering the beach at Tumble Down Dick, not half a mile to the south of the landing – de Bouillé's soldiers of France and the Irish of Dillon and Walsh marshalled themselves at the foot of the only conceivable upward route, and in the urgent silence, one following another, began their ascent: a train of torches snaking slowly up the cliff-face.

*   *   *

Before 5 o'clock in the morning, in the first light of the day, they reached the top. The town lay little more than three miles further south. To reach it, they would be led by their guides, the eager Chaberts and de Bouillé's own man, Malcolm, following a rough track running along the coast.

Just beyond Tumble Down Dick was the hill called Panga, now the

British look-out post renamed Signal Hill. Marching quickly, and still in silence, the main assault force skirted this, but left a detachment of thirty of the Royal Comtois to secure the height: and continued on towards the town and Fort George.

Signal Hill

At the summit of Signal Hill there were only the goats and the wheeling birds for company: but from that seven hundred foot vantage, the signalmen could overlook most of the island, save for the coast and inland areas obscured by the ranges to the northwest and south. Jenkins' Bay was thus screened from their view by day, although, on the windward side, their glasses could sweep the Atlantic: if they were to continue that sweep, around to the leeward side, they scanned the Caribbean Sea.

The post had been a concession by Vaughan to the alert Rodney and had been established to give warning of all approaching ships. To further this, a twelve-pounder carronade had been added.

Currently, the post was to have been manned by a junior NCO, Corporal Henderson, with two artillerymen, Bombardier Pettigrew and a lowly gunner James Pickering. The bombardier however, had been obliged by a nod and wink from Henderson on the 25th and had left for a convivial excursion into the town, less than an hour's walk from Signal Hill, although the poor state of the narrow, stony path did nothing to make the journey easier. But he had failed to return to the Hill as promised, and, as the hours went by and Pettigrew's absence became increasingly disturbing, Henderson and Pickering feared that the bombardier had been taken up.

* * *

Pettigrew had indeed been taken up in the town, not having sufficiently considered that as one of only twenty-seven artillerymen among several hundred red-coated infantry, his blue coat might – as it surely did – draw the attention of his detachment commander, Captain Garstin, who had imagined the bombardier to be at his post at Signal Hill. The NCO had been unable to account for his presence in the town and the furious Captain Garstin had summoned the Picket to march the offender off to the Fort. There, on the morning of 26 November, Pettigrew awaited the Captain's further displeasure: but in the event, it was to be curiously delayed.

* * *

For the two men on the crown of the Hill, the bombardier's absence meant that there was less time to doze by turns in the tiny shed erected to shelter them from the sun. This was also a place in which to keep the flags overnight, that they might not be damaged by the ever-inquisitive goats.

According to Standing Orders, the signalmen were to remain vigilant at the hilltop during the hours of daylight '. . . for as long as objects could be perceived at sea . . .' and they were to make an appropriate hoist – to be answered by a pendant flown at the Fort – for sails which might appear in any quarter. There was less sea-traffic now since the heady days of Sir George's 'Great Capture' but enough to keep the signalmen at the task of raising and lowering colours . . . 'for a sail in the Northern quarter a flag, Blue White and Red: for the Northwest, a flag half Blue and half White: to the Southeast a flag, Blue with a Red Cross and in the Southwest, a flag, Red White and Blue. And if the sails were those of line-of-battle ships, they were to fly a White Pendant over the flag, and for frigates, the White Pendant underneath the flag . . .'

At nightfall, when the soldiers were permitted to go down the slopes to their quarters – a house at the foot of the hill – there was nothing to do except to talk a little, to eat a meal prepared from their rations and to sleep. Thus did the Corporal and the gunner retire to their billet on the night of Sunday, the 25th, with the prospect of resuming their duty at first light.

* * *

Soon after daybreak at a quarter after five o'clock, Henderson was shaken awake by his landlady's servant to be told that there were 'people' at the top of the hill, come to steal her animals. The old lady had seen the glitter of their arms – Henderson must go and send them away: he must get up, quickly . . .

So rudely awakened, it would have been difficult for the corporal to imagine who could possibly be at the top of the hill at this, or any other time, for this was one of the most remote places on the island. The only 'people' in the vicinity were the men at the adjacent battery at Tumble Down Dick – the Corporal and three men whom Cockburn had deemed sufficient to serve nine eighteen pounders. Yet it was, of course, possible that one or more of them might be at some mischief: Henderson therefore despatched Pickering to investigate.

It was some considerable time later that the Corporal realised that yet another of his tiny command had failed to reappear. At the landlady's urging, Henderson too, plodded to the hilltop: to become the second prisoner taken by the soldiers of the Royal Comtois that day. In the farcical sequel occasioned by Henderson's disappearance the old lady sent up a third enquirer, a Mulatto servant who was likewise apprehended: and then a fourth, who took in the situation and in haste, descended the slopes to proclaim – but to an audience of one, only – the presence of the French.

MIRACLE

At a quarter before six o'clock that morning, as the attackers entered the town, Lieutenant-Colonel Cockburn was granted his miracle. He was not immediately aware of its advent since he had risen at sun-up at the sound of the morning gun, mounted his horse and begun his customary ride. As he remembered the events of that day, he had ridden to the south of the island before reining in to look about him. He then saw three large vessels just clearing the North point of the island, opposite Saba and realised at once that these were enemy ships. Thereupon he wheeled his horse and galloped back to order the drummers to beat the general alarm and the troops to get under arms. He entered the Town without seeing an officer, hearing on his way 'a few popping shots of musketry.'

* * *

Of the garrison in the town, the first witnesses of the miracle were Sergeant-Major William Robinson, of the 13th Foot and the thirty recruits whom he exercised in the nearby meadow, now used as a drill field. The appearance on the scene of Count Dillon's Irish soldiers, apparently wearing the British red coat, drew no especial attention from the Sergeant-Major but at the order, Dillon's men fired a volley into his ranked men. These – the 'popping shots' heard by Cockburn – killed and wounded a number of the recruits.

At their fall, the shocked Robinson shouted for the remainder to scatter, although no urging could have been necessary: they were already lost, having drilled without ammunition or even flints in their muskets. They did have their bayonets, but they were less than thirty and the Irish, according to Robinson – now a prisoner with the surviving recruits – 'about fifty'.

Cockburn, still alone, headed towards the sound of firing. As he passed the Fort he called out to the sentry at the drawbridge to order the alarm guns to be fired and at the same time, meeting a company of the 13th Regiment which had been quartered nearby, shouted to them to throw themselves into the Fort without waiting to arm and to draw up the bridge. This order was not to be obeyed in the manner intended by Cockburn but he himself was now in jeopardy. He continued to shout the alarm as he rode through the town at the gallop, passed his house 'without stopping' and had debouched onto the Grand Parade before his horse was brought up by an Irish officer, Captain O'Connor, who caught hold of the bridle but lost his grip as Cockburn kicked the horse on and rode forward. He was fired on by O'Connor's men but remained unharmed, although his escape was to be short-lived: for, as he 'turned about again in an endeavour to get a few men together, I found myself in a narrow pass between two columns of the enemy, and was made prisoner . . .'

*　　*　　*

The men of the garrison fared no better. In the remarkable absence of their officers, almost all still abed (to be rounded up in their turn), and with so many of the men so widely dispersed in their quarters: above all, with neither gun nor drum to sound a general alarm, there was no hint of organised resistance in the streets. Indeed, Major George Henderson, then a captain of the 13th Regiment, accounted for only three shots in the defence of St Eustatius: '. . . the barrack-Guard of the 15th Regiment, a Sergeant and six men, were alarmed, and . . . the Sergeant gave the French one fire. The sentinel at the drawbridge in the Fort (being, as one supposes, alarmed by the Barrack-Guard of the 15th,) fired his musket: and the Sergeant of the Barrack-Guard of the 13th withdrew his guard within the churchyard wall, and also gave one fire. That is all the resistance the Major ever heard of.'

But the Fort, with its drawbridge still down since it had been lowered at the morning gun, represented some illusion of safety. Thence fled the men of the 13th and 15th Regiments pursued by the French: among the British however, were the few who found sufficient courage to make an attempt to raise the bridge, although this was foiled by the onrushing attackers and one man of the 13th, toiling desperately at the windlass, was shot through the body as the French entered the Fort.

It was over within minutes. The bridge was raised indeed, but this time for the purpose of sealing the British within their stronghold: at which, de Bouillé reported . . . 'the whole garrison threw down their arms. All the prisoners [were] paraded in the Fort, and we found on examination, that we had lost only ten men in killed, drowned, or wounded. The enemy lost 32.'

The British had lost something else. Major Henderson came to the Fort later that morning, on military business, and had difficulty in expressing his feelings on seeing the defeated troops. It was not in his power, he said, to describe their miserable situation: he 'never saw such heavy distress and misfortune painted in men's countenances as he saw there: they seemed almost in a state of distraction. They tore the cockades from their hats, pulled their lapels off their clothes and disfigured themselves as much as they could: Some reviled, some reproached – nothing certain could be collected from them – all lamented the heavy misfortune fallen upon them, and directed their reproach against the Commandant.'

And yet more: for Bredin's *History of the Irish Soldier* includes the claim that some 350 of the British garrison immediately took service with the French, in the regiments of Dillon and Walsh.

*   *   *

To proclaim the victory, the British flag was struck down and the flag of France rose above Fort George. Prudently, it did not remain there: de Bouillé employed Rodney's ruse and hoisted the union flag once more to divert enquiry until the capture was consolidated. Meanwhile, a force of 300 men was brought to St Martin's by the *Amazone* and one sloop and took possession of the island. No resistance was offered and the three British officers and their 53 NCO's and men were ferried ignominiously back to Statia as prisoners. On that day too, Saba surrendered as soon as called upon to do so: and on the next day, the 27th, the flag of the United Provinces was hoisted above the Fort – now again Fort Orange – to signal the restoration of the island to the Dutch and the formal reverse of Rodney's Great Capture.

*   *   *

No time was lost in de Bouillé's consolidation. The officers and men of the British garrison found themselves en route for Martinique to be disposed in accordance with custom: parole (but for the officers, only), exchange, rank for rank, or prison for the less fortunate, namely the men. As for the new order on Statia, Texier's stepson, Chabert was rewarded with the post of the displaced de Graaff, and became the new civil Governor of St Eustatius, St Martin's and Saba. Lieutenant-Colonel Fitzmaurice, Captain Commandant of Walsh's battalion was appointed as the military Governor. One of his earliest petitioners was the urbane Richard Downing Jennings, who required permission to sail for England for certain purposes – we shall come to those soon – and perhaps a little assistance from Fitzmaurice in the matter of essential contacts in London.

On the day after the surrender, all the vessels in the Bay were sold 'by public vendue' for the benefit of the new captors. The product of these auctions was added to the hoard found in the King's Chest, hitherto so carefully safeguarded by Cockburn, and the whole distributed among the French force on the following day. According to Cockburn (by the testimony of a French officer), the chest contained some sixty thousand

191

pounds, but, 'to their great surprise, it exceeded that sum more than double.'

The historian Philippe Moret estimates this 'prize money' to be in the region of one and a half million livres and lists the respective shares thus: for de Bouillé, 120,000 livres (six thousand pounds), to Dillon, Damas and other senior officers, 20,000 livres each: captains, 4,000 and soldiers and sailors – 200 – the equivalent of ten guineas each. But, save for that demolished garrison, the happiness was widespread. Nothing was more indicative of the light brought by the new order than de Bouillé's decision to return the plundered wealth of the Dutch merchants to the rightful owners. All who had given up their money and property under Cockburn's malignant proclamations had only to attend the Headquarters once more to have these possessions restored to them.

This gesture provided a searing contrast with the régime of Rodney and Vaughan and all of those whom the *Newport Mercury* had described as their 'gruesome crew.' Nor was the opportunity to point the moral neglected by Britain's enemies or by her critics in the House, either at the time or in subsequent references.

It was indeed a happy outcome. Courteous and generous in the aftermath of the adventure, de Bouillé had acceded at once to Cockburn's plea that part of the money in the King's Chest was his own. This was at once paid to him in the presence of a French officer who told Ensign Rogerson – now about to come into his own as Cockburn's Nemesis – that it amounted to three thousand Johannes, (or, as estimated by Moret, 264,000 livres or thirteen thousand two hundred pounds).

None of the respect and attention shown by the French toward the British officers could salve their humiliation: but it was the most junior among them, Rogerson, who had embarked on his military career with such faith in those set above him and such eagerness to serve them, for whom de Bouillé's generosity to Cockburn added another bitter wound. Neither his view of the surrender, nor de Bouillé's extraordinary kindness to Cockburn were matters which Rogerson proposed to keep to himself. How deeply felt was his sense of betrayal and what furious emotion now burned within Rogerson's breast was made plain in a reply to Brigadier General Christie after the Ensign eventually made his way to Barbados.

What was the general opinion of the Officers and late garrison of St Eustatius, relative to the surrender? It was that the Commandant had actually sold the island, or that some treacherous proceedings had taken place.

ROGERSON

It was December before the first of the late garrison presented himself at Christie's Headquarters in Barbados. The resignation of Lieutenant Webster of the 13th regiment had created an opportunity for Ensign Rogerson and de Bouillé, informed of this and not wishing to retard Rogerson's promotion, had granted him the opportunity of an early exchange. Rogerson's happiness at this however, was considerably diminished by the prospect of the ordeal now before him, of being interviewed by an officer whose fury at the turn of events was heightened for the young man by Christie's intimidating rank.

Seething, Christie heard the Ensign out: but on that day, the 11th, wrote him an angry letter desiring further information. As Rogerson '. . . had come without bringing from the late Commander of His Majesty's Troops in that garrison, a single scrap of paper or any satisfactory account from either of the two Lieutenant-Colonels next in command there, relative to the dishonourable surrender of that important island, and of St Martin's by a handful of French troops, the former with a garrison of 723 men and the latter (with) 63 effective men, making 786 of as good troops as are in His Majesty's service . . . therefore, to enable me to state for the King's information the particulars of so singular an event, I do require and desire you not only to give answers in writing to the questions hereto annexed, but also, to add thereto every other particular you can think of, to throw light on this important business.'

* * *

There were twenty-one questions. Rogerson conscientiously worked his way through the list, returned his replies as ordered and equally conscientiously damned Cockburn with every possible sin of negligence for which, Rogerson proposed, there could be only one possible motivation. All the questions were penetrating and all of Rogerson's answers potentially injurious to Cockburn: but two replies especially summed the gravity of the situation now awaiting Cockburn when he should at last appear:

When was Lieutenant-Colonel Cockburn informed of the landing of the enemy, and what steps did he take thereon?

Lieutenant-Colonel Cockburn was not, to my knowledge, informed of the landing of the enemy until he was taken prisoner. A report universally prevailed that an Orderly Sergeant of the 15th Regiment acquainted him, by the information of a negro, at eleven o'clock the preceding night, that the French were then landing. He took little notice of this report and dismissed the Sergeant directly. Lieutenant-Colonel Cockburn took no steps whatever to prevent the enemy's taking possession of the garrison, he being taken prisoner on horseback 'on his return from bathing.'

We already know how Rogerson had answered a further question. Nothing could explain the astonishing loss of St Eustatius save that blunt accusation that the Commandant had actually sold the island: or that some treacherous proceedings had taken place.

* * *

Christie had heard enough. The matter must be placed before Germain and Rogerson must be the messenger: he could additionally carry Christie's despatches. Rogerson was advanced enough money to sustain him until he could draw pay, then – no sooner than Hood had agreed that he should be given an urgent passage – hurried peremptorily away to the *Ranger* brig, about to sail for England. The vessel waited no longer than was necessary to take the Ensign up from his boat, then, on Sunday 16th, weighed and made sail.

'. . . Came on board an Officer belonging to the 13th Regiment with despatches for England.' wrote the Master. 'Came to sail in Company of us, the *Sybil* and *Champion* Frigates . . .'

Rogerson had spent six extremely tense days in Barbados. He would now spend twenty-four days at sea – albeit in squall and rain and with all the discomforts and perils of the voyage – but mercifully, without the dreadful presence of the Brigadier. He could make use of the time to still his unquiet nerves and compose his account of the disaster for other ears.

* * *

Cockburn arrived at Christie's Headquarters on the 17th, full of bluster and condemnation of the officers and men of his late command. He was appalled to find that Rogerson had not only anticipated him and thus destroyed Cockburn's hope of deflecting blame with this explanation, but in addition, had been hustled aboard the *Ranger*, which had already sailed. Foreboding of what this might mean for himself clearly preoccupied the Lieutenant-Colonel for the period he remained at Barbados, which was, in Christie's opinion, (expressed in an additional report to Germain, on 20th December), unduly prolonged:

. . . I am not very clear of the intention of the late Commandant of St Eustatius. Health and other pretences are thrown out to gain time, but if any opportunity of a vessel of War going to England, I believe I shall apply to the Admiral for a Passage for him.

In fact the 'health and other pretences' succeeded in keeping Cockburn in Barbados until early in March, by which time he revealed that not only had he been betrayed by the cowardice of the garrison, but also, that Brigadier General Christie now plotted his downfall out of sheer malevolence. On the 10th of that month, shortly before he too, took his reluctant passage to England, Cockburn complained to the Commander-in-Chief in the West Indies, General Mathew, at St Lucia, at the same time sending copies to two publications, the *New York Gazette* (where his grievances appeared on 8 May, 1782) and the *Political Magazine*, which published his letter in July.

He had delivered his report of the events at St Eustatius to Christie, Cockburn wrote: but Christie had told him that it was unlucky that he had not arrived sooner, for the *Ranger* sloop-of-war had sailed two days before, for England . . . and that Ensign Rogerson was aboard her. 'Upon being told this,' added Cockburn darkly, 'I immediately suspected some foul play: however, I took my leave for that time, promising to return for dinner.'

By which time he had learned more unhappy tidings, from 'many respectable persons.'

Mr Christie had repeatedly closeted that Ensign Rogerson (. . . an Officer ill-spoken of by his own corps) and wrote out a list of queries, to which he extorted answers from him, altogether false and tending to destroy my character. I was further told that Mr Christie had even given money to the Ensign, to support him home . . .

And though Rogerson had so much honesty left as to say that I might be expected here hourly, yet, so far from detaining him until my arrival, Mr Christie hurried him away the quicker, giving him in charge to an Officer of his family, to see him into the boat, that I should have no opportunity of confronting him and doing myself justice.

General Mathew was spared nothing of Cockburn's recital of the unjust treatment inflicted on him by Christie – a Spanish inquisitor, in Cockburn's words, who had never looked an enemy in the face. The Brigadier had prejudged him, set him aside from his appointment as Quartermaster-General and lied to him: had even been hypocritical enough to deny that he had given Rogerson 'one syllable' to take home concerning St Eustatius, 'only the usual returns, duplicates and private letters.' The Brigadier, alleged Cockburn, claimed that these had been entrusted to Rogerson merely because he happened to be a passenger. 'This declaration he repeated in the presence of Lieutenant-Colonel Stopford, Captain Garstin, Ensign Watson and others: notwithstanding all this, knowing the man, I had my doubts of his veracity, and the event has fully justified my suspicion.'

Which doubtless left General Mathew unimpressed, save that in September he ensured that the correspondence, which now included a five-page refutation from Christie, would be transmitted to the Secretary of State.

* * *

Cockburn's witnesses had arrived at Headquarters at the same time as himself, paroled 'not to serve against the French King or his Allies till exchanged, with leave to proceed to England . . .' Christie duly interrogated them but was far from being enlightened by their explanations. He had, of course already sent one report to Germain by the *Ranger*: now, in the letter of 20th December, he added what he had gleaned from these latecomers.

Among the details of the Commandant's omissions, of the similarly culpable behaviour of Lieutenant-Colonels Stopford and Edhouse, and of other paroled officers 'loitering their time away (instead of going home), in some of the islands' – now ordered to depart therefrom immediately, for England, Christie included an important item obligingly contributed by Captain Garstin: namely, that Garstin had ridden out with Count Dillon who had told him that the Marquis de Bouillé had 'given Lieutenant-Colonel Cockburn three thousand Joes – that is half Johanne's of Eight Dollars each' – claimed by him as his property. Also, that the Marquis had returned to the owners all the Purses containing private property of individuals residing at St Eustatius, which had been taken from them: the rest of the Treasure was shared between himself, Count Dillon, the other officers and troops under his command, in certain proportions.'

There was enough here to furrow brows in Whitehall and at the War Office: quite enough to pave the way for Cockburn's reception in London, whenever he could no longer postpone that moment.

* * *

So too, ended Rogerson's brief respite when *Ranger* anchored in Portsmouth harbour on 9 January. Disembarked, the Ensign made his way to London to make his report at the War Office.

Writing to Christie – now Major-General – on 12 August, in order to declare his readiness to contradict Cockburn's version of the interviews at Barbados, as well as to thank Christie for recommending him for the vacant Lieutenancy in the 13th Regiment, Rogerson described his own reception in London:

> . . . The disagreeable news, of which, by your desire, I was the messenger, did not fail of creating much surprise among his Majesty's Ministers, as well as the King himself, who visibly showed his displeasure on perusing the report of the capture of St Eustatius. I confess, that at the time, I felt myself so delicately situated that I almost considered myself responsible for the misfortune I had to account for: time, and I judge, a change in His Majesty's Councils, assisted greatly towards drowning the stigma that then prevailed, for after six weeks had elapsed, the subject began to lay dormant, and the Officer commanding the Garrison anxiously expected home. It was not till now that I was permitted to visit my friends in the country, and then with orders to return at a moment's notice . . . since that time a universal silence has been observed, owing I conclude, to the absence of Lieutenant-Colonel Cockburn . . .

But no doubt that silence was also due in part to some contemplation of what Rogerson had told them on 24 January. Fresh from yet another searing interrogation at the War Office, Rogerson had thankfully sought out the nearby Salopian Coffee House: but he was soon calling for pen and paper for an urgent afterthought. He wrote:

> '. . . I recollect more, . . . that some time previously, Mr Gordon, late a Sergeant in Colonel Cockburn's own Corps, the 35th, was sent by him in a small vessel for Barbados . . . unaccountable to say, by some means or other, on a fine night, pleasant weather, was cast away on a bold shore on the Island of Guadaloupe, being made a prisoner and well-known to some people who had come here from St Eustatius. He was sent to Martinique, set at large, and had frequent interviews with the Marquis de Bouillé . . . and afterward allowed to proceed to his desired Port, where he soon after arrived. After making some stay there, he returned to his Patron, Colonel Cockburn, who received him and his wife with open arms . . . (I fancy this might be 3 weeks preceding the capture.)

Cockburn, added Rogerson:

> '. . . provided them with an elegant house and immediately, in addition to the appointments he then held, conferred on him several new ones, which brought him in considerable advantages – I must leave you to draw your own conclusion.'

– 8 –

HORSE GUARDS

The Headquarters of the British Army known as the Horse Guards had recently been built on that open ground known by the Tudors as The Tiltyard. But even with its prime location fronting Whitehall and with the elegant vista of St James's Park at the rear, this was a remarkably unprepossessing structure. So much so indeed, that it was later to be described as 'one of the ugliest edifices devoted to His Majesty's Service.' The comment came long after Lieutenant-Colonel Cockburn had passed through its arched entrance, but he too, could not have viewed a more depressing prospect.

It was here on 12 May, 1783, a full year and four months since he had appeared at Christie's Headquarters, that Lieutenant-Colonel Cockburn at last stood as the accused to hear the charges read to him by the newly promoted Lieutenant William Rogerson.

That period of grace had been granted by the need to await the arrival in England of the officers of the garrison of St Eustatius and of certain NCO's who would also be required to give evidence. The months had gone by too, as the Judge-Advocate General, Sir Charles Gould and his staff considered the charges and while they agreed on the five Generals and ten Colonels who would serve as Cockburn's judges. They settled at length on Lieutenant-General Sir Robert Hamilton, who would be President, Lieutenant-Generals Hugh, Earl Percy, and William Taylor, and Major-Generals John Douglas and Joseph Brome.

The Colonels were an equally formidable group: the Earl of Suffolk, Lord Spencer Hamilton and the Honourable Chapel Norton: Guydickens, Leland, Hotham, Hill, Dixon and Hulse. They would try Cockburn fairly enough, but they could not have been unaware of his aspersions on Christie and Rogerson in the *Political Magazine* and the *New York Gazette*: nor of their blistering replies which had also become public knowledge.

Cockburn had succeeded only in priming members of the Court Martial with an unfortunate impression of his temperament. Typically, his comment that Rogerson was an officer 'ill-spoken of by his own corps' had provoked the young man to appeal to his brother officers of the 13th Regiment and as a result, Lieutenant-Colonel Edhouse and eighteen officers obliged him with their collective approval of his conduct and character. Further to damage Cockburn, this letter of 8 October, 1783, was published in the *Morning Herald* and 'in the Magazines.'

It fell to Rogerson to open the proceedings. He told the Court that as the officer who first brought the intelligence of the surrender to Major-General Christie and from him to His Majesty's Ministers, he had been expressly ordered by the Judge Advocate General to the prosecution. It was not his inclination, he said, for '. . . I stand before you in the most disagreeable and invidious light that an officer can appear in.' But it was his duty. He asked for the 'countenance and protection' of his brother officers for, he said, he had neither fortune, rank or abilities to support him. Similarly, he asked for the patience of the Court since he had never before served as witness, prosecutor or accused on so solemn an occasion.

Yet he had acted because he had heard that the whole of the garrison was accused of neglect, supineness and want of courage, and even, it had been said, that His Majesty would dismiss the two regiments from his service for ever. Hearing this:

> . . . conscious as he was of the gallantry, alertness and attention of his unfortunate brother soldiers and of many whose conduct it had been his whole ambition to copy and whose friendship he was proud to deserve . . . The Honourable Court should believe that whatever his narrative contained and whatever he had said or signed relative to the loss of St Eustatius, if it tended to incriminate any particular individual, was not due to pique or personal resentment but was rather, a conscientious discharge of his duty to vindicate the character and honour of the garrison – who until that unfortunate day had deserved only the most honourable applause . . .

Rogerson did not wish to offer any evidence but he would be happy to reply to any questions put to him by Lieutenant-Colonel Cockburn. For the moment however, Cockburn had none.

*   *   *

Cockburn was charged on two counts. The first of these was that:

> While commanding-in-chief His Majesty's Forces in the Island of St Eustatius, he was guilty of culpable neglect in not taking the necessary precautions for the defence of the said island, notwithstanding he had received

intelligence of an attack intended by the enemy upon the same. And farther, that he did, on the twenty-sixth day of November, 1781, suffer himself to be surprised by an inferior body of French troops, which landed on the said island, without any opposition: and that he did shamefully abandon and give up the Garrison, Posts and Troops which were under his command . . .

On the second charge, Lieutenant-Colonel James Cockburn was also accused of:

Scandalous and infamous behaviour, unbecoming the character of an Officer and a Gentleman, in claiming and obtaining from the Commander-in-Chief of the French troops, a sum of money, not his own, upon the ground of it being his own private property.

Evidence for the Prosecution

Lieutenant Rogerson may have professed his personal distaste for the role thrust on him: nevertheless, the appointment lent him the courage to out-face one reluctant witness far above him in rank. So much so, that when Sir Charles Gould wrote to him on 2 May and asked for his opinion on the matter, Rogerson firmly opposed Colonel Stopford's appeal to the Judge Advocate that he might be excused from attending the court martial on the grounds of ill-health.

I have the honour to acknowledge the receipt of yours, and I must beg leave to say, if Colonel Stopford's health is in such a situation that a journey to London would in any degree injure it, I should be very sorry to require his attendance. However disagreeable my situation may be as a man in respect to the Court Martial, I must now, as an officer, consider myself discharging a duty which I owe to His Majesty and the Garrison I have had the honour to serve with. On that account I think that the testimony of Lieutenant-Colonel Stopford who commanded the 15th Regiment of Foot cannot with any propriety be dispensed with.

In the event, both Stopford and Edhouse attended, although they were treated with an unwarranted delicacy. They were questioned on the strength of the two regiments on the island, the reduction of the guard and on the other measures which had followed Cockburn's assumption of the command. They were questioned on the importance of Tumble Down Dick as a potential landing place and on the nature of the road from Tumble Down Dick to the town: on the fact that the troops were issued with only 'five or six' rounds of ball 'in order to save ammunition', and that they were dispersed in barracks located in different parts of the island . . .

Edhouse further confirmed that at no time during his command had Cockburn assembled the troops at their alarm posts '. . . or taken any particular steps to stimulate the troops to a greater degree of attention and alertness (if possible,) when on and off duty . . .' There were more questions on what Cockburn had done or not done to prepare the garrison against the possibility of an attack but none of the replies were helpful to Cockburn's defence. The scales were further loaded against him when Edhouse agreed that although he was Second-in-Command of the garrison, the Prisoner had not communicated to him any intelligence he had received relative to the designs of the enemy. But no member of the Court, it seemed, thought fit to ask Lieutenant-Colonel Edhouse or Lieutenant-Colonel Stopford why they themselves had made no provision against this contingency and why indeed, they had been taken prisoner while still abed and without offering the enemy any resistance.

They were followed in the course of the next three weeks by a succession of witnesses: the officers and NCO's of the garrison. Again, little was offered in Cockburn's favour and that only in cautious terms carrying little conviction when set against the entire catalogue of default. The Court sat stonily as the Adjutant of the 15th, Lieutenant Bathe, explained that while it was true that each man had been issued with six rounds, this had been by order of General Vaughan. The General had made provision for sixty rounds and three good flints per man, but it was also his order that the remainder of the ammunition should be '. . . carefully lodged in the regimental store.'

The Court chose not to pursue this. It was easier to focus on the more positive evidence of Captain Garstin. Cockburn had told him late in October of the letter from Mr Ross warning of the possibility of a French landing on the eastward side of the island, at English Quarter. With Cockburn's encouragement, he had accordingly begun the construction of a battery of three eighteen pounders to command the site '. . . which was nearly completed, with a guard-house and magazine, when the island was surprised.' He had also surveyed the whole of the island and had especially noted Jenkins' Bay. The enemy could possibly land there, he informed Cockburn, but they would find it difficult to get up the rock – 'almost perpendicular, near three hundred feet: a few men posted there would keep off numbers . . .'

And in consequence of this report, came the question, 'Was there a guard or a single soldier posted there?'

'No', said Garstin. 'I never knew or heard of any.'

Captain Garstin's replies were no more helpful to Cockburn after an adjournment.

Following the survey, did Lieutenant-Colonel Cockburn ever ask for his opinion on the most probable means of defending the difficult approaches to Fort George from Jenkins' Bay, or from Tumble Down Dick or from English Quarter . . . for the purpose of establishing an interior defence to the island?

'I don't recollect he ever did,' said Garstin. Nor, following the survey, had he ever visited any of the batteries in company with Lieutenant-Colonel Cockburn or any of the difficult approaches to Fort George from the several practicable landing places. Neither had he at any time received orders from Cockburn to establish night signals at the different posts at which guns or artillerymen were planted to give alarm on the approach of an enemy.

But if he had commanded one or two companies at or near the narrow pass between Jenkins' Bay and Signal Hill, did he think he could have stopped an enemy long enough for the garrison to have got under arms?

Captain Garstin did think so. It was this implication of negligence which remained as the essence of all of the evidence, for where the witnesses were not openly hostile to Cockburn – Major Henderson made quite plain his anger and contempt for him – they were obliged to concede Cockburn's omissions.

Henderson added to these by describing the ill-omened changes initiated by Cockburn following the death of Brigadier General Ogilvie. The Court had already heard some of this from Lieutenant-Colonel Edhouse: nevertheless, Henderson was taken over the same ground. The detachment at Tumble Down Dick had previously consisted of one Subaltern, four NCO's and twenty privates – and, Henderson believed, 'an artilleryman,' but 'almost immediately' Cockburn had decided that the guard should be reduced to a Corporal and three privates. Cockburn had also converted the outlying picket to an inlying picket quartering these soldiers in widely dispersed barracks. The effect, Henderson told the Court, was that: '. . . they must come in from the different barracks in a straggling manner . . .' and thus suffer delay in assembling as a useful body. As to the batteries, and particularly the one under construction at English Quarter, Cockburn had told him nothing. What information Henderson had, he had obtained from Captain Garstin. Nor had Cockburn spoken to him of the letter from Mr Ross, which he knew of only from hearsay. Following the receipt of that warning, Cockburn had not issued any orders to alert the garrison to the possibility of an attack . . .

'No,' said the Major, in reply to a further question: it did not appear to him from the whole proceedings of Lieutenant-Colonel Cockburn during his command, and particularly during the last month of his command, that he had acted as an able and vigilant officer. He seldom saw the Lieutenant-Colonel except in his own house.

And was it the opinion of Major Henderson, enquired the prosecutor, that Lieutenant-Colonel Cockburn had shamefully abandoned and given up the garrison, posts and troops under his command?

The question remained unanswered. The Court did not think it proper to require the witness to reply.

In their turn, two NCO's of the 13th Regiment fuelled Cockburn's discomfiture. Sergeant William Pontsbury confirmed that he had been in his barrack with his men when he had been told of the attack by a fleeing Corporal. No officer had joined them and although he had prepared to defend the barrack, he had received an order at about seven o'clock from Lieutenant-Colonel Cockburn that he was to surrender the post. Adjutant Smith had brought that order to him.

Bad enough, but worse to come: for Sergeant Major Robinson contradicted Cockburn's assertion that he had 'galloped past his own house' as he had ridden for the Grand Parade. Robinson remembered seeing the Lieutenant-Colonel 'opposite to his own door, sitting on his horse and calling for his sword.'

One after the other, the remaining witnesses gave their evidence, but little of it of much comfort to the prisoner. Lieutenant Bathe told of the orders promulgated in March and in May of 1781 during Brigadier Ogilvie's tenure of command, which specified the assembly points for the garrison in case of an alarm and the firing of alarm guns from Fort George. Thus, dispositions had been made, at least by Ogilvie: but of course, this served merely to emphasise that there had been no patrols or guards to give the alarm on the morning of the landing. Bathe was followed by Lieutenant Scott of the 13th Regiment who escaped with a brief examination on the manner of quartering the officers – upon the different private families, he explained, and yes, these families did consider it to be an act of oppression.

Captain Madden of the 15th Regiment endorsed all that had been said about the absence of guards between the landing site and the outskirts of the town: no guard had been stationed at Jenkins' Bay, either by General Vaughan or by Brigadier Ogilvie: neither were any troops posted on the road from Jenkins' Bay to the garrison.

Madden was followed by a naval officer, Captain Maclaurin. He had brought the *Triton* frigate into St Eustatius, with victuals for the 13th Regiment, and had also carried a memorandum from Brigadier General Christie, duly produced and read to the Court.

Captain Maclaurin is requested, if consistent with the service and (if) Brigadier Prescott desires it, to put a single company of the 13th Regiment, now at Antigua, on board the vessel . . . to convey them to St Eustatius: this is only conditional, in case a representation has been made to him from Colonel Cockburn that he wants more men at St Eustatius.

Maclaurin then repeated Cockburn's reply: '. . . he did not want any reinforcement but complained generally of part of the troops which were under his command, saying, he had vagabonds enough and did not want for any more.'

Here, Cockburn made one of his few interjections. Could Captain Maclaurin positively swear that he had made use of the word 'vagabonds?' The question was an unfortunate one, for Maclaurin could indeed swear to it and obliged the Court by repeating the Lieutenant-Colonel's contemptuous phrase. But he offered a gleam of hope for the prisoner when questioned on the absence of a ship of war to patrol Statia's approaches. A vessel of superior force to the enemy would have been of service. A lesser vessel might need to be covered from the island, but both '. . . might have discovered the approach of an enemy and given warning by signal to the garrison.' Similarly, guard boats rowing in the area of Jenkins' Bay and Tumble Down Dick would have been able to give an alarm of an attempted landing . . . but there had been no such guard boats.

Cockburn seized on this. Did Maclaurin remember that when he arrived at St Eustatius the Lieutenant-Colonel had asked him whether he was to be stationed there, as Cockburn '. . . had been promised one or two frigates?'

Captain Maclaurin believed that he had been asked that question but could not recollect anything further on that subject. Or whether Cockburn had applied to Admiral Rodney for a frigate to remain on station at St Eustatius for general defence of the island . . .

* * *

Captain Garstin's fellow artillery officer, Lieutenant Lewis, described the post at Signal Hill and agreed that there had not been a similar one above Jenkins' Bay. Had there been one, no enemy could have passed without being discovered. When pressed, he recalled that a stone wall had been erected by Ogilvie, between the Grand Parade and the coastal battery at Fort Amsterdam, some few hundred metres north west of Fort George. Yes, this had been demolished during the time of Cockburn's command, but, Lewis said, he had not seriously thought of it as a potential check to an enemy. He would hardly call it a wall – just loose stones one upon the other: a wall erected without mortar. It would not impede the enemy since '. . . they might pass it by going some few yards about . . .'

The enemy must come through a narrow pass between Jenkins' Bay and Fort George, a 'hollow way' which Lewis supposed to have been gulled by torrents of water from the hills. But he knew of no measures taken to oppose the enemy at this pass: 'there could be none,' he offered: 'They had possession of the town before it was known that the enemy had landed.' As for the men at Tumble Down Dick, they too could not have defended that post. There were nine guns. Nine guns sounded formidable enough to the Court until Lewis replied to the next question: how many Artillery men were stationed at the post?

Only one, answered the Lieutenant, and in reply to an opportune question prompted by Cockburn, added that even if the Subaltern, the four NCO's and twenty men had remained at Tumble Down Dick, they would have been unable to repel the attack because they were still insufficient to serve nine guns. The Court was on firm ground in such matters of military efficiency: its members found themselves entering a swamp however, when they examined another officer of the 15th, Lieutenant George Mackenzie: although his replies, apart from providing an entertaining view of certain aspects of the war, must certainly have gratified the prosecution.

Mackenzie had been with Mr Ross, he deposed, who told him of the information he had given to Lieutenant-Colonel Cockburn that the enemy proposed an expedition against St Eustatius . . . that they meant to make a landing at the back of the island – to Windward – and that Cockburn had damned the information.

And did Lieutenant Mackenzie know that Mr Neagle, 'who lived in Lieutenant Cockburn's family' went several times to Martinique, previous to the surprise in question?

Yes, said Mackenzie. He did know. He thought that Neagle had gone there about a month before the surprise.

And how did he know this?

Because he [Mackenzie] had bought some mahogany furniture for the Marquis de Bouillé by permission of the Commanders-in-Chief. He had had no opportunity to send this to the Marquis and therefore had 'frequent' occasion to write to Martinique to apologise. Neagle, it seemed, knew of this correspondence. He had told Mackenzie that he was going to Martinique 'privately' and that only Lieutenant-Colonel Cockburn – and now Mackenzie – knew of it. It must be kept secret, Neagle said: he was cleared out for St Lucia, but of course, had no intention of going there. He sailed that evening, carrying another of Mackenzie's letters to Martinique.

The Court required Mackenzie to explain his familiarity with the

French island and its Governor. During his service in the West Indies, the Lieutenant said, he had been sent to Martinique 'on public business' – presumably to deal with prisoner-of-war exchanges – on three occasions; twice by General Grant and once by General Vaughan. And yes, he did '. . . speak the French language:' but he did not know whether the Marquis de Bouillé had been encouraged to plan the assault on St Eustatius by any intelligence he might have received concerning the negligence and inattention of the Governor . . .

*　*　*

The members of the Court were left to make what they could of the mysterious Irish merchant, Mr Neagle, despite the helpful appearance of the Commissary-General, Matthew Forster, who might not have been entirely distressed by the turn of events. However, he described Neagle as 'a loyal good subject.' He knew Texier and his son-in-law Chabert, Forster said, but nothing of the allegation that Chabert had planned the expedition against St Eustatius.

More was to be learned from Mr Houlton Harries, late Surgeon of the 13th Regiment. Chabert was Mrs Texier's grandson: it was Chabert who led one of the principal columns of the French. As for Texier's part, that gentleman had shown Harries letters indicating that he was the only person consulted by the Marquis de Bouillé.

The Court was similarly curious but remained unsatisfied about the origins and allegiances of the unheeded Mr Ross. But the probing went on until the end of May, by which time the Court had gathered consistent evidence on the landing, the route followed by the assault force, their seizure of the post at Signal Hill and their unhindered march from Jenkins' Bay to Fort George. The recital, in new testimony or brought to light in re-examination of the witnesses, laid bare every deficiency of the garrison under Cockburn's command, and not least, the lack of either frigate or guard boats to alarm the island. 'Not a canoe' said Cockburn bitterly, during his own defence. 'They did not leave me even a canoe.'

Evidence for the Defence

In the opening words of his defence, on Friday 23 May, Lieutenant-Colonel Cockburn reminded the Court of his substantial record as a soldier.

'I am now in the thirty-sixth year of my service,' he began, '. . . without an hour's remission from it. I have served in every war that has happened within that time, and have often been wounded . . .' and, until 'this unfortunate accident' his reputation had been unblemished. Indeed, several General Officers would appear to testify to his conspicuous zeal for the service. This was – or had been? – self-evident: yet it was significant of an unhealed scar that Cockburn now recalled his soldierly conduct in the aftermath of another defeat, hitherto mercifully dimmed by the passage of some twenty-five years.

'. . . in 1757, when I was Lieutenant and Adjutant of the 35th Regiment, and of the garrison of Fort William Henry that surrendered to the French, I was one of those who petitioned the King through the then Commander-in-Chief, for leave to serve, though contrary to the terms of capitulation which we looked upon as infringed by the French. The King approved, and I served, though as it were with a halter about my neck, the Marquis de Montcalm having declared that he would put to death every (such) Officer he took in service.'

And in a further reminder of his long experience, he added: 'I saw that great officer fall in the field.'

The reference to Quebec may have evoked its reflex of respect from the officers of the Court but they were now concerned with a very different affair. There would be less room for comradely understanding, but in an endeavour to enlist something of this, Cockburn sought to portray himself as the victim of a spiteful plot by Christie and Rogerson – above all, by Rogerson – and by Lieutenant Mackenzie and that cowardly Sergeant-Major Robinson. It had been the misfortune of many officers of higher rank and abilities than himself to have been surprised, he said, but 'none had ever been held out as a traitor to his country and persecuted for eighteen months' as he had been.

As the Commander of St Eustatius he had done everything his judgement suggested for the protection of the island – 'for the honour and advantage of the King's service.' He had not spent his time in idleness or debaucheries, rising at gunfiring and taking his rounds . . . on one of which sorties, on the morning of the assault, he had seen the enemy vessels 'clearing the north point of the island.'

Cockburn's next words could not have served him well,

. . . I might as well have expected an enemy to have fallen from the clouds as where they did: . . . no appearance of vessels of any kind around the island so long as light could give a view, therefore it could never have been supposed that the few hours between that and day-break could have brought such an armament. One vessel stationed at the island would have been sufficient to have prevented a surprise . . .

The Court then heard how Cockburn had immediately turned about and galloped back towards the Town; of his unavailing attempts to alarm his unsuspecting and, he claimed, disobedient soldiers and call them to arms; and of how, despite everything he could do, he had come to be captured by the Irish officer, Captain O'Connor. That was the fortune of war: but he could at least deal with all of the allegations of neglect or worse brought against him by previous witnesses, and indeed, much of what Cockburn then explained was logical, if indeed, the fault lay with others. Whether, in the light of what they had already heard, the Court would be convinced of this was yet to be seen.

Because of the extensive nature of Statia's coast, Cockburn said, it was impossible to place a force at every post strong enough to repel an attack. His plan, therefore, had been to set small detachments at the batteries '. . . sufficient to give the alarm, with the principle of keeping together as large a body as I could, with which I could march to the place attacked.'

But nothing, of course, had come of this plan. Again, Cockburn denounced the perfidious soldiers of the 13th. They had disobeyed him in not throwing themselves into the Fort at his shouted order: nor had the detached company of this regiment done their duty since they might have taken the enemy in the rear as they emerged from the mountain defile and came into the plain. '. . . That would have made the alarm general and given me an opportunity of assembling even a few men, with which I would have attacked the first body (of the enemy) I met . . .'

* * *

Cockburn spoke of the information he had received from Ross. Firstly, he had not chosen to divulge this to the garrison out of common prudence, 'surrounded as he was by a host of enemies within.' And even though Mr Ross's intelligence was founded on vague and uncertain report, he had paid proper attention to it. He freely confessed that he had never confidentially consulted his second-in-command, Lieutenant-Colonel Edhouse: 'but with all public orders and measures he must be acquainted.' However, he had always consulted Captain Garstin in the most confidential manner. Garstin, he thought, was an able officer and a man of honour.

It had been said that he had not reconnoitred the island, but he had already done that in Brigadier Ogilvie's time, with the Army Engineer. When General Vaughan had left St Eustatius he had withdrawn the Engineer and had ordered that no more works (i.e. batteries) were to be constructed: but Cockburn's uneasiness about the security of the island had prompted him – for the first time in his life – to disobey. He therefore erected two new batteries and repaired a third – all this under the direction of Captain Garstin who acted as Engineer.

At this point, the logic became submerged by Cockburn's anger:

> . . . When the conduct and merit of an officer of thirty-six years' experi-
> ence, acquired by the toils of fourteen campaigns are to be rated by the
> opinion of those who have neither years nor service on their side . . . nor
> ever had an opportunity of being called out into active service – then the
> discipline of the Army must certainly be in danger.'

The judges making no comment, Cockburn resumed his defence. He
had intended, he said, that after the new battery at English Quarter had
been manned he would have detached a small picket from the main body
and stationed them on the height above Jenkins' Bay, and at other places
as necessary, as soon as any sort of shelter could have been provided for
them. '. . . Every person acquainted with the West Indies must know that
the consequences to men lying out all night without cover was most certain death – particularly to men already melted down by the climate . . .'
Therefore he had concentrated on measures to defend the most accessible places.

Yes, he had refused Christie's offer of reinforcements and with good
reason. The four flank companies which had been the flower of the garrison had been taken from him long before the offer had been made. The
proposed reinforcement had consisted only of one Battalion company of
the 13th Regiment and they had been 'both weak and sickly.' Some sinister significance had also been read into the reduction of the detachment
at Tumble Down Dick: but Ogilvie had strengthened that post only
because of Admiral Hood's reverse on 7 May. In consequence, the
Brigadier had been apprehensive for the safety of St Eustatius but after
Rodney and Vaughan had sailed in the *Sandwich* to join Hood, the threat
was removed.

Bluntly, Cockburn denied that Ogilvie had ever established an outlying picket. In fact, he said, there was a house in the Town that they lay
in until dismissed at gun-firing: they were allowed a tour of guard duty,
but the sickness of the garrison obliged him to order them to lie in their
respective barracks, 'which saved the men a guard.' In his stride now,
Cockburn commenced to attack his defaulting officers. The Court had
heard that the men had only five rounds each: the remainder of the allocation of sixty rounds per man was kept in the store of each Regiment,
thus, if any of the men were in need of ammunition it must be the fault
of their Commanding Officers. Edhouse and Stopford had much else to
answer for, Cockburn suggested, for even though he himself had become
a prisoner, that should not have prevented the two Field Officers from
sounding the alarm – which was not the case, 'for I believe every officer
except myself was made prisoner in his quarters.'

Lieutenant Mackenzie became the next target. Cockburn expended considerable fire on this witness, not only contradicting Mackenzie's evidence, but in addition, claiming that if there was to be any suggestion of treachery, it was here that the taint lay most strongly. Cockburn knew of the 'very particular intimacy' between de Bouillé and the Lieutenant, and because of this – and in order to make his own report – he had asked Mackenzie to obtain all the information he could from the Marquis and his officers regarding the French expedition.

Mackenzie had complied and 'given me a paper in his own handwriting.' This was offered for the Court's inspection: lest that was not enough to support the allegation of a 'particular intimacy', Cockburn expressed the hope that the Court had observed the pointed and prejudiced manner in which Lieutenant Mackenzie had given his evidence. For example, Mackenzie had sworn that the warning from Ross had been verbal and given to Cockburn on the Wednesday before the surprise: but Captain Garstin could confirm that the intelligence came in the form of a letter, which Cockburn had shown to him as soon as he had received it.

Mackenzie had also insinuated that Mr Ross had been Cockburn's agent in a traitorous correspondence with the enemy. To refute this, Cockburn explained the presence of Mr Neagle in his house and the relationship with the ejected Texier who owned it. Neagle – 'a native of Ireland' – had been a resident of St Eustatius long before the arrival of the British. He had traded in partnership with a Mr Dawes, a British subject. Their characters were considered to be so good that they had been spared from the general confiscations and their property had been secured to them by the Commanders-in-Chief. When the French residents had been ordered off the island, Texier – an old friend of Neagle – had asked Forster and Cockburn to permit Neagle to live in the house with them so that he could care for Texier's property if Forster and Cockburn should themselves leave St Eustatius. So Neagle had moved in. Indeed, he had so impressed the Lieutenant-Colonel and the Commissary-General as a man of principle and honour – Forster, of course, had already testified to this effect – that they had invited him to share their table, to which proposition he was so good as to agree.

Here, Cockburn emphatically endorsed Forster's opinion: he believed that the King had no more honest subject and that if Mr Neagle had been able to procure or give intelligence, it would have been in the interest of His Majesty, King George. He would produce affidavits and other proofs for the Court which would demolish the 'black insinuations' of Lieutenant Mackenzie. If Neagle had been secretly employed by Cockburn he would not have told Mackenzie or anyone else, and if any correspondence had been carried on between St Eustatius and

Martinique, then it must have been conducted by the 'intimate friend' of the Marquis de Bouillé, Lieutenant Mackenzie himself.

Mackenzie's behaviour had been curious in other circumstances. As a paroled officer, he had asked for a passage on a vessel bound for France. The Marquis had answered that because their friendship was so well known, it would not 'look well' if he sailed without brother officers. This was accordingly arranged. There had also been some peculiar conduct after the surrender of the garrison, when both Cockburn and Mackenzie were dining with the Marquis. De Bouillé had produced a pocket book in which he had listed the names and strengths of the British regiments in the West Indies. He had given this to Mackenzie – 'with a pencil' – and asked the Lieutenant to correct it. 'Mackenzie undertook this task to my great mortification,' said Cockburn, 'but as the Marquis understood English very well, I could only give dumb hints to Mr Mackenzie to desist, which he did not take.' But he told de Bouillé that 'Mackenzie did not have the same opportunity of knowing the strength of the army that I had and I could assure him that the regiments in that list were double the number they were set down at.'

*　　*　　*

Cockburn began the final stage of his defence by attacking Lieutenant-Colonel Edhouse and Sergeant-Major Robinson. Edhouse, he said, had sworn that Cockburn had continued in the command of St Eustatius from the day of Ogilvie's death to the day of the French assault. In saying this, Edhouse must have been deceived by a very treacherous memory: he had forgotten that Brigadier Fraser had been sent from Barbados to take the command until a new disposition was made. If it had been wrong to reduce the guard at Tumble Down Dick, or if there had been anything wrong with any other of Cockburn's dispositions, why had Brigadier Fraser condoned these measures?

As for Robinson, he was both a liar and a coward and the Court should see his evidence in its true light. The Sergeant-Major had claimed that after Cockburn had been taken prisoner, he had sent him to Captain Garstin with orders not to fire. Yet he had also said that no one had heard the Lieutenant-Colonel give those orders, nor had he told anyone else of them. But, Cockburn assured the Court, had he been in any position to give such orders he would not have employed such a man as the Sergeant-Major to carry them. Robinson had 'fled from the enemy upon a few shots when he had bayonets, without making the least resistance: I believe it to be without example, particularly as his numbers were little inferior to the enemy.'

There had been a suggestion that Adjutant Smith, who had been killed during the attack, might have given such orders, but if that was so, Cockburn was totally ignorant of them. Not that it would have mattered, he said. By that time, it was notorious that the whole garrison were prisoners in the Fort.

It was Rogerson's turn and now Cockburn's anger and bitterness overflowed. The Lieutenant had spent much effort in convincing the Court that he had not volunteered to be the Prosecutor, but was there in obedience to an order. I should be glad to ask, said Cockburn savagely, why he was a volunteer in Barbados, '. . . where the most wicked combination was formed for my destruction.' The Court should know of circumstances which would convince them that Rogerson's malicious and cruel persecution stemmed 'entirely from personal pique and resentment to me and not from any generous motive for the public service.'

There was little else to offer the Court. Cockburn referred again to the defaulting company of the 13th Regiment before making his last submission. That company quartered above Amsterdam Fort had been placed there by order of General Vaughan. Their task was to assist the artillery and to serve as a reserve in the case of an emergency. One subaltern 'at least' had been ordered to remain constantly at the post: Cockburn had provided quarters accordingly and Ogilvie had kept this disposition in being, as he himself had done, always holding the Commanding Officer of the duty Regiment as responsible . . .

* * *

Cockburn could add nothing more to his narrative, save for an emotional plea to the Court: and whatever truths they would arrive at, following all they had listened to there can be no doubt of Cockburn's sincerity at this point.

'Notwithstanding my long service,' he declared, 'I was obliged to purchase most of my commissions, my Company and my Majority particularly. My present rank I obtained from Sir William Howe in the field of battle, upon the fall of my Lieutenant-Colonel by my side.'

He knew of the rage against him felt by the 13th Regiment but he was confident that their opinions were not shared by the 15th. In a tribute which must have come as a considerable surprise and relief to a justifiably worried Lieutenant-Colonel Stopford, Cockburn said that the 15th Regiment was inured to war and subject to strict discipline. And *they* had never thought his conduct reprehensible. Yet because of all this, he had suffered greatly. He had been ordered under arrest from 6 November and although with the privilege of being at large, it had been attended with the most disagreeable circumstances.

I have also been set aside in my rank, Cockburn said, which was a circumstance truly distressing, as it conveyed an appearance of guilt. He trusted however, to the candour and equity of the Court, that its judgement would restore him to the countenance of his Sovereign, and the same good opinion of his brother officers that he had hitherto experienced. And that, upon mature consideration of the evidence they have already received, they would find it amounted to nothing more than *hearsay* and *matter of opinion*, and as such, *was not to be regarded*.

* * *

It was an impressive tribute to James Cockburn's military record that no less than five Generals attended in order to speak well of his conduct as an officer. Their very names illuminated the campaigns of the past twenty-five years and in all of these, Cockburn, they deposed, had played an honourable role. Prisoner and supplicant though he was in this room at the Horse Guards, the terse narrative of his previous service could only evoke admiration and respect.

Cockburn himself had reminded the Court of that first terrible episode at Fort William Henry, but the years which followed had been no less fraught with hardship and sacrifice. Jeffrey, Lord Amherst, had known Lieutenant-Colonel Cockburn since 1758, first as the Adjutant of the 35th Regiment, then part of his Lordship's command during the siege of Louisburg. He recollected that Cockburn had then gone with the Regiment up the St Lawrence, under Major-General Wolfe; that in 1760, Cockburn had been at Montreal under Brigadier Murray and that in the next year, the 35th had been at Staten Island and had embarked from there with Major-General Monckton's expedition against Martinique. And afterwards, to the Havannah, under Lord Albemarle, and then to disease-ridden Florida in 1763, that dread place from which so few of the 35th had returned.

In all of this time, through all of these ordeals, Lieutenant-Colonel Cockburn, to the best of Lord Amherst's recollection and knowledge, had conducted himself as 'a very active, diligent, good officer.'

Amherst's words were endorsed by General the Honourable Thomas Gage, who from his own long knowledge of Cockburn, additionally described him as 'a gallant officer.' Gage was followed by General James Murray who had also known Cockburn since the siege of Louisburg, and as the Adjutant of the 35th. He had thought so highly of Cockburn that he had chosen him as his Aide-de-Camp at the battle of Quebec. The General had reviewed the 35th and had found the Regiment to be in excellent order – due, he was told by its Colonel (now Lieutenant-General) Campbell, to Cockburn's assiduity . . .

Which good order had also been particularly noted by Lieutenant-Generals William Tryon and Daniel Jones. Tryon had commanded the troops at Kingsbridge in 1757. The strictest discipline had been preserved in the 35th Regiment 'which he attributed to the diligence and attention of their Commanding Officer, Lieutenant-Colonel Cockburn, whom he esteemed and respected as a very excellent officer.' And so testified Daniel Jones, formerly commanding the troops at New York and the islands in the Spring of 1778. The Lieutenant-Colonel had been very observant of the orders given and both he and the Regiment had done their duty with great care and diligence. And Jones' response to a question from the Court was that had he been in General Vaughan's situation (in the West Indies), he would have had no objection to giving Cockburn a command.

* * *

There were two further interpositions from which Cockburn could derive some much-needed pride at this time. In the first, he told the Court that Lieutenant-General Sir William Howe and Sir Henry Clinton had intended to bear witness to his good conduct while under their respective commands. They had both attended for that purpose during the early part of the trial but were not now present. However, in the absence of Sir William, Colonel Matthew Dixon, a member of the Court, offered his own knowledge of Cockburn's conduct at that time. Duly sworn in, Dixon referred to the manner of Cockburn's promotion in the field at the battle of White Plains. Following the death of his commanding officer, Lieutenant-Colonel Carr, Cockburn had shown gallantry in forming up the disordered regiment and marching up the hill to engage the enemy. Sir William had given Cockburn his promotion over officers of more seniority in acknowledgement of this spirited conduct which had been a frequent topic of conversation among the officers . . .

It was left to Lieutenant Rogerson as the Prosecutor to offset any favourable emotions generated by these tributes. More at issue of course, was the matter in hand and Rogerson abruptly reminded the Court of that by countering Cockburn's implied slur on Lieutenant Mackenzie. For this purpose he called eight officers who respectively spoke of Mackenzie as an officer of merit and of the strictest honour and veracity. With little variation, these words were repeated by Lieutenant-Colonels Edhouse and Stopford, by Major Henderson, by the Captains, Madden, Garstin, Freeman and Goldfrap and by the Lieutenants, Lewis and Scott. Madden added that he had sailed on the same ship with de Bouillé and Lieutenant Mackenzie – 'as good an officer as any in his line' – and had had every opportunity of noting any improper communication between them. But there had been none, he declared: he had not perceived any.

Rogerson called on Henderson to rectify two other injustices. The Major deposed that, on hearing that Cockburn had spoken disrespectfully of the behaviour of the 13th Regiment, Henderson's own Corps, he had challenged Cockburn on the truth of this in the presence of Edhouse and Major Roberts of the 28th Regiment. Possibly Henderson's demeanour, as well as the provision of two witnesses – and potential seconds – had encouraged Cockburn to deny that he had ever spoken badly of any officer or soldier of the 13th Regiment, 'except that villain Rogerson, who has assassinated my character.'

And finally, there had been Cockburn's vilification of Sergeant-Major Robinson. Henderson remembered that Robinson had come to the Regiment in 1763, out of General Rufane's Regiment at Hillsea Barracks. The Sergeant-Major had always been regarded as a very good soldier and a man of very fair character. Henderson himself held a very high opinion of him and believed that that was the opinion of every officer in the Corps. Indeed, agreed the Major when asked, Robinson had the reputation of a spirited and brave man and he had never heard anything to the Sergeant-Major's disadvantage in this respect.

The statement brought an acid query from Lieutenant-Colonel Cockburn. Had Major Henderson ever seen the Sergeant-Major tried under fire? 'No,' said Henderson: 'I never did.'

Verdict

The tributes had not been enough to sway the members of a Court which had already come to a decision. That much was evident, for on that same day of Saturday, 24 May, Lieutenant-Colonel James Cockburn heard himself pronounced 'Guilty' of the whole of the first charge, and with that, the sentence ending his career as a professional soldier.

The Court, he was informed, had considered the evidence for the prosecution and had weighted this against his defence. In their opinion he was guilty of:

> . . . culpable neglect while Commanding-in-Chief of His Majesty's Forces in the island of St Eustatius, in not taking the necessary precautions for the defence of the island, notwithstanding that he had received intelligence of an attack intended by the enemy . . . and of having on the 26th day of November 1781, suffered himself to be surprised by an inferior body of French troops: which landed on the said island without any opposition. He had shamefully abandoned and given up the Garrison, Posts and Troops under his command . . .

Lieutenant-Colonel James Cockburn was therefore to be cashiered and declared unworthy of serving His Majesty in any capacity whatsoever: further, this sentence was to be read out to him 'publicly' at the head of the 13th and 15th Regiments of Foot who were under his command at the time of the surprise – if that was convenient – or otherwise at the head of whichever of the said Regiments His Majesty saw fit to direct. It was adjudged, in addition, that the charge of which the prisoner had been convicted, together with the sentence . . . should be declared in public orders and circulated to every Corps in His Majesty's service.

*　　*　　*

There were two riders. The Court thought it just to vindicate Lieutenant George Mackenzie – who during his examination at the bar had conducted himself with temper and propriety – from the insinuations made by Lieutenant-Colonel Cockburn. Mackenzie had naturally called on the honourable testimony of several respectable officers to counter these remarks; but: '. . . there had not been adduced a tittle of proof which detracted from the character of Lieutenant Mackenzie as an Officer, or to impeach his credit as a witness.'

The Court thought it proper to do justice to that Company of the 13th Regiment which had been quartered near the Fort. There had been no evidence that they had received any order from Lieutenant-Colonel Cockburn in which he had been disobeyed, as the prisoner had alleged during his defence.

*　　*　　*

The Court adjourned for seven days, for His Majesty's approval of the proceedings. Duly obtained, the Royal views were given to the Court by the Judge-Advocate General on Saturday 31 May, and on two counts, in his sea of misery, Cockburn had reason to be thankful. His Majesty had concurred with the Court in all respects, save that he had decided to dispense with the public humiliation of the prisoner at the head of the 13th and 15th Regiments, or of one of them, it being not convenient to assemble them for the purpose.

The sentence would also relieve Cockburn from the necessity of facing the second charge, namely of 'Scandalous and infamous behaviour unbecoming the character of an Officer and a Gentleman in claiming from the Commander-in-Chief of the French troops a sum of money not his own, upon the grounds of it being his private property.' If this had been proved, said the Judge Advocate, then the prisoner could only be punished by being cashiered. But he had already suffered that sentence on

216

the first charge, thus precluding any additional investigation. It was His Majesty's command therefore, that the Court should be discharged from any further proceeding against Lieutenant-Colonel Cockburn, and that the Court should thereupon be dissolved.

There remained some final wounding for Cockburn, first a formality which must have cost him much to meet with the dignity he showed at that moment. 'I am under the painful necessity' the President told him, 'of telling you, Sir, that you are no longer to consider yourself as an Officer of His Majesty's service.'

'The sentence tells me so, Sir' said Cockburn: but then had the added mortification of hearing the President's next words, addressed to Lieutenant Rogerson:

I have received your letters and laid them before the Court: and it comes from me, merely as President, to tell you Sir, that there is not the least shadow of imputation upon you in any shape whatever. I hope that delivering this in this public manner, will satisfy you, *and clear you to the world.*'

EPILOGUE

All the characters of this story deserve their chroniclers. Some very few of that strange parade already have them. British biography is rich in its coverage of such men as Germain and Burke and of Ministers and politicians in office at the time of the American War of Independence. It has given us equally rewarding lives of the Admirals, Rodney, Hood, Hotham – indeed, he became an Admiral, dying in 1813 and of the soldiers Clinton, Burgoyne and to a point – because the view is of his campaigns and not his personality – Vaughan. France, Holland and America have recorded the achievements of their own great figures of the conflict but in all of these countries, so many spear-carriers yet unsung await their discovery by other historians. Their existence is acknowledged here by an author truly conscious of these gaps: but we should not leave the key figures of the St Eustatius affair without learning a little more of them.

* * *

Cockburn first. Not lacking in surprises, the Dictionary of National Biography mentions Mrs Letitia Cockburn's letter of thanks to General Vaughan for having appointed her husband as Quartermaster-General, but says that 'this was an appointment he appears never to have taken up.' The DNB does, however, accurately record the fact of his court martial at the Horse Guards and the sentence passed on him at the close of the trial. The reference is completed with the dour comment that Cockburn 'died soon afterwards' – information which betrayed this researcher into a long and entirely profitless blind alley since no confirmation of Cockburn's death could be found within the notional period suggested.

In fact, James Cockburn refused to oblige society with an early death but lived to succeed to the title on the death of his cousin, Sir William James Cockburn, the 4th Baronet, of Langton, who died in 1800. James Cockburn enjoyed the role of 5th Baronet for another four years before the *Kelso Mail* reported his death: 'At his house on Hillingdon Heath, on

Friday sennight, Sir James Cockburn, of Langton, Baronet, aged 73.'

The announcement also appeared in the Annual Register of 1804, although confusion is piled high by an entry in Burke's Peerage and Baronetage (1980 edition), which gives the date of Cockburn's death as 9 June, 1809. This authority piles confusion even higher by asserting Lieutenant-Colonel James Cockburn, of the 35th Regiment to be 'Brigadier General and Quartermaster-General in North America.'

The unusual brevity of the announcements indicated a past better left unearthed, but tears of a kind did come from an unlikely source. In 1782, Edward Drewe, himself cashiered at St Lucia in 1780 through the agency of James Cockburn and now living at Exeter, had published and then withdrawn his own account of that court martial, although, he wrote, he was 'not influenced by a recent event.' Literate, and with a ready wit, Drewe thereafter turned to writing lampoons and essays which he published under the title of '*Military Sketches*' in 1784. He also used the opportunity to repeat his claim to have been Cockburn's victim, albeit he seasoned this with a pious sympathy for his oppressor.

The Preface included references to 'my dispute with the unfortunate Governor of St Eustatius and the ruin of my Military Fortune . . . You will see at a glance, Drewe declared to his readers: '. . . what I was and what I would have been, had I met with favour instead of enmity: but my adversary has fallen also, and on the very day which blended me with the peaceful. Rest to his military remains! In no period of his misfortunes have I indulged myself in acrimony or triumph. I am the victim of his faults, yet I have never detracted from his merits . . .'

Or so we are to believe, for Drewe must surely have been tempted.

Françoise-Claude-Amour de Bouillé died in 1800. His brilliant career in the West Indies was capped by two further momentous incidents after he had returned to France, namely, his ruthless suppression of the mutiny of the army at Nancy, in 1790 and, in June 1791, his resourceful but unsuccessful attempt to engineer the escape of Louis XVI and his family to the relative safety of Montmédy, Lorraine, on the frontier of Luxembourg. In the event, de Bouillé's plan was defeated by a vigilant and vengeful postmaster who personally ensured that the King's coach would be halted at Varennes, where Louis and his family were seized by the National Guard and returned to Paris as prisoners.

*   *   *

Those other Prisoners of State, Samuel Curson and Isaac Gouverneur were escorted from the *Vengeance* and taken to London. With them, of course, went those notorious books and papers. Helen Augur, in *The Secret War of Independence*, tells us that the papers and the two

Americans were put under the special charge of Undersecretary William Knox, 'who soon realised the importance of keeping the revelations they afforded a dead secret. In July, 1781, Curson and Gouverneur were tried for high treason in an examination prudently held within the offices of the American Department. Sir Sampson Wright acted as magistrate and Knox, who happened to be justice of the peace for Middlesex County, attended the trial. The Americans were remanded to jail, still under Knox's charge, and nobody was allowed to see them without his special order . . .'

Augur continues . . . 'Meanwhile Knox had a trusted clerk working several weeks making copies of the Curson and Gouverneur letters, and three others of the Department making a precis of the other papers from Statia'. Readers will shortly meet Knox's trusted clerk and what he has to tell us will be of interest.

But '. . . by March, 1782, it was apparent that the British authorities would soon release the Americans and Knox was afraid he would be blamed for their imprisonment. (Curson died not long after his release.) Knox accordingly appropriated that part of their correspondence which he felt proved their term in jail quite justified.' And in Auger, 1955 as in Spinney, 1968, et al, *and what happened to these papers later on nobody could discover.'*

* * *

The last entry in the Army List for William Rogerson is for 30 March, 1789, wherein he appears as a Captain of the 9th Regiment of Foot (East Norfolk.) He does not appear in the Army List for 1793, in the index to Active Officers, in the Half Pay List or in the Records of Casualties or Alterations. Although these are the most important sources, there may possibly be references to Rogerson in the muster rolls for the 9th Foot, the Monthly Returns of the British Army or in miscellaneous service records. The records of resignations from the Army (PRO class WO 31) begin in 1793 and Rogerson may have given up his commission at an earlier date. Clearly, however, he saw neither further prominence nor advancement. He had informed the members of the court martial that he 'had neither fortune, rank or abilities to support him' and this has proved true enough to screen him, so far, from further discovery.

* * *

There are other figures of the island's story who remain to be noted here, but yet again, fortune's gifts to them were capricious and took little account of their entitlement. Lieutenant-General Sir John Vaughan made a better showing of surviving the affair than his partner in the Great Capture, Sir George Brydges Rodney. Anxious to be done with the incessant badgering of the lawsuits, Vaughan disgorged the fancied profits from the expedition as speedily as the lawyers advised and encouraged Sir George to do likewise. Defending himself in the House of Commons (in 1781 of course, and while he was also the member for St Johnstown in the Irish Parliament), Vaughan asserted on his honour and was prepared to take oath that he had never made a 'single shilling' out of the confiscations. Unfortunately for both of the Commanders-in-Chief, the claimants ensured that this was true.

He was compensated for all the ill-humour, nevertheless. He had been promoted to the rank of Lieutenant-General in 1782, became a Knight Commander of the Bath in 1792 and thereafter, Commander-in-Chief of the Leeward Islands. He died suddenly at Martinique on 3 June, 1795, at the age of 58, unmarried.

* * *

Johannes de Graaff returned to Statia in 1782, as a private resident after the consolidation of the occupation by the French. He died in 1813 and, despite his place in Statia's history and the existence of a magnificent portrait by an unknown artist, Dr John Hartog's *History of St Eustatius* informs us that the burial place of Johannes de Graaff is also unknown.

So too, is the answer to the question of whether Commissary-General Matthew Forster had permitted a little of the wealth of St Eustatius to stick to his fingers. Nevertheless, it is one of the pleasures of historical research that we may nurse our own suspicions. It appears that the postwar careers of both Matthew Forster and Sergeant William Gordon were untroubled by inconvenient investigation. Both men succeeded in fading into a civilian anonymity and in Forster's case, it seems that the direct accusations of fraud levelled by Brigadier General Christie and Captain Saxton of the *Invincible* were not pursued. The French capture of St Eustatius would in any event have made it difficult to challenge Forster's version of his stewardship and, as with certain other matters of potentially damaging embarrassment, the ending of that terrible war enabled much to go by default.

William Gordon achieved a remarkable transmogrification, for he appeared as a witness in 1787 during the interminable legal process associated with Rodney and Vaughan's defence against the claims of the Statian merchants. At this hearing – the 'General Case on Petition, in Objection to the Register's Report' – the erstwhile Sergeant described himself as 'a merchant of Exeter' leaving open yet another question of how this status was achieved on the savings from his miserable pay as a soldier.

Cuftom-Houfe, London, February 3, 1794.

FOR SALE,

BY Order of the Honourable the Commiffioners of His Majefty's Cuftoms, in purfuance of an Act of Parliament of the Third Year of His prefent Majefty, on Wednefday the 12th, Thurfday the 13th and Friday the 14th Inftant, at Three o'Clock in the Afternoons of the faid Days, in the Long Room, Cuftom-Houfe, London,

The following Goods,

Which are allotted in fmall Quantities, for the better Accommodation of the feveral Dealers, as well as private Perfons, who chufe to become Purchafers.

For Home Confumption.

Tobacco, Snuff, Brandy, Rum, Geneva, Cordials, Wine, Tea, Coffee, Sugar, Currants and other Grocery, Skins, Hones, Horns, Watches, Prints, Snuff Boxes, Cornelian Stones, Mother of Pearl, a Veffel, with her Tackle, Apparel and Furniture, Boats, Coals, Hemp, Materials of Veffels, Woollen Cloth, Spa Ware, Bows, and Wood for Arrows, Copper Plates, Marble Mortars, Extract of Bark, Glafs, Cuttings of Lofs Hides, Mats, Wafte Silk, Cobalt, Tobacco Afhes, and Cinders.

Alfo fuch Goods as have remained in His Majefty's Warehoufe upwards of Three Months, not cleared or the Duties paid, viz.

Pictures, Hardware, Perfumery, Wearing Apparel, Drugs, Chocolate, Leather Shoes, Worfted, Preffing Paper, Plated Copper, Wool, Chip Hats, Optical Glaffes, Pocket Books, Linen ; and fundry other Sorts of Goods, as mentioned in the Catalogues,

Clear of all Duties.

The Tobacco, Snuff, Tobacco Afhes, and Cinders, may be viewed at the King's Tobacco Warehoufe, Tower-Hill ; the Veffels, Boats, Coals, &c. at the Tobacco Ground, near Greenland Dock, Rotherhithe ; and all the other Goods at His Majefty's Warehoufe, Cuftom-Houfe, London, on Monday the 10th and Tuefday the 11th of February, from Nine to One in the Forenoons, and in the Mornings before the Sale ;

Where Catalogues will be delivered.

ISLAND of St. EUSTATIUS.

THE great Variety of Claims for Reftitution of Property feized in February, 1781, at the Capture of the faid Ifland and it's Dependencies, being at length adjufted, the Agents for the Fleet and Army employed on that Service hereby give Notice, that they will diftribute 64.000l. to the Perfons entitled to fhare therein, or their legal Reprefentatives ; which Sum is nearly the Amount of what is at this Time in their Hands, referving only a Fund for difcharge of Law and other Expences ftill remaining unfatisfied.

The faid Sum will be divided in the Proportions prefcribed by His Majefty's Inftructions of the 30th of March, 1781, and the Order in Council dated the 17th of July, 1793, before which laft mentioned Date no Diftribution could poffibly take Place.

The Proportions are as follows ; viz.

Two Sixteenths to the Commanders in Chief by Sea and Land, to whofe prompt and vigorous Exertions in the Execution of their Orders, the Capture was afcribed, (the ufual Proportion allotted to them being judged by His Majefty too fmall ;) and the fubfequent Allotments out of the remaining Fourteen Sixteenths as hereafter mentioned, viz.

One Sixteenth to the Commanders in Chief.

One Ditto to the Flag and General Officers.

Four Ditto to the Captains of the Navy and Field Officers.

Two Ditto to the Lieutenants of the Navy, Captains of the Army and Marines.

Two Ditto to the Warrant Officers of the Navy, Subalterns of the Army and Marines.

Two Ditto to the Petty Officers of the Navy, Non-Commiffioned Officers of the Army, and Marines.

Four Ditto to the Sailors, Soldiers and Marines.

The Sum to be paid to each Clafs will be,

To the Commanders in Chief by Sea and Land, each 5,750 l. - - - -	11,500 l.
To the Flag and General Officers - -	3,500 l.
To the Captains of the Navy and Field Officers - - - - - - -	14,000 l.
To the Lieutenants of the Navy, Captains of the Army and Marines, each 49 l. 12 s. 10 d. - - - -	7,000 l.
To the Warrant Officers of the Navy, Subalterns of the Army and Marines, each 26 l. 4 s. 4 d. - -	7,000 l.
To the Petty Officers of the Navy, Non-Commiffioned Officers of the Army, and Marines, each 7 l. 15 s. 2 d.	7,000 l.
To the Sailors, Soldiers, and Marines, each 1 l. 8 s. 5 d. - - - -	14,000 l.
	64,000 l.

The Payment for the Fleet will be made at the Sign of the White Lion in Wych-Street, as follows ;

To the Alfred, Barfleur, Belliqueux, Invincible and Sybil, on Monday the 3d of March.

Monarch, Princeffa, Torbay, Blaft, Salamander, Etna and Vefuvius, on Tuefday the 4th of March :

And the Shares not then paid will be recalled at the fame Place the Firft Wednefday in every Month for Three Years to come, under the Direction of Mr. Francis Wilfon, of the Navy-Office.

To the Sandwich, Alcide, Gibraltar, Panther and Convert, on Wednefday the 5th of March.

To the Refolution, Shrewfbury, Prince William, Barbuda, Swallow and Sylph, on Thurfday the 6th of March.

And the Shares not then paid will be recalled at the fame Place the laft Saturday in every Month for Three Years to come, under the Direction of Mr. John Druce, of the Navy-Office.

George Jackfon, } Agents for the Fleet.
William Pagett,

N. B. Claims from Reprefentatives or Attornies will not be admitted, until the Authorities under which the fame are made have been approved and certified by the Infpector of Seamens Wills and Powers, at the Navy Pay-Office, Somerfet-Place, purfuant to an Act of Parliament of the Thirty fecond of His prefent Majefty.

The Payment of the Claims on the Agents for the Army will be made at the fame Place on Saturday the 8th of March ; and the Shares not then paid will be there recalled the Firft Wednefday in every Month for Three Years to come, under the Direction of Mr. Francis Wilfon, of the Navy-Office.

George Jackfon, } Agents for the Army.
John Lloyd,

The final shares of the St Eustatius booty.
(*Crown copyright. PRO ZJ1/90. Reproduced by courtesy of the Controller, Her Majesty's Stationery Office*)

And lastly, the man who called this history into being, Rodney. It is impossible to reduce the quality of his service to a few lines of epilogue and it would be an impertinence to attempt it. For those who wish to know the Admiral as a magnificent professional, a patriot and a human being of depth and feeling, there is the incomparable biography by David Spinney. Here, we note only the splendid aftermath of the huge morass represented by St Eustatius, for Sir George went on to fight his last and greatest battle against de Grasse, the battle of the Saints on 12 April, 1782. No victory could have been more welcome to his country, dazed by Graves' failure at Chesapeake, by the surrender of Cornwallis and recently, by the fall of St Kitts. The threat now was to Jamaica and for that project, De Grasse, with thirty-six sail of the line and five thousand troops under the indefatigable de Bouillé, bided his time at Martinique. He sailed on 8 April, unleashing an eager Rodney from St Lucia with thirty-seven sail.

The resulting encounter at the Saints Passage demolished the French beyond hope of renewed challenge: combined with the failure of a joint French and Spanish attack on Gibraltar in September, these actions restored British pride and gave Britain her strongest cards in negotiating the Treaty of Versailles in the following year. This was Rodney at the peak of his genius as a sea-officer: but Hood ran true to form in attempting to sour Rodney's triumph by denigrating Sir George's refusal to pursue the shattered French fleet after the decisive engagement. Hood's share of the battle is described in the DNB as 'particularly brilliant' and it was to his ship *Barfleur* that De Grasse struck his colours. There were to be other compensations for this bitter man however, for after further notable service in the Mediterranean, he lived on to become an Admiral, then Viscount Hood, Governor of Greenwich Hospital and a Knight Grand Cross of the Order of the Bath. He died in 1816.

* * *

No relief came to Sir George in his final years. Despite the honours and the Freedom of great cities and the peerage which came in 1782, the rest was indeed what Spinney has called a 'bleak glory.' It was not enough that the most treasured relationship of husband and wife could not sustain the Admiral and Lady Henrietta in retirement. By mutual agreement, and for their own reasons, Lady Rodney chose to live apart. But in addition, and for what remained of his life, there was the acid of the lawsuits to erode the Admiral's personal substance and his spirit, until that too, left him: he died under his son's roof at Hanover Square, in London on 24 May 1792.

Lady Rodney had gone to live in France but was unfortunate enough to be displaced herself by the upheaval of the Revolution. Spinney recounts that '. . . in a pathetic letter to Pitt dated 1 October, 1792, she described her situation – utterly destitute, her pension precarious and all the English gone, except herself.' It seems . . . 'that her cries were heard, for the Dowager Lady Rodney was not left to face the Terror but brought home at the eleventh hour, to survive for many years' – in fact, until 28 February 1826 when she died, aged ninety-one.

* * *

A last word was promised from that Dutch sailor, Cornelius de Jong, once Rodney's prisoner at St Eustatius and now a Captain of the Dutch Navy. It is a poignant memory, for it tells of de Jong's encounter with Lady Rodney and her two daughters at Den Helder, in 1799, when they were on their way to England to claim Lady Rodney's pension. De Jong had calculated that in the course of Rodney's activities, the British had seized some 170 vessels in the Dutch West Indies, at St Eustatius, Essequebo, Barbice, Demarara and Surinam. 'According to the English custom, one eighth of their value – the equivalent of twenty-one ships with their cargoes – belonged to the Admiral. In addition, he had captured Van Byland's frigate *Mars* and the smaller vessel of the same name and accrued the prize entitlement . . . and who knows how much the rich warehouses of Statia must have brought in for him?'

These spoils, mused de Jong, must have endowed the Admiral with princely treasures: no matter how much suffering the war had caused, it appeared to Cornelius de Jong that Rodney had been made rich by it.

The Dutch officer thought it most strange, therefore, that the three ladies '. . . were plainly not in circumstances at all appropriate to the heiresses of this happy Admiral. They were accompanied only by a single female servant and everything about them revealed scantiness instead of abundance.' That pathetic trio caused de Jong to wonder where all those treasures had gone. Had they flown away or sunk? Or whatever had their possessor done to become bereft of them in such a short time?

This book has endeavoured to answer some, at least, of those questions: not only the matters of where the money came from and what happened to it, but also, how this episode touched the lives of all those others who came to St Eustatius or who were in some way concerned with this small island. Sleeping in the sun of the Antilles, host now to its own people and to the willing exiles who have chosen to live there, Statia searches for a future: but always, it reminds us that such greatness as it once owned was brought down by the English Admiral, Sir George Brydges Rodney – and finally by the emerging trading patterns which invalidated its 18th Century *raison d'être*.

* * *

A tiny flame flickered among the embers of this story some five years afterward. It will be remembered that Rodney and Vaughan had been unable to produce the evidence of the English traders' treachery, since their confiscated books and papers had disappeared without trace from the Treasury. This matter has remained a mystery, although Spinney closed his own reference to the affair by quoting an abortive offer to produce the books 'for a consideration' made by one Thomas Digges, of Dublin – 'a not very respectable individual' – in a letter dated 2 August, 1786, to be found in the papers of Lord Shelburne. And there the matter has rested: 'From that day to this, no further word has been heard of them, so the case of Rodney and Vaughan failed.'

Yet there *is* that glimmer, although the relevant document in Rodney's Papers has previously gone unnoticed. Brought to light now it will tell us the name of the persons who ensured that Rodney and Vaughan would be deprived of their essential evidence.

* * *

It may have been by appointment, but 'in June or July, 1786' two respectable gentlemen of London, the Reverend Dr Samuel Peters and his brother, Colonel John Peters, met a somewhat less respectable person, one Arthur Savage, in St James's Park. Strangely, their conversation turned to the riddle of Lord Rodney's missing papers and on this subject, Arthur Savage was anxious to enlighten them. So successfully did he do this, that the brothers noted down all he told them, and solemnly appended their signatures in witness.

It seemed, they wrote, that Savage had been employed by Lord George Germain 'with Daniel Leonard and others' to make extracts from the papers which 'were enough to 'criminate many merchants in England, Scotland and America of an illicit trade in favour of Congress.' So vile did this treachery appear to Arthur that there 'opened before him a Scene of Iniquity such as he had never dreamed of, or thought the world could be guilty of' – a statement which indicates a realization on his part that under certain circumstances, the papers might possibly provide him with something more than the salary of a copyist. Such thoughts, however, were withheld from the Peters brothers, possibly because they were capable of drawing their own conclusions. Or possibly, no such unworthy considerations had yet suggested themselves.

The papers were at that time lodged in the custody of Lord George Germain's office, and at some point the task was halted and all the copyists dismissed: as this occurred, according to Savage, about the time that Lord North's government fell and Lord Rockingham took office in March 1782, these developments can be placed fairly accurately.

It cannot have been chance which brought a visitor from St Eustatius to the small house in Brompton occupied by Arthur's brother, John, particularly since the visitor was Richard Downing Jennings, who had arrived in England in October and to whom Arthur – another chance visitor – was now introduced, although as 'Mr Ginnings,' in which manner he is consistently noted throughout the Peters' document.

Here again, the topic of conversation was the traders' papers, now believed to be in the Treasury, and which, so Jennings told John Savage, he greatly wanted out of the Secretary of State's office. He had come, therefore, to seek advice from John Savage as to how this might be achieved . . .

While this was being pondered by his listeners, Jennings produced the final encouragement: so anxious was he to have those papers in his own hands that he would willingly exchange them for Ten Thousand Pounds. The vision of this unimaginable sum had no sooner filled the minds of his incredulous listeners than Jennings added carelessly . . . 'or Guineas.'

We are left to our own enjoyment of that moment. But it was John who gestured towards his brother and proposed that Arthur might be able to help Jennings to secure the papers 'as well as any Person in England.' And with due modesty, Arthur agreed that this was so and that, in view of the incentive, he would undertake to serve Mr Jennings as he desired.

*　　*　　*

It is clear that Arthur now proceeded to operate as if he were still employed by the government. His first move was to obtain a note from the Secretary of State, Lord Shelburne, to Mr Nepean, desiring that gentleman to give 'a writing' to Arthur Savage, permitting him to retrieve the papers from the Treasury and to 'deliver them to Mr Jennings.' Lord Shelburne's amiability in this and Jennings' presence in London is purportedly explained in a memorandum to Lord Rodney from his lawyer, which also advises him of various claims pending:

Tis well known that after the Marquis de Bouillé left the island of St Eustatius, that he was succeeded by Colonel Fitzmaurice in the command, *a near relation* to Lord Shelburne, and that *he* despatched Mr Jennings, well recommended to Lord Shelburne, for those Papers that have been given up.

However, this does nothing to explain the efforts which Jennings found necessary to his plan, and the huge inspiration dangled before Arthur and John Savage. Arthur gave few details to the Peters of his search for the papers in the Treasury, save that it took him two or three days to find the 'Boxes of Papers.' Two weeks after that meeting, however, on 27 April, 1787, Dr Peters was able to add more information, in reply to a note left at his house by the lawyer, Mr Hutton.

'Mr Arthur Savage said that Lord Shelburne ordered Mr Nepean to write a note to the Clerk, or Keeper of the Books of Mr Jennings, in the Treasury, to deliver the said Books to Arthur Savage . . .'

With this authority, Arthur sought out Mr Pollock, an official of the Treasury, only to be told by him that the papers were not in his care: Savage should find the person who held the key to the appropriate room, but of both of those matters, Mr Pollock confessed his ignorance. With admirable persistence, therefore, Arthur 'went from place to place and finally found the Person who held the key' – who did as Nepean's note bid him, unlocked the door, and thereupon left Arthur to conduct his search alone.

Not quite alone, however. Arthur had hired a hand cart, and having rummaged for 'a considerable time' among the Treasury's piled miscellany, the correct boxes and papers were found and with the help of the cart man, carried out of the building, loaded on to the cart, and trundled to a rendezvous with Jennings, 'in or near Oxford Street.' It is worth savouring that journey, also, as the barrowload of stolen secrets, pushed by a sweating carter and urged on by a furtive thief, made its unsteady way along Whitehall and all the way to Oxford Street, to halt finally before an extremely pleased Richard Downing Jennings. Who gave Arthur two shillings with which to pay the carter, and saw the load transferred into his own keeping – presumably into a coach.

And thereafter, to disappear from the lives of Arthur and John Savage.

*　*　*

It was not long before both men agreed that some essential part of the transaction was still outstanding. It is possible that subsequently, there was an attempted correspondence – at least addressed to Jennings at Statia – but nothing has come to light and it is more than probable that any such appeal which reached him from the Savages was cast contemptuously aside. What is certain, however, is that by 'June or July, 1786', the Savage brothers had abandoned any hope of seeing a single penny of the promised fee or of seeing Jennings and his fellow traders undone by a government not in the least anxious to reopen the wounds of the American Revolution.

It was then that Arthur took himself to St James's Park to unburden himself to Dr and Colonel Peters, who assuredly – since the Peters' document, as mentioned earlier, is in the Rodney Papers – reported the interview to Lord Rodney.

It is surprising that neither that document, nor any of the numerous references to Arthur Savage in the Shelburne Papers have previously attracted an inquisitive historian. It is indeed a farcical interlude: yet it is as much part of Statia's story as are any of the people who lived there, or who came so sternly, as soldiers or sailors, to call the island their own, albeit for the blink of history's eye.

INDEX

240

Monarch, xii, 14, 17, 109, 115, in chase of Krul, 117, comes up with convoy, 121, 122, 123

Monckton, Major General Robert, 28, 43, 213

Money, 127, 128

Monmouth Court House, 31

Monmouth, 84

Monro, Lt. Colonel George, 39, 40, 41

Montagu, 25, 96, 178, 181

Montcalm, Marquis de, 39, 40, death of, 43, 207

Monteil, M., 105

Monteserratt, 109

Montreal, 43, 213

Moonlight Battle, 15, 25, 98

Moore, Mr, 137

Morales, David, 73

Moret, Philippe, xiii, 192

Morne Fortune, 32, 81, 84, 86, barracks, 87, Morning Herald, 199, troops housing, 87, hospitals and magazines on, 87, cannon on, 90, 91, hurricane damage at, 96, Cockburn leaves, 97

Mosley, Captain, 71

Mosquito and fever, 87

Motherbank, transports at, 106

Motte Piquet, Admiral Toussaint-Guillaume, Comte de la, 168, 169, intercepted convoy, 170, 171, 173

Munday, G.B.M., xi

Mundy, Basil, 121

Murray, Brigadier General, James, 213

Murray, Lt-General the Hon Thomas, 28

Musgrave, Lieutenant Colonel Thomas, 86

Muster Book, 6, 125, 142, 144, 145

Muster Rolls, xii, 221

Mutineers, 11, 138

Mutiny, 12

N

Namur, 13

Nancy, 220

National Army Museum, xiv

Naval and Military stores, 137, 150

Naval War College, Rhode Island, xii

Navy Board, 22

Navy Office, 19

Navy victuallers, 102

NCO's, 6, 36, 91, 94, 132, 187, 191, 198, 201, 202, 203, 205

Neagle, Mr., 125, 126, 175, 205, 206, 210

Negro, 194

Negroes, 100, 101, 102, 129, 136, 182

Nelson, Admiral Lord, 7

Nemesis, 172

Nepean, Mr., 227, 228

Netherlands Antilles, 5

Netherlands, 2, 3, 49

Nevis, 109

New Jersey Militia, 39

New York Gazette, 195, 198

New York, State of, 26, 30, 31, 32, 33, Cockburn sends son to England from, 35, Muster taken, 35, 38, 66, Cockburn quartered in, 81, 82

Newcastle, Duke of, 13, 17

Newfoundland, 17

Newfoundland Banks, 55

Newport Mercury, xii, 147, 192

Newport, Rhode Island, xii, 61, Historical Society, xiii

Varennes, 220
Vaughan Papers, xii
Vaughan, Sir John, xi, xii, 9, 22, 26, 27, as Major-General, 28: at Esopus, 28, 29, 30: 33, 38, 43, to be consulted by Rodney, 59, 86, date of return to England, 87, arr. St Lucia, 87, Army sick etc., reported to, 88, pleas from officers, 89, requires money for army, 90, courts martial within command, 91, orders court martial of Drewe, 92, during hurricane, 95, reports to Germain on, 95, report from Hotham, 96, solicits aid for Bradshaw's widow, 97, lack of achievement, 98, disappointment of St Vincent, 102, summoned by Rodney, 107, de Graaff surrenders to, 114, disembarks troops, 117, 133, Rodney, requires horse, 121, present during extortion, 127, reports Specie to Germain, 128, requires money for troops, 128, Articles of Agreement, 130, booty bestowed on by HM, 137, legal actions against, 137, on soldiers' shares, 140, 141, on 'depredations', 141, Petitions to, 142, rescinds deportations, 142, evasion on Curaçao, 156, 157, status as MP, 158, de Graaff appeal to, 159, sends Fraser to St Eustatius, 175, sails from St Eustatius, 175, instructs Cockburn to place money aboard *Montagu*, 178, 'blameless', 184, issue of ammunition, 200, 'no guards stationed', 203; 206, 209, 219, later career and death of Vaughan, 222

Vaughan, Wilmot, third Viscount Lisburn, 27
Vendue, Master, 132, 150
Vendue, 191
Venezuela, Gulf of, 4
Vengeance (American privateer), 33
Vengeance, HMS, xii, 96, 133, 166, Curson & Goveneur taken aboard, 167, sails with convoy, 168, 169, reaches Beerhaven, 171, 172
Venice, 65
Venus, 167, 168
Vere, Lord, 10
Versailles, 54, 79, Treaty of, 224
Vestal, frigate, 55
Vesuvius Bomb, 160
Vigie, the, 84, 85
Vigilant, 160
Villains arrested, 133
Virgin Islands, 3, 121
Virginia, 60, 70, 74
Visman, Captain Pieter, 125
Vosper, Edna, xii, 26
Vriend Schap, 173

W

Wallace, Sir James, 29
Walsh, 185, 186, 191
Walters, John, 161
Walton-on-Thames, 10
War Invalids, 173
War Office, 196, 197
War supplies, 51
Warehouses, 137, 139, burgled, 141
Warren (American privateer), 33
Warrowarow Bay, 99, 100
Warwick, 59

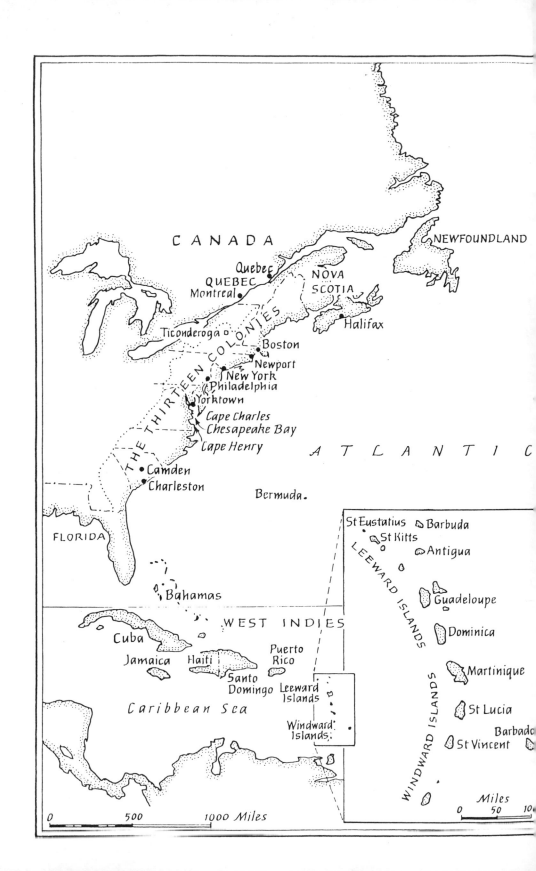

CANADA

NEWFOUNDLAND

Quebec
QUEBEC
Montreal

NOVA
SCOTIA

Halifax

Ticonderoga

Boston
Newport
New York
Philadelphia
Yorktown
Cape Charles
Chesapeake Bay
Cape Henry

THE THIRTEEN COLONIES

ATLANTIC

Camden
Charleston

Bermuda.

FLORIDA

St Eustatius · Barbuda
St Kitts
Antigua

LEEWARD ISLANDS

Guadeloupe

Dominica

Bahamas

WEST INDIES

Cuba

Jamaica   Haiti
Santo
Domingo Leeward
Islands

Puerto
Rico

Martinique

St Lucia

Barbado

Caribbean Sea

Windward
Islands.

WINDWARD ISLANDS

St Vincent

Miles
0   50   10

0   500   1000 Miles